Teaching Social Studies to English Language Learners

Teaching Social Studies to English Language Learners provides readers with a comprehensive understanding of both the challenges that face English language learners (ELLs) and the ways in which educators might address them in the social studies classroom. The authors offer context-specific strategies for the full range of the social studies curriculum, including geography, U.S. history, world history, economics, and government. These practical instructional strategies will effectively engage learners and can be incorporated as a regular part of instruction in any classroom. An annotated list of web and print resources completes the volume, making this a valuable reference to help social studies teachers meet the challenges of including all learners in effective instruction.

Features and updates to this new edition include:

- An updated and streamlined Part 1 provides an essential overview of ELL theory in a social studies-specific context.
- "Teaching Tips" offer helpful suggestions and ideas for creating and modifying lesson plans to be inclusive of ELLs.
- Additional practical examples and new pedagogical elements in Part 3 include more visuals, suggestions for harnessing new technologies, discussion questions, and reflection points.
- New material that takes into account the demands of the Common Core State Standards, as well as updates to the web and print resources in Part 4.

Bárbara C. Cruz is Professor of Social Science Education at the University of South Florida, USA.

Stephen J. Thornton is Professor and Chair of the Department of Secondary Education at the University of South Florida, USA.

Teaching English Language Learners Across the Curriculum
Series Editors: Bárbara C. Cruz, Stephen J. Thornton, and Tony Erben

Teaching Mathematics to English Language Learners
Gladis Kersaint, Denisse R. Thompson, and Mariana Petkova

Teaching English Language Learners in Career and Technical Education Programs
Victor M. Hernández-Gantes and William Blank

Teaching English Language Learners through Technology
Tony Erben, Ruth Ban, and Martha Castañeda

Teaching Social Studies to English Language Learners
Bárbara C. Cruz and Stephen J. Thornton

Teaching Language Arts to English Language Learners
Anete Vásquez, Angela L. Hansen, and Philip C. Smith

Teaching Science to English Language Learners
Joyce Nutta, Nazan U. Bautista, and Malcolm B. Butler

Teaching the Arts to Engage English Language Learners
Margaret Macintyre Latta and Elaine Chan

Teaching Social Studies to English Language Learners

Second Edition

BÁRBARA C. CRUZ
AND
STEPHEN J. THORNTON

Routledge
Taylor & Francis Group

NEW YORK AND LONDON

Second edition published 2013
by Routledge
711 Third Avenue, New York, NY 10017

Simultaneously published in the UK
by Routledge
2 Park Square, Milton Park, Abingdon, Oxon OX14 4RN

Routledge is an imprint of the Taylor & Francis Group, an informa business

First edition published by Routledge 2009

Library of Congress Cataloging in Publication Data
Cruz, Bárbara.
  Teaching social studies to English language learners/Bárbara C. Cruz and Stephen J. Thornton. – 2nd ed.
     p. cm. – (Teaching English language learners across the curriculum)
     Includes bibliographical references and index.
  1. Social sciences–Study and teaching–United States. 2. English language–Study and teaching–Foreign speakers. 3. Curriculum planning–United States. I. Thornton, Stephen J. II. Title.
  H62.5.U5C78 2013
  300.71'273–dc23   2012036649

ISBN: 978–0–415–63495–3 (hbk)
ISBN: 978–0–415–63496–0 (pbk)
ISBN: 978–0–203–09416–7 (ebk)

Typeset in Minion and Helvetica
by Swales & Willis Ltd, Exeter, Devon

Printed and bound in the United States of America
By Edwards Brothers Malloy on sustainably sourced paper.

We dedicate this book to
James S. Agarpao and Kevin A. Yelvington,
for their support and encouragement throughout the process.

Contents

List of Figures xii

List of Tables xiv

Series Introduction xv

Acknowledgments xvii

Introduction 1
Teachers and ELLs 3
Who Can Benefit from this Book? 3
How to Use this Book 4

PART 1 — Your English Language Learner *Tony Erben* 7

1.1 — Orientation 9

1.2 — The Process of English Language Learning and What to Expect 12
Principle 1: Give ELLs Many Opportunities to Read, to Write, to Listen to, and to
Discuss Oral and Written English Texts Expressed in a Variety of Ways 13
Principle 2: Draw Attention to Patterns of English Language Structure 14
Principle 3: Give ELLs Classroom Time to Use Their English Productively 15
Principle 4: Give ELLs Opportunities to Notice Their Errors and to Correct Their
English 15
Principle 5: Construct Activities that Maximize Opportunities for ELLs to Interact
with Others in English 17
Constructing a Curriculum with Language Needs in Mind 17

1.3 — Deciding on the Best ESOL Program 21

1.4 — Teaching for English Language Development 26

1.5 — Not All ELLs Are the Same 30
Stages of Cultural Adjustment 32
Cultural Practices at School 34

1.6 — Culturally Responsive Pedagogy 35

1.7 — Not All Parents Are the Same: Home–School Communication 38
Ideas: On Fostering Access 39
Ideas: On Fostering Approachability 39
Ideas: On Achieving Good Follow-Through 40

1.8 — English Language Learners with Special Needs 41
Gifted ELL Students 43
Conclusion 44

PART 2 — Principles of Social Studies Teaching and Learning 45

2.1 — Principles of Social Studies Teaching and Learning 47
Elements of an Instructional Program 47

2.2 — How Instruction Unfolds 52

2.3 — Social Studies-Focused ELL Research 54
Classroom Environment 54
Pedagogical Orientation, Practice, and Reflection 55
Culturally Sensitive Pedagogy 55
General Approaches for Teaching Social Studies to ELLs 56
Language Use 57
Content-Centered Instruction 58
Sheltered Instruction 59
Individualized and Differentiated Instruction 59
Technology-Based Instruction and Learning 60
Discussion and Questioning 61
Discovery and Exploration 62
Cooperative Learning Skills 63

2.4 — Enacting the Social Studies Curriculum 64
Textbooks and Trade Books 64
Graphic Organizers and Realia 65
Demonstrations and Total Physical Response 66
Role Playing and Simulations 67
Visual Resources 67

Assessment 68
Conclusion 70

PART 3 — Teaching Social Studies **73**

3.1 — Introduction **75**

3.2 — Geography **80**
Kinesthetic Learning and Stratified Questioning: The Concept of Scale (Levels 1–4) 82
Kinesthetic Learning and Visual Aids: Africa: Physical Geography and Population
Distribution (Levels 3 and 4) 84
K–W–L–Q–H, Visual Aids, Guided Imagery, and Stratified Questioning: Women's
Work in Southern India (Levels 2–4) 87
Discovery Exercise Using Visual Aids and Stratified Questioning: Adaptation of
the Environment: Place Where Native Americans Lived (Levels 1–4) 90

3.3 — U.S. History **95**
Visual Aids, Stratified Questioning: Lewis and Clark Expedition (Levels 1–4) 97
Visual Aids, Cartography, and Critical Thinking: Lewis and Clark Activity 2:
Cartography (Levels 3 and 4) 100
Dioramas, Kinesthetic Learning, and Cooperative Learning: Lewis and Clark
Extension Activity: Creating a Diorama (Levels 1–4) 100
Cooperative Learning, Peer Teaching, and Primary Documents: Lewis and Clark
Activity 3: Primary Documents Using Cooperative Learning (Levels 3 and 4) 101
Bar Graphs and Historical Photograph Analysis: City Life 1860–1920s (Levels 2 and 3) 103
Timelines and Stratified Questioning Strategy: Woodrow Wilson (Levels 1–4) 105
Modified Text, Visual Aids, Picture Books, Stratified Questioning, and Music:
Women in WWII (Levels 1–4) 107
Eisenhower's Military–Industrial Complex Speech, 1961: Simplifying Text and
Role Playing (Levels 3 and 4) 117

3.4 — World History **122**
Culturally Sensitive Pedagogy, Visual Aids, Stratified Questioning, and Research
Skills: World Origins of Our Class (Levels 1–4) 124
Visual Aids, Guided Observation, Word Wall, and Stratified Questioning: The
Agricultural Revolution (Levels 1 and 2) 126
Realia, Word Wall, and Visual Aids: The Renaissance (Levels 1–4) 128
Visual Aids and Primary Source Documents: Cultural Encounter and Exploration
(Levels 3 and 4) 134
Simplified Text and Concept Map: The Enlightenment (Levels 2–4) 137
Visual Aids, Stratified Questioning, and Guided Discussion: The Industrial
Revolution: The Cases of Great Britain and Japan (Levels 1–4) 139
Visual Aids, Role Playing, Guided Reading, and Stratified Questioning: Japanese
Americans During WWII (Levels 1–4) 147
Role Playing and Cooperative Learning: Factory Life in the Twentieth Century
(Levels 2–4) 153

3.5 — Government and Civics 157
Graphic Organizers and Visuals: The Duties, Responsibilities, and Rights of
United States Citizens (Levels 1 and 2) 158
Peer Teaching and Visual Aids: Political Cartoons (Levels 2–4) 161
Teaching with Primary Sources (Levels 2–4) 163
Using Bilingual Dictionaries and Graphic Organizers: Voting Rights (Levels 3 and 4). 165
Language Development through Simplifying Complex Text and Using Visual Aids:
Women's Suffrage (Levels 3 and 4). 168
Cooperative Learning, Computer Technology, and Alternative Assessments:
Political Bumper Stickers (Levels 1–4) 172
Visual Aids and Graphic Organizers: Executive Powers (Levels 1–4) 174

3.6 — Economics. 177
Visuals and Simplified Text to Develop Key Vocabulary (Levels 1 and 2) 178
Graphic Organizers and Role Playing: "Half a Loaf is Better than None":
International Trade and Development (Levels 3 and 4) 179
Visual Aids, Realia, Total Physical Response, and Stratified Questioning Strategy:
Goods and Services (Levels 1–4) 183
Visual Aids and Cooperative Learning: The Economic Concept of Scarcity (Levels 2–4) . . . 184
Cooperative Learning: Setting Priorities and Making Choices: A Lesson in Personal
Budgeting (Levels 3 and 4) 186
Graphic Organizers and Cooperative Learning: Consumer Credit and Debt (Levels 2–4) 188
Visual Aids and Stratified Questioning Strategy: Advertising (Levels 1–4) 189

3.7 — Anthropology, Sociology, and Psychology 191
Cooperative Learning and Visual Aids: Mental Cartography (Levels 1–4) 192
Visuals, Graphic Organizer, and Modified Assessment: Religions of the World
(Levels 1 and 2) 193
Visual Aids, Realia, Object-Based Learning: Archaeological Artifacts (Levels 1 and 2). 194
Simplifying Complex Language: Cultural Anthropology: Seeing Through Others'
Eyes (Levels 3 and 4) 195
Alternative Assessments: Sociology: Surveys and Opinion Polls (Levels 2–4) 197
Visual Aids, Graphic Organizer, and Effective Closure: Psychology: Identity
Formation (Levels 1–4) 199

3.8 — Controversial Issues in the Social Studies Classroom 204
Cooperative Learning, Kinesthetic Activities, and Stratified Questioning Strategy:
The Paper Chase (Levels 1–4). 206
Using Technology, Audio-Visual Materials, and Cooperative Learning: Controversial
Issues at Home and Abroad (Levels 2–4) 208
Political Cartoons, Values Clarification, and Role Playing: Immigration: Whom
Should We Allow In? (Levels 1–4) 210
Simplified Text, Guided Note Taking, Visual Aids, and Cooperative Learning:
Human Rights (Levels 2–4). 214
Kinesthetic Learning and Critical Thinking: Taking a Stand (Levels 2–4) 216
Cooperative Learning, Critical Thinking, and Research Skills: The Dead–Red Sea
Canal (Levels 3 and 4) 218

Resources **221**
Internet Resources for Teachers 221
Print and Associated Resources for Teachers 228
Resources for Students 237

Glossary **244**

Notes **246**

References **248**

Index **259**

Figures

1.1 The number of English language (EL) learners in the United States 10

1.2 The growth of the English language (EL) learner population in the United States between 1998/1999 and 2008/2009 10

1.3 Three databases 19

1.4 Stages of adjustment 32

2.1 Standard format for responding to readings 70

3.1 How big is Africa? 86

3.2 A pueblo 91

3.3 A chickee 92

3.4 The United States, showing extent of settlement in 1790 98

3.5 America becomes urbanized 103

3.6 A photograph of city life 104

3.7 Woodrow Wilson's political biography 106

3.8 "I'm proud . . . my husband wants me to do my part" 108

3.9 "Women in the war—We can't win without them" 108

3.10 The poster of "Rosie" was created for Westinghouse by J. Howard Miller in 1942 109

3.11 "Women Learn 'War Work'" 111

3.12 "Long Beach Plant, Douglas Aircraft" 112

3.13   Hunters and gatherers getting food. 126

3.14   Farmers getting food 127

3.15   The Parthenon, Athens. 130

3.16   Notre Dame Cathedral, Paris 131

3.17   St. Peter's Basilica, Rome 131

3.18   Portuguese discoveries in Africa, 1340–1498 134

3.19   Concept map 138

3.20   Christ Church and Coal Staith, Leeds, 1829. 140

3.21   Textile industries, George Spill & Co., 1855 143

3.22   Japanese internment poster 148

3.23   Relocation centers map. 151

3.24   "Obeying the law" 159

3.25   "Voting in elections" 160

3.26   "Ballot" 160

3.27   "Freedom of speech and right to assemble". 161

3.28   The apotheosis of suffrage 170

3.29   Men looking in the window of the National Anti-Suffrage Association headquarters 171

3.30   Women's Suffrage Headquarters, Cleveland, Ohio 171

3.31   U.S. presidency brainstorm 174

3.32   Vocabulary chart: Exchange 178

3.33   Caribbean web activity 179

3.34   The world's religions and the percentages of their followers 194

3.35   Exit ticket. 201

3.36   Tweets of the day 213

3.37   Collage of human rights. 215

Tables

1.1   Generalized patterns of ESOL development stages 13

1.2   Types of ESOL programs in the United States 22

1.3   Cummins' Quadrants 28

3.1   Four levels of speech emergence 77

3.2   Lesson plan with ELL modifications 78

Series
Introduction

No educational issue has proven more controversial than how to teach linguistically diverse students. Intertwined issues of ethnic and cultural differences are often compounded. What is more, at the time of writing, summer 2012, public policy regarding immigration and how immigrants and their heritages *ought* to fit with the dominant culture is the subject of rancorous debate in the United States and a number of other nations.

However thorny these issues may be to some, both legally and ethically, schools need to accommodate the millions of English language learners (ELLs) who need to be educated. Although the number of ELLs in the United States has burgeoned in recent decades, school programs generally remain organized via traditional subjects, which are delivered in English. Many ELLs are insufficiently fluent in academic English, however, to succeed in these programs. Since policymakers have increasingly insisted that ELLs, regardless of their fluency in English, be mainstreamed into standard courses with all other students, both classroom enactment of the curriculum and teacher education need considerable rethinking.

Language scholars have generally taken the lead in this rethinking. As is evident from Part 1 of the volumes in this series, language scholars have developed a substantial body of research to inform the mainstreaming of ELLs. The primary interest of these language scholars, however, is almost by definition the processes and principles of second language acquisition. Until recently, subject matter has typically been a secondary consideration, used to illustrate language concerns. Perhaps not surprisingly, content-area teachers sometimes have seen this as reducing their subjects to little more than isolated bits of information, such as a list of explorers and dates in history or sundry geological formations in science.

In contrast, secondary-school teachers see their charge as effectively conveying a principled understanding of, and interest in, a subject. They look for relationships, seek to develop concepts, search for powerful examples and analogies, and try to explicate principles. By the same token, they strive to make meaningful connections among the subject matter, students' experience, and life outside of school. In our observations, teacher education programs bifurcate courses on content-area methods and (if there are any) courses designed to instill principles of teaching ELLs. One result of this bifurcation seems to be that prospective and in-service, content-area teachers are daunted by the challenge of using language principles to inform their teaching of subject matter.

But there are educators who are experimenting with ways to improve the preparation teachers receive. For example, Gloria Ladson-Billings (2001) has experimented with how to prepare new teachers for diverse classrooms through a teacher education program focused on "diversity, equity, and social justice" (p. xiii). Teachers in her program are expected, for instance, to confront rather than become resigned to low academic expectations for children in urban schools. From Ladson-Billings's perspective, "no matter what else the schools find themselves doing, promoting students' academic achievement is among their primary functions" (p. 56).

The authors in this series extend this perspective to teaching ELLs in the content areas. In *Teaching Language Arts to English Language Learners*, the authors offer proven techniques that teachers can readily use to teach reading, writing, grammar, and vocabulary as well as speaking, listening, and viewing skills. *Teaching Science to English Language Learners* was written specifically for pre- and in-service teachers who may not have been trained in ELL techniques, but still find themselves facing the realities and challenges of today's diverse classrooms and learners. The authors of *Teaching Mathematics to English Language Learners* provide simple and straightforward advice on how to teach mathematics to the ELLs in the classroom, offering context-specific strategies for everything from facilitating classroom discussions with all students, to reading and interpreting math textbooks, to tackling word problems. In *Teaching Social Studies to English Language Learners,* the full range of the social studies curriculum, including geography, U.S. history, world history, economics, and government, is explored. *Teaching English Language Learners in Career and Technical Education Programs* explores the unique challenges of vocational education, using the authors' teaching framework and case studies that draw from common settings in which career and technical educators find themselves working with ELLs—in the classroom, in the laboratory or workshop, and in work-based learning settings. Written for prospective and practicing visual arts, music, drama, and dance educators, *Teaching the Arts to Engage English Language Learners* offers guidance for engaging ELLs, alongside all learners, through artistic thinking. Last, *Teaching English Language Learners through Technology* can be used by all teachers since the authors explore the use of computers and digital technology as a pedagogical tool to aid in the appropriate instruction of ELLs across all content areas.

The purpose of this series is to assist current and prospective educators to plan and implement lessons that do justice to the goals of the curriculum and make sense to and interest ELLs. If the needs of diverse learners are to be met, Ladson-Billings (2001) underscores that innovation is demanded, not that teachers merely pine for how things once were. The most obvious innovation in this series is to bring language scholars and specialists in the methods of teaching particular school subjects together. Although this approach is adopted more frequently than a decade ago (e.g., CREATE, 2012), it remains relatively uncommon. Combining the two groups brings more to addressing the problems of instruction than could be obtained by the two groups working separately. Even so, these volumes hardly tell the reader "everything there is to know" about the problems addressed. But we do know that our teacher education students report that even modest training in teaching ELLs can make a significant difference in the classroom. We hope this series extends those successes to all the content areas of the curriculum.

Acknowledgments

The authors would like to acknowledge the efforts and contributions of several key individuals who helped bring this project to fruition:

- Caroline Parrish, whose research assistance helped us in the initial stages of writing and who generously allowed us to modify and use two lesson plans she created for English language learners;
- Clay Kelsey, who assisted us in formatting some of the original visuals for the book;
- Dr. Roy Winkelman, who kindly shared his historical map and photograph collection with us;
- Carmela Fazzino-Farah and Kellie Cardone, who facilitated the use of many of the visuals in the book and who generously shared their knowledge and expertise in the field;
- Jill Korey O'Sullivan, Roberta Stathis, and Patrice Gotsch, who pushed us to think deeply and creatively about how students acquire and master language;
- Dr. Phil Smith, who forwarded valuable information and cutting-edge research and provided feedback on some of our work.

Introduction

Thanh had been in the United States for only a week when he entered my 10th-grade World History classroom. Even though he spoke no English, I could tell immediately that he was an especially intelligent youngster. As a first-year teacher, however, I did not have the experience, knowledge, or skills to fully appreciate his aptitude or help him develop his language skills.

Freshly out of an undergraduate teacher preparation program, I had Thanh sit along the side of the class, towards the back, remembering all I had been told about adolescents—especially "different" ones—that they could be easily embarrassed in front of peers. Much to my surprise, Thanh came up to me at the end of class after a few days and pointed to a seat in the front row. As I still didn't comprehend what he was asking, he sat himself down, clearly indicating that that was where he wanted to be. I showed him my seating chart, erased his name from the side/back seat, and rewrote it in the empty space in the front row. He smiled broadly, thanking me with his beaming face.

His Vietnamese–English dictionary was Thanh's constant companion; he repeatedly consulted it throughout the class. He often motioned me to write out words I said on the board so he could look them up in his dictionary. He asked for additional readings. He checked out films from the school library on the topics we were studying. In short, he intuitively knew what I should have been doing as his teacher, but wasn't.

By the end of the year Thanh was constructing and stringing together simple sentences, completing all homework as well as or better than his peers, and producing social studies projects that reflected not only his high academic ability but also his particular cultural perspectives on a number of issues. Although I learned much from Thanh about Vietnam that year, two things are clear to me as I reflect on my experience of that first year of teaching: that I certainly learned more from Thanh than he did from me, and that Thanh—and other English language learners like him—often learn in spite of teachers, not always because of them. I seemed to embody Clair's (1995) observation that, teachers are, by and large, "learning to educate these students on the job" (p. 194).

The story of Thanh is repeated countless times in U.S. classrooms every day. About 14 million children are either immigrants or the American-born children of immigrants. Demographic data show that this population—and in particular Hispanic immigrants—is the fastest-growing student population (Rumbaut & Portes, 2001; National Center for Education Statistics, 2008). But are we as social studies educators equipped to educate this special needs population? Given our experiences and conversations with teachers, the answer is a resounding "no." This book is an attempt to provide teachers with some of the tools necessary to be effective social studies teachers of the English language learner (ELL[1]) student.

Although Part 1 of this book was drafted by a language scholar, we come to this task as social studies educators. Thanh's story is but a striking example of our experiences in teaching social studies to ELLs. Between us, for example, we have taught Spanish-speaking adolescents in Miami, Tampa, and the San Francisco Bay area, ELLs from around the globe preparing for graduate schools in the United States, and Japanese teachers of English in Tokyo. One of us was an ELL in the mid-1960s, before much ELL support was provided in schools.

But we are not language specialists. This presents advantages and disadvantages. The obvious disadvantage, which we hope is somewhat compensated for by working with a language scholar, is our spotty knowledge of language acquisition. But we believe there is also a considerable advantage to having struggled to teach social studies to ELLs as we encountered many of the obstacles and opportunities we address in this book.

These encounters taught us some things, some of which we later learned were supported by research. For example, we learned to speak slowly, use simple words, avoid too many clauses in one sentence, make definite connections in a sequence of ideas, enunciate clearly, and say the same thing in more than one way. Wherever possible we used examples that might be culturally familiar to ELL students or asked them to provide related illustrations from their own cultures. Most of all, we tried to capitalize on language and cultural diversity in our classrooms to enrich the curriculum rather than regarding them as distractions. We most definitely rejected the "deficit" model of ELL education in the social studies. But our path to such insights was far from systematic.

It is with this perspective in mind that we approach Parts 2–4 of this book. We have tried to build a methods book for a targeted population—social studies educators who design and teach school programs for ELLs—that is rich in content. From what we can see, language educators for whom the particular subject matter frequently seems a secondary consideration write most of the guidance that exists for teaching ELLs. But social studies teachers' task is to engage students with a *particular* body of subject matter.

The learning activities we describe sample the kinds of topics actually taught in secondary school social studies curricula. Although we cannot possibly deliver a comprehensive treatment of the topics taught in social studies, we hope the activities on the topics we do treat can be transferred or adapted to other topics. That is, we hope that the learning activity on the concept of scale in Chapter 3.2 (Geography) might be suggestive for teaching other map concepts or that the activity in the same chapter on the relationships between climatic conditions and agricultural practices in India provides some clues for doing the same with the topic of sub-Saharan Africa.

In a sense, we hope the activities herein are like good recipes—not to be followed slavishly but to be adapted, flavored with what ingredients are available locally, the talents and time available to the chef, and to the tastes of the people who will eat it. The activities are, then, a point of departure and their utilization will be properly conditioned by any given teacher's (or curriculum developer's) available time, energy, imagination, and knowledge of the topic as well as the particular students to be taught.

Teachers and ELLs

The number of ELL students continues to grow both in terms of total numbers and as a percentage of the total student population in the United States. Whereas 41 percent of teachers report having had ELLs in their classrooms, estimates of how much ELL instruction those teachers have received range from just 13 percent to 30 percent (Menken & Antunez, 2001; National Center for Education Statistics, 2002; Ballantyne *et al.*, 2008). In a study of 25 popular preservice teacher education texts, Watson *et al.* (2005) discovered that less than 1 percent of the text included useable content related to the teaching of ELLs; in many cases, the topic of ELLs was not identified at all.

Meeting the needs of such students can be particularly challenging for social studies teachers given the often text-dependent nature of the content area. The language of the social sciences is often abstract and includes complex concepts calling for higher-order thinking skills. Additionally, many ELLs do not have a working knowledge of American culture that can serve as a schema for new social learning. As Cho and Reich (2008) point out, in comparison with other subject areas, "the content of social studies is particularly culturally embedded and incremental" (p. 238). Finally, unlike other content areas such as math and science, social studies classrooms have seldom been well equipped with manipulatives and hands-on instructional materials (Short, 1993).

Who Can Benefit from this Book?

Although there are excellent generic ELL books, they are often more appropriate for English to speakers of other languages (ESOL) teachers than for social studies teachers who have ELLs in their classrooms. This book focuses on the instructional issues inherent to social studies and is specifically useful for:

- *preservice social studies teachers* who want to become better prepared to meet the challenges of their future classrooms;
- *practicing social studies teachers* who would like a "refresher" or perhaps never received ELL training in their teacher preparation program;
- *ESOL aides and support staff* who would like to learn more about issues, strategies, and content related to social studies education;
- *social studies teacher educators* who would like to address ELL instruction in their methods courses;

- *ESOL teacher educators* who would like to infuse their methods courses with content-specific information and strategies;
- *exceptional student education teachers* who may have ELLs in their classroom or who may find language scaffolding approaches useful for their special needs students;
- *district curriculum supervisors* who are responsible for curriculum development, modification, and teacher training;
- *administrators* such as school principals, assistant principals, and subject area leaders who would like to improve the quality of instruction for ELLs in their schools and offer support for teachers.

How to Use this Book

The central purpose of this book is to provide social studies teachers with practical methods that should be effective not only with ELLs, but with all students. The book is aimed at grades 6–12 (middle and high school). It is organized to facilitate easy and quick location of key concepts and strategies. Additionally, we have included a glossary of the major terms associated with ESOL. You will note, too, that the Table of Contents is rather more detailed than is common and, therefore, we did not feel it would be useful to repeat all of this detail in the index.

Following this introduction, Part 1 of this book which was originally drafted by the language scholar Tony Erben, presents an overview of theory and research on English language teaching and learning. Part 1 reviews research with an eye to providing guidance for the design and teaching of school programs. In the first edition, Part 1 was almost entirely pitched at principles at a general level—that is, not at social studies in particular. In this revised edition, we have updated this part of the book and give more social studies examples to illustrate the general principles.

Part 2, which contains Chapters 2.1–2.4, forms a transition between the parts before and after. Chapter 2.1 lays out our sense of what a desirable instructional program in social studies looks like. Our intention is not to be comprehensive, but to suggest some salient themes and trust the reader to generalize. These themes are built on throughout Part 2, where we look at the limited base of social studies-focused ESOL research. We try to identify where this work parallels research treated in Part 1 as well as what appears to be specific about teaching social studies (versus mathematics, science, language arts, etc.). Part 2 has been considerably revised, reflecting that there is a good deal more research connecting ESOL and the social studies than when we prepared the first edition in 2007. This new research has served to confirm our already strong conviction that what matters most in education is the quality of instruction (Calderon *et al.*, 2011). The revisions in Part 2 also reflect some of the lessons learned while we worked on *Gateway to Social Studies,* a classroom social studies textbook specifically designed for middle school ELLs.

Part 3 contains chapters with illustrative learning activities in the main areas of the social studies curriculum. In this new edition, we have added a number of learning activities in the chapters. Many of these new activities were included to give greater attention to the earliest levels of English acquisition, preproduction and early production. Throughout Part 3, we adopt the same approach detailed in Part 2, such as an emphasis on active learning and conceptual understandings. Chapters 3.2 through 3.5 treat, respectively, the main areas of the secondary curriculum: geography, U.S. history, world history, and government and civics. Chapters 3.6 through 3.8 cover areas that are widely taught, although frequently only as electives rather than required—economics, sociology, anthropology, and psychology—as well as controversial issues that span across the social studies. Although it is tempting to just read the chapter that corresponds to the discipline you teach, you should also read other chapters, since many of the teaching strategies can be modified to other content areas. For example, in Chapter 3.7 (Anthropology, Sociology, and Psychology), the activity on archaeological artifacts could easily be a learning exercise in a World History course. Similarly the lesson on places where Native Americans lived in Chapter 3.2 (Geography) could readily be used in a United States or World History course.

The three sections in the Resources chapter provide direction to materials for teachers and ELL students. Although we identify methods articles, websites, curriculum materials, and the like throughout Part 3, the Resources chapter summarizes many of these as well as including additional sources.

Finally, this book is written in the spirit of experimentation. Readers looking for a tightly scripted set of methods may be disappointed. Rather, we agree with Nel Noddings (2006), when she warns against too much prescription of methods in teacher education and urges instead to "try things out, reflect, hypothesize, test, play with things" (p. 284). When we began working on this book, we now realize, we expected more from language scholars than we should have expected. Certainly they can be a great guide on language, but ultimately social studies educators must still answer the primary educational question for their own subject: What is worth teaching?

Part 1
Your English Language Learner

Tony Erben
University of Tampa

with

Bárbara C. Cruz
Stephen J. Thornton
University of South Florida

1.1
Orientation

English language learners (ELLs) represent the fastest-growing group at all levels of schooling in the United States. (We will use the term "English language learner" throughout the book, mostly because of its widespread use and acceptance, although the term "English learner" is increasingly being used.) The U.S. Census Bureau (2010a) reports that between the years of 1980 and 2007 the percentage of non-English language speakers in the United States increased by 140 percent. (Figure 1.1 shows the number of ELLs in the United States and Figure 1.2 shows the growth.) As a result, the number of ELLs in the nation's schools has more than doubled (National Clearinghouse for English Language Acquisition, 2006). In several states, including Texas, California, New Mexico, Florida, Arizona, North Carolina, and New York, the percentage of ELLs within school districts ranges anywhere between 10 and 50 percent of the school population. In sum, there are over 10 million ELLs in U.S. schools today. According to the U.S. Census Bureau (2010b), one out of five children aged 5 to 17 years old speaks a language other than English at home. Although many of these children and adolescents are heritage language learners (those exposed to a language other than English at home) and are proficient in English, many others are recent immigrants with barely a working knowledge of the language, let alone a command of academic English. Meeting their needs can be particularly challenging for all teachers given the often text-dependent nature of content areas. The language of the curriculum is often abstract and includes complex concepts requiring critical reading and thinking skills. Additionally, many ELLs do not have a working knowledge of American culture that is necessary for understanding key social studies concepts or that can serve as a schema for new learning.

But let's now look at these ELLs. Who are they and how do they come to be in our classrooms?

ELL or, sometimes, English learner, is the term used for any student in an American school setting whose native language is not English. Their English ability lies anywhere on a continuum from knowing only a few words to being able to get by using everyday English. But they still need to acquire academic English so that they can succeed educationally at school. All students enrolled in an American school, including ELLs, have the right to an equitable and quality education.

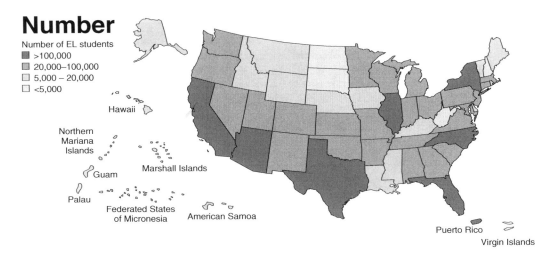

FIGURE 1.1. The number of English language (EL) learners in the United States.

Source: National Clearinghouse for English Language Acquisition, 2011.

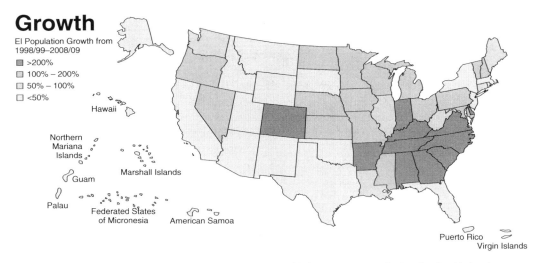

FIGURE 1.2. The growth of the English language (EL) learner population in the United States between 1998/1999 and 2008/2009.

Source: National Clearinghouse for English Language Acquisition, 2011.

Traditionally, many ELLs were placed in stand-alone English to speakers of other languages (ESOL) classes and learned English until they were deemed capable of following the regular curriculum in English in a mainstream classroom.

However, with the introduction of federal and state legislation such as the 2001 *No Child Left Behind Act*, Proposition 227 in California, and other English-only legislation in other states, many school systems started requiring that ELLs receive their English instruction through their curriculum content classes rather than through stand-alone ESOL classes.[1] This "mainstreaming" approach has become the most frequently used method of language instruction for ELL students in U.S. schools. Mainstreaming involves placing ELLs in content-area classrooms where the curriculum is delivered in English; typically, curricula and instruction are not modified in these classrooms for non-native English speakers (Carrasquillo & Rodriguez, 2002). According to Meltzer and Hamann (2005), placement of ELLs in mainstream classes occurs for a number of reasons, including assumptions by non-educators about what ELLs need, the scarcity of ESOL-trained teachers relative to demand, the growth of ELL populations, the dispersal of ELLs into more districts across the country, and restrictions in a growing number of states regarding the time ELLs can stay in ESOL programs. ELL specialists (e.g., Coady *et al.*, 2003) predict that, unless these conditions change, ELLs will spend their time in school with: (1) teachers inadequately trained to work with ELLs; (2) teachers who do not see meeting the needs of their ELLs as a priority; and (3) curricula and classroom practices that are not designed to target ELLs' needs. As we shall see, of all possible instructional options to help ELLs learn English, placing an ELL in a mainstreamed English-medium classroom where no accommodations are made by the teacher is the least effective approach. It may even be detrimental to the educational progress of ELLs.

But have the thousands of curriculum content teachers across the United States, who now hold the collective lion's share of responsibility in providing English language instruction to ELLs, had adequate preservice or in-service education for the task? Are they able to modify, adapt, and make the appropriate pedagogical accommodations within their lessons for this special group of students? Affirmative answers to these questions are essential if ELLs are to make academic progress commensurate with grade-level expectations. It is also important that teachers feel competent and effective in their professional duties.

The aim of Part 1 of this book is to provide an overview of the linguistic mechanics of second language development. Specifically, as teachers you will learn what to expect in the language abilities of ELLs as their proficiency in English develops over time. Although the rate of language development among ELLs depends on the particular instructional and social circumstances of each ELL, general patterns and expectations will be discussed. We will also outline the learning outcomes teachers might expect in what ELLs typically accomplish in differing ESOL programs as well as the importance of maintaining first language development. Because school systems differ across the United States in the ways in which they try to deal with ELL populations, we describe the pedagogical pros and cons of an array of ESOL programs. We also clarify terminology used in the field. In addition, Part 1 profiles various ELL populations that enter U.S. schools (e.g. refugees vs. migrants, special needs) and shares how teachers can make instruction more culturally responsive. Finally, we survey what teachers can expect from the cultural practices that ELLs bring to the classroom and ways in which both school systems and teachers can enhance home–school communication links.

1.2
The Process of English Language Learning and What to Expect

It is generally accepted that anybody who endeavors to learn a second language will go through specific stages of language development. According to some second language acquisition theorists (e.g., Krashen, 1981; Pienemann, 2007;), the way in which language is produced under natural time constraints is very regular and systematic. Pienemann's (1989, 2007) work has centered on one subsystem of language, namely morphosyntactic structures, that is, a given language's linguistic units such as words, parts of speech, or intonation. It gives us an interesting glimpse into how an ELL's language may progress (Table 1.1). Just as a baby needs to learn to crawl before it can walk, so too a second language learner will produce language structures only in a predetermined psychological order of complexity. What this means is that an ELL might utter "homework do" before being able to utter "tonight I homework do" before ultimately being able to produce a target-like structure such as "I will do my homework tonight." Of course, within terms of communicative effectiveness, the first example is as successful as the last example. The main difference is that one is less English-like than the other.

Researchers such as Pienemann (1989, 2007) and Krashen (1981) assert that there is an immutable language acquisition order and, regardless of what the teacher tries to teach to the ELL in terms of English skills, the learner will acquire new language structures only when he or she is cognitively and psychologically ready to do so. Even still, teachers can very much affect the *rate of language development and acquisition* by providing what is known as an "acquisition-rich" classroom. Ellis (2005), among others, provides useful research generalizations that constitute a broad basis for "evidence-based practice." Rather than repeat them verbatim, here we synthesize them into *five principles for creating effective second language learning environments.* They are presented and summarized below.

TABLE 1.1 Generalized patterns of ESOL development stages

Stage	Main features	Example
1	Single words; formulas	My name is _____. How are you?
2	Subject–verb object word order; plural marking	I see school I buy books
3	"Do"-fronting; adverb preposing; negation + verb	Do you understand me? Yesterday I go to school. She no coming today.
4	Pseudo-inversion; yes/no inversion; verb + to + verb	Where is my purse? Have you a car? I want to go.
5	3rd person –s; do-2nd position	He works in a factory. He did not understand.
6	Question-tag; adverb–verb phrase	He's Polish, isn't he? I can always go.

Source: Pienemann (1988).
ESOL, English to speakers of other languages.

Principle 1: Give ELLs Many Opportunities to Read, to Write, to Listen to, and to Discuss Oral and Written English Texts Expressed in a Variety of Ways

Camilla had only recently arrived at the school. She was a good student and was making steady progress. She had learned some English in Argentina and used every opportunity to learn new words at school. Just before Thanksgiving her civics teacher commenced a new unit of work on the executive branch of the federal government. During the introductory lesson, the teacher projected a photo of the president sitting to the right of his advisory cabinet on the whiteboard. She began questioning the students about the members of the executive branch. One of her first questions was directed to Camilla. The teacher asked, "Camilla, tell me what you see on the right hand side of the cabinet." Camilla answered, "I see books and pencils."

Of course the teacher was referring not to the cabinet which is next to the whiteboard, but to the cabinet projected on to the whiteboard. Though a simple mistake, the example above is illustrative of the fact that Camilla has yet to develop academic literacy.

Meltzer (2001) defined academic literacy as the ability of a person to "use reading, writing, speaking, listening and thinking to learn what they want/need to learn AND [to] communicate/ demonstrate that learning to others who need/want to know" (p. 16). The definition is useful in that it rejects literacy as something static and implies agency on the part of a learner who develops an ability to successfully put his or her knowledge and skills to use in new situations. Proficiency in academic literacy requires knowledge of a type of language used predominantly in classrooms without which students may fail to learn the content of a lesson. As illustrated in the classroom vignette above, understanding multiple-meaning words, as they relate to a given content area, is crucial for learning the academic content. It is extremely important for ELLs to attain academic literacy, and content teachers should provide explicit instruction in it (Hakuta, 2011).

Currently, there is much research to suggest that both the discussion of texts and the production of texts are important practices in the development of content-area literacy and learning. For ELLs this means that opportunities to create, discuss, share, revise, and edit a variety of texts will help them develop content-area understanding as well as recognition and familiarity with the types of texts found in particular content areas (Boscolo & Mason, 2001). Classroom practices that are found to improve academic literacy development include teachers improving reading comprehension through modeling, explicit strategy instruction in context, spending more time giving reading and writing instruction as well as having students spend more time with reading and writing assignments, providing more time for ELLs to talk explicitly about texts as they are trying to process and/or create them, and helping to develop critical thinking skills as well as being responsive to individual learner needs (Meltzer & Hamann, 2005).

The importance of classroom talk in conjunction with learning from and creating texts cannot be overestimated in the development of academic literacy in ELLs. In the case of Camilla above, rather than smiling at the error and moving on with the lesson, the teacher could have further developed Camilla's vocabulary knowledge by taking a two-minute digression from the lesson to discuss with the class some other examples of words they will encounter at school, such as *right* and *rule,* and how their everyday meaning and academic meanings differ.

Principle 2: Draw Attention to Patterns of English Language Structure

In order to ride a bike well, a child needs to actually practice riding the bike. Sometimes, training wheels are fitted to the back of the bike to help the younger child maintain balance. The training wheels are taken away as the child gains more confidence. As this process unfolds, parents also teach kids the rules of the road: how to read road signs, to be attentive to cars, to ride defensively. Although knowing the rules of the road won't help a child learn to ride the bike better in a physical sense, it will help the child avoid being involved in a road accident. Knowing the rules of the road—when and where to ride a bike—will make the child a more accomplished bike rider. Why use this example? Well, it is a good metaphor to explain that language learning needs to unfold in the same way. An ELL, without much formal schooling, will develop the means to communicate in English. However, it will most likely be only very basic English. Unfortunately, tens of thousands of adult ELLs across this country never progress past this stage. School-age ELLs have an opportunity to move beyond a basic command of English—to become accomplished communicators in English. However, this won't happen on its own. To do so requires the ELL to get actively involved in classroom activities, ones in which an ELL is required to practice speaking.

As mentioned above, early research into naturalistic second language acquisition has shown that learners follow a "natural" order and sequence of acquisition. What this means is that grammatical structures emerge in the communicative utterances of second language learners in a relatively fixed, regular, systematic, and universal order. Teachers can take advantage of this "built-in syllabus" by implementing an activity-centered approach in which ELLs are provided with language-rich instructional opportunities. They should also have explicit exposure and instruction related to language structures that they are trying to utter but with which they still have trouble.

Principle 3: Give ELLs Classroom Time to Use Their English Productively

A theoretical approach within the field of second language acquisition, called the interaction hypothesis, was developed primarily by Long (1996, 2006). From this perspective, acquisition is facilitated through interaction when second language learners are engaged in negotiating for meaning. That is, when ELLs are engaged in talk they make communication modifications that help language become more comprehensible and they more readily solicit corrective feedback, leading them to adjust their own use of English.

The discrepancy in the rate of acquisition shown by ELLs can be attributed to the amount and the quality of input they receive as well as the opportunities they have for output. Output means having opportunities to use language. Second language acquisition researchers agree that the opportunity for output plays an important part in facilitating second language development. Skehan (1998), drawing on Swain (1995), summarizes the benefits to ELLs' output from using language with others. ELLs will: (1) obtain a richer language contribution from those around them; (2) be forced to pay attention to the structure of language they listen to; (3) be able to test out their language assumptions and confirm them through the types of language input they receive; (4) better internalize their current language knowledge; (5) by engaging in interaction, work towards better discourse fluency; and (6) be able to find space to develop their own linguistic style and voice.

Teachers should plan for and incorporate ELLs in all language activities in the classroom. Of course an ELL will engage with an activity based on the level of proficiency he or she has at any given time, which the teacher should take into account when planning for instruction. Under no circumstances should ELLs be left at the "back of the classroom" to linguistically or pedagogically fend for themselves.

Principle 4: Give ELLs Opportunities to Notice Their Errors and to Correct Their English

Throughout the day, teachers prepare activities for students that have the sole intent of getting them to learn subject matter. Less often do teachers think about the language learning potential that the same activity may generate. This can be applied to ELLs: teachers encourage them to notice their errors, to reflect on how they use English, and to think about how English works, which plays a very important role in their language development. In a series of seminal studies, Lyster and his colleagues (Lyster, 1998, 2001, 2004, 2007; Lyster & Ranta, 1997; Lyster & Mori, 2006) outline six feedback moves that teachers can use to direct ELLs' attention to their language output and in doing so help them correct their English.

Example 1: Explicit Correction

Student: "The heart hits blood to se body. . ."
Teacher: "The heart pumps blood to the body."

In the above example, an ELL's utterance is incorrect, and the teacher provides the correct form. Often teachers gloss over explicitly correcting an ELL's language for fear of singling out the student in class. However, *explicit correction* is a very easy way to help ELLs notice the way they use language.

Example 2: Requesting Clarification

Student: "I can experimenting with Bunsen burner."
Teacher: "What? Can you say that again?"

By using phrases such as "Excuse me?", "I don't understand," or "Can you repeat that?", the teacher shows that the communication has not been understood or that the ELL's utterance contained some kind of error. *Requesting clarification* indicates to the ELL that a repetition or reformulation of the utterance is required.

Example 3: Recasting

Student: "After today I go to sport."
Teacher: "So, tomorrow you are going to play sports?"
Student: "Yes, tomorrow I am going to play sport."

Without directly showing that the student's utterance was incorrect, the teacher implicitly *recasts* the ELL's error, or provides the correction.

Example 4: Providing Metalinguistic Cues

Teacher: "Is that how it is said?" or "Is that English?" or "Does that sound right to you?"
Without providing the correct form, the teacher provides a *metalinguistic clue*. This may take the form of asking a question or making a comment related to the formation of the ELL's utterance.

Example 5: Eliciting

Teacher: "So, then it will be a . . ." (with long stress on "a")

The teacher directly gets the correct form from the ELL by pausing to allow the student to complete the teacher's utterance. *Elicitation* questions differ from questions that are defined as metalinguistic clues in that they require more than a yes/no response.

Example 6: Repetition

Student: "The two boy go to town tomorrow."
Teacher: "The two boys go to town tomorrow." (with teacher making a prolonged stress on "boy")
Repetitions are probably one of the most frequent forms of error correction carried out by teachers. Here a teacher repeats the ELL's error and adjusts intonation to draw an ELL's attention to it.

Using these corrective feedback strategies helps to raise an ELL's awareness and understanding of language conventions used in and across content areas.

Principle 5: Construct Activities that Maximize Opportunities for ELLs to Interact with Others in English

One day, when we had visitors from up north, our daughter came home very excited and said that the teacher had announced that her class would soon start learning Spanish. Our friend, ever the pessimist, said, "I learned Spanish for four years in high school, and look at me now, I can't even string a sentence together in Spanish." What comes to mind is the old saying, "use it or lose it." Of course, my friend and I remember our foreign language learning days being spent listening to the teacher, usually in English. We were lucky if we even got the chance to say anything in Spanish. Since we never used Spanish in class (or outside school), our hopes of retaining any Spanish diminished with each passing year since graduation. My daughter's 20-year-old brother, on the other hand, had the same Spanish teacher that my daughter will have. He remembers a lot of his Spanish, but also that his Spanish classes were very engaging. A lesson would never pass in which he didn't speak, listen to, read, and write in Spanish. He was always involved in some learning activity and he always expressed how great it was to converse during the class with his friends in Spanish by way of the activities that the teacher had planned.

These observations can apply to ELLs as well. In order for ELLs to progress with their English language development, a teacher needs to vary the types of instructional tasks that the ELL will engage in. Student involvement during instruction is the key to academic success whereas constant passive learning, mostly through traditional lecture-driven lessons, can impede any language learning efforts by an ELL.

Our five principles provide a framework with which to construct a curriculum that is sensitive to the language developmental needs of ELLs. However, to further solidify our understanding of an ELL's language progress, it is necessary to have a clear picture of what ELLs can do with their language at different levels of proficiency and its implications for instruction. Although several taxonomies exist that seek to categorize the developmental stages of second language learners, many education systems throughout the United States have adopted a four-tier description. The four stages are called preproduction, early production, speech emergence, and intermediate fluency (Krashen & Terrell, 1983). Table 3.1 on page 77 summarizes each level.

Constructing a Curriculum with Language Needs in Mind

The *preproduction* stage applies to ELLs who are unfamiliar with English. They may have had anything from one day to three months of exposure to English. ELLs at this level are trying to absorb the language, and they can find this process overwhelming. In a school context, they are often linguistically overloaded, and get tired quickly because of the need for constant and intense concentration. An ELL's language skills are at the receptive level, and he or she enters a "silent period" of listening. ELLs at this stage are able to comprehend more English than they can produce (if you have ever tried to learn a new language, you have probably experienced this phenomenon yourself). Their attention is focused on developing everyday social English. At the preproduction stage, an ELL can engage in nonverbal responses; follow simple commands; point and respond with movement; and utter simple formulaic structures in English such as "yes," "no," "thank you," or use names. ELLs may develop a receptive vocabulary of up to 500 words.

By the time ELLs enter the *early production* stage, they will have had many opportunities to encounter meaningful and comprehensible English. They will begin to respond with one- or two-word answers or short utterances. ELLs may now have internalized up to 1,000 words in their receptive vocabulary and anything from 100 to 500 words in their active vocabulary. In order for ELLs to begin to speak, teachers should create a low-anxiety environment in their classrooms. At this stage, ELLs are experimenting and taking risks with English. Errors in grammar and pronunciation are to be expected. Pragmatic errors are also common. Teachers need to model or demonstrate with correct language responses in context. Redundancies, repetitions, circumlocutions, and language enhancement strategies are important for teachers to use when interacting with ELLs at this level (see Table 3.1 on page 77).

At the *speech emergence* stage, an ELL will begin to use the language to interact more freely. At this stage, ELLs have a 7,000-word receptive vocabulary. They may have an active vocabulary of up to 2,000 words. By this time, ELLs may have had between one and three years' exposure to English. It is possible that they have a receptive understanding of academic English; however, in order to make content-area subject matter comprehensible, teachers are advised to make great use of advance organizers. Teachers should make explicit attempts to modify the delivery of subject matter, to model language use, and to teach metacognitive strategies in order to help ELLs predict, describe, demonstrate, and problem solve. Because awareness of English is growing, it is also important for teachers to provide ELLs at this stage with opportunities to work in structured small groups so that they can reflect and experiment with their language output.

At the stage of *intermediate fluency*, ELLs may demonstrate near-native or native-like fluency in everyday social English, but not in academic English. Often teachers become acutely aware that, even though an ELL can speak English fluently in social settings (e.g., the playground, at sport functions), the ELL will experience difficulties in understanding and verbalizing cognitively demanding, abstract concepts taught and discussed in the classroom. At this stage ELLs may have developed up to a 12,000-word receptive vocabulary and a 4,000-word active vocabulary. Teachers of ELLs at the intermediate fluency level need to proactively provide relevant content-based literacy experiences such as brainstorming, clustering, synthesizing, categorizing, charting, evaluating, journaling, or log writing, including essay writing and peer critiquing, in order to foster academic proficiency in English.

At the University of South Florida, we have developed online ELL databases that have been created to provide pre- and in-service teachers with annotated audio and video samples of language use by ELLs who are at each of the four different levels of language proficiency. The video and audio files act as instructional tools that allow teachers to familiarize themselves with the language ability (speaking, reading, and writing) of ELLs who are at different stages of development. For example, teachers may have ELLs in classes and not be sure of their level of English language development, nor be sure what to expect the ELL to be able to do with English in terms of production and comprehension. This naturally affects how a teacher may plan for instruction. By looking through the databases, a teacher can listen to and watch representations of ELL language production abilities at all four levels (preproduction, early production, speech emergence, and intermediate fluency). In addition, the databases feature interviews with expert ESOL teachers, examples of tests used to evaluate the proficiency levels of ELLs, and selected readings and lesson plans written for ELLs at different levels of proficiency. Lastly, they provide case studies that troubleshoot pedagogical problem areas when teaching ELLs.

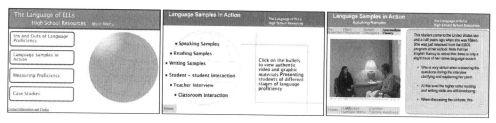

FIGURE 1.3. Three databases.

There are three databases: one that features ELLs at the elementary school level, one featuring ELLs at the middle school level, and one featuring ELLs at the high school level.

The three ELL databases can be found at:

- http://esol.coedu.usf.edu/elementary/index.htm (elementary school language samples);
- http://esol.coedu.usf.edu/middleschool/index.htm (middle school language samples);
- http://esol.coedu.usf.edu/highschool/index.htm (high school language samples).

It is important to remember that a lack of language ability does not mean a lack of concept development or a lack of ability to learn. Teachers should continue to ask inferential and higher-order questions (questions requiring reasoning ability, hypothesizing, inferring, analyzing, justifying, and predicting) that challenge an ELL to think. However, the phrasing of such questions needs to be suitably modified as will be discussed.

Teaching Tip

- For two good websites that outline ways to enhance questioning using Bloom's taxonomy, see http://www.ascd.org/publications/educational-leadership/summer08/vol65/num09/Asking-Good-Questions.aspx and www.nwlink.com/~donclark/hrd/bloom.html (Clark, 1999). The latter gives a further detailed breakdown of Bloom's learning domains in terms of cognitive, affective, and psychomotor key words and how these can be used to foster an ELL's language learning.

Zehler (1994) provides a list of further strategies that teachers can use to engage ELLs at every stage. These include:

- asking questions that require new or extended responses;
- creating opportunities for sustained dialogue and substantive language use;
- providing opportunities for language use in multiple settings;
- restating complex sentences as a sequence of simple sentences;
- avoiding or explaining use of idiomatic expressions;
- restating at a slower rate when needed, but making sure that the pace is not so slow that normal intonation and stress patterns become distorted;

- pausing often to allow students to process what they hear;
- providing specific explanations of key words and special or technical vocabulary, using examples and non-linguistic props when possible;
- using everyday language;
- providing explanations for the indirect use of language (for example, an ELL student may understand the statement, "I like the way Mary is sitting" merely as a simple statement rather than as a reference to an example of good behavior).

1.3
Deciding on the Best ESOL Program

This section outlines the learning outcomes that ELLs typically accomplish in differing ESOL programs and the importance of the maintenance of first language development. Although school systems differ across the United States in the ways in which they try to deal with ELL populations, this chapter describes the pedagogical pros and cons of an array of ESOL programs and clarifies terminology used in the field.

There are several factors that influence the design of an effective ELL program. These include the ELL student demographics to be served, district resources, and individual student characteristics. The MLA Language Map at www.mla.org/map_main provides an interactive look into the distribution of languages spoken in the United States. The online maps are able to show numbers as well as percentages by state, district, and zip code. Over 30 languages may be geographically represented and compared. The MLA Language Map shows graphically that not all districts are the same. ELL populations differ across the country. Some areas may have an overwhelming majority of Spanish-speaking ELLs whereas other districts may have an equally large numbers of ELL students but speaking 50–100 different languages. On the other hand, some districts may have very few ELLs while other districts experience an influx of ELLs of whose language and culture the area's schools have little knowledge (for example, Hmong in Marathon County in Wisconsin, Haitian Creole in Palm Beach, Broward, and Dade counties in Florida, and Somali/Ethiopian in Hennepin and Ramsey counties in Minnesota). Cultural and linguistic differences, as well as factors such as size, age, and mobility of community members, very much influence the types of ESOL instructional programs that school districts choose to develop. Refer to *English Language Learner Programs at the Secondary Level in Relation to Student Performance* (http://www.eric.ed.gov) for a wonderful research-based yet easy-to-read outline of how the implementation of different ELL programs in schools affects the language learning gains of ELLs. In this Routledge series, you can also find descriptions of successful programs around the nation (see the volumes on Language Arts, Science, Mathematics, Career and Technical Education, and the Arts).

As noted, not all ELLs are the same. ELLs may enter a school with vastly different educational backgrounds. Some enter U.S. schools with a strong foundational knowledge in their first language. This means that they may have had schooling in their first language, have literacy skills in their first language, and/or have developed social everyday language competency as well as academic proficiency in their first language. Other ELLs may have had less or even no academic schooling in their first language. Many ELLs, especially refugees, may have attended school in their homeland only for it to have been interrupted by, for example, famine or war or persecution for political or religious reasons. Some ELLs arrive in the United States with their families at a very young age and, although they speak their first language at home, they may have never developed reading or writing proficiency in it. As will be discussed in the next chapter, it is of great importance to uncover the nature of an ELL's first language development since this has a profound bearing on how an ELL manages to acquire English.

Another factor that influences program design, according to the Center for Applied Linguistics (www.cal.org), is the resources that a district has at its disposal. Some districts may have a cadre of qualified ESOL specialists working in schools, whereas other districts may only be able to use paraprofessionals and yet others draw on the surrounding community for help. Based on these constraints, one can classify different ESOL programs into what Baker (2001) terms strong and weak forms of bilingual education. Table 1.2 provides an overview of the merits of the many types of ESOL programs operating across the United States.

According to Gold (2006), "there is no widely accepted definition of a bilingual school in published research in this country" (p. 37). As a rule of thumb, they are widely understood to be schools that promote bilingualism and literacy in two or more languages as goals for students (Baker, 2001; Crawford, 2004).

TABLE 1.2 Types of ESOL programs in the United States

Type of program	Target ELLs and expectations	Program description	What research says
Submersion	All ELLs regardless of proficiency level or length of time since arrival. No accommodations are made. The goal is to reach full English proficiency and assimilation	ELLs remain in their home classroom and learn with native speakers of English. The teacher makes no modifications or accommodations for the ELL in terms of the curriculum content or in teaching English	States such as Florida have in the past faced potential litigation because of not training teachers to work with ELLs or modifying curriculum and/or establishing ELL programs. In order to avoid submersion models, Florida has established specific ELL instructional guidelines (Consent Decree, 1990)
ESL class period	As above, though usually in school districts with higher concentrations of ELLs	Groups ELLs together, to teach English skills and instruct them in a manner similar to that used in foreign language classes. The focus is primarily linguistic and ELLs visit these classes typically 2 or 3 times per week	This model does not necessarily help ELLs with academic content. The effect is that these programs can tend to create "ESL ghettos." Being placed in such programs can preclude ELLs from gaining college entrance-applicable credits (Diaz-Rico & Weed, 2006)

TABLE 1.2 Continued

Type of program	Target ELLs and expectations	Program description	What research says
ESL-plus (sometimes called submersion with primary language)	ELLs who are usually at speech emergence and/or intermediate fluency stage. The aim is to hasten ELLs' ability to integrate and follow content classroom instruction	Includes instruction in English (similar to ESL class period and pull-out) but generally goes beyond the language to focus on content area instruction. This may be given in the ELL's native language or in English. Often these programs may incorporate the ELL for the majority or all of the school day	According to Ovando & Collier (1998), the most effective ESL-plus and content-based ESL instruction is where the ESL teacher collaborates closely with the content teacher
Content-based ESL	As above	ELLs are still separated from mainstream content classes, but content is organized around an academic curriculum with grade-level objectives. There is no explicit English instruction	See above
Pull-out ESL	Early arrival ELLs. Usually in school districts with limited resources. Achieving proficiency in English fast is a priority so that the ELL can follow the regular curriculum	ELLs leave their home room for specific instruction in English: grammar, vocabulary, spelling, oral communication, etc. ELLs are not taught the curriculum when they are removed from their classrooms, which may be anything from 30 minutes to 1 hour every day	This model has been the most implemented though the least effective program for the instruction of ELLs (Collier & Thomas, 1997)
Sheltered instruction or SDAIE (specifically designed academic instruction in English). Sometimes called structured immersion	Targets all ELLs regardless of proficiency level or age. ELLs remain in their classrooms	This is an approach used in multilinguistic classrooms to provide principled language support to ELLs while they are learning content. Has same curriculum objectives as mainstream classroom in addition to specific language and learning strategy objectives	ELLs are able to improve their English language skills while learning content. Exposure to higher-level language through content materials and explicit focus on language fosters successful language acquisition (Brinton, 2003)

TABLE 1.2 Continued

Type of program	Target ELLs and expectations	Program description	What research says
Transitional bilingual	Usually present in communities with a single large ELL population. Geared towards grades K–3. Initial instruction in home language and then switching to English by grade 2 or 3	ELLs enter school in kindergarten and the medium of instruction is in the home language. The reasoning behind this is to allow the ELL to develop full proficiency in the home language so that the benefits of this solid linguistic foundation may transfer over to and aid in the acquisition of English. Intended to move ELL students along relatively quickly (2–3 years)	Of all forms of traditional bilingual programs, the transitional model entails the least benefit to ELLs in terms of maintaining and building CALP in their home language
Maintenance bilingual	As above, but the ELL continues to receive language and content instruction in the home language along with English	As above, but are geared to the more gradual mastering of English and native language skills (5–7 years)	ELLs compare favorably on state standardized tests when measured against achievement grades of ELLs in transitional bilingual programs or ESL pull-out, ESL class period and ESL-plus programs (Hakuta *et al.*, 2000)
Dual language/ two-way immersion	This model targets native speakers of English as well as native speakers of other languages, depending which group predominates in the community	The aim of this program is for both English native speakers and ELLs to maintain their home language as well as acquire another language. Curriculum is delivered in English as well as in the ELL's language. Instructional time is usually split between the two languages, depending on the subject area and the expertise of the teachers	Dual language programs have shown the most promise in terms of first and second language proficiency attainment. Research results from standardized assessments across the United States indicated that ELLs can outperform monolingual English children in English literacy, mathematics, and other content curriculum areas. Has also many positive social and individual affective benefits for the ELL (Genesee, 1999)

TABLE 1.2 Continued

Type of program	Target ELLs and expectations	Program description	What research says
Heritage language	Targets communities with high native population numbers, e.g. Hawaii, Native Americans in New Mexico. Community heritage language maintenance is the goal	In heritage language programs, the aim can be to help revitalize the language of a community. Sometimes English is offered as the medium of instruction in only a few courses. Usually the majority of the curriculum is delivered in the home language	Language diversity can be seen as a problem, as a right, or as a resource. Heritage language programs are operationalized through local, state, and federal language policies as emancipatory (Cummins, 2001)

ESOL, English to speakers of other languages; ELLs, English language learners; ESL, English as a second language; CALP, cognitive/academic language proficiency.

1.4
Teaching for English Language Development

This section explains the practical implications of research on bilingualism for classroom teachers as it relates to a context where many ELLs are learning English as their second, third, or even fourth language. One key objective of this section is to help teachers understand how they can positively and purposefully mediate an ELL's language development in English.

A very prevalent conception of academic English that has been advanced and refined over the years is based on the work of Jim Cummins (1979, 1980, 1986, 1992, 2001). Cummins analyzed the characteristics of children growing up in two language environments. He found that the level of language proficiency attained in both languages, regardless of what they may be, has an enormous influence on and implications for an ELL's educational success. One situation that teachers often discover about their ELLs is that they arrived in the United States at an early age or were born in the United States but did not learn English until starting school. Once they begin attending school, their chances for developing their home language are limited, and this home language is eventually superseded by English. This phenomenon is often referred to as limited bilingualism or subtractive bilingualism. Very often ELLs in this situation do not develop high levels of proficiency in either language. Cummins has found that ELLs with limited bilingual ability are overwhelmingly disadvantaged cognitively and academically from this linguistic condition. However, ELLs who develop language proficiency in at least one of the two languages derive neither benefit nor detriment. Only in ELLs who are able to develop high levels of proficiency in both languages did Cummins find positive cognitive outcomes.

The upshot of this line of research on bilingualism seems counterintuitive for the lay person, but it does conclusively show that, rather than only providing ELLs with more English instruction, it is also important to provide ELLs with instruction in their home language. By reaching higher levels of proficiency in their first language, an ELL will be able to transfer the cognitive benefits to learn English more effectively.

Of course, it is not always feasible to provide instruction in an ELL's home language, so it behooves all teachers to be cognizant of the types of language development processes that ELLs undergo. Cummins (1981) also posited two different types of English language skills. These he called BICS and CALP. The former, basic interpersonal communication skills (BICS), correspond to the social, everyday language and skills that an ELL develops. BICS is very much context-embedded in that it is always used in situations that have real-world connections for the ELL, for example in the playground, at home, shopping, playing sports, and interacting with friends. Cognitive academic language proficiency (CALP), by contrast, differs from BICS in that it is abstract, decontextualized, and scholarly in nature. This is the type of language required to succeed at school or in a professional setting. CALP, however, is the type of language that most ELLs have the hardest time mastering exactly because it is not everyday language.

Even after being in the United States for years, ELLs may appear fluent in English but still have significant gaps in their CALP. Teachers can be fooled by this phenomenon. What is needed is for teachers in all content areas to pay particular attention to an ELL's development in the subject-specific language of a school discipline. Many researchers (Hakuta *et al.*, 2000; Hakuta, 2011) agree that an ELL may easily achieve native-like conversational proficiency within two years, but it may take anywhere between five and ten years for an ELL to reach native-like proficiency in CALP.

Since Cummins's groundbreaking research, there has been a lot of work carried out in the area of academic literacy. An alternative view of what constitutes literacy is provided by Valdez (2000), who supports the notion of *multiple literacies*. Scholars holding this perspective suggest that efforts to teach academic language to ELLs are counterproductive since it comprises multiple dynamic and ever-evolving literacies. In their view, school systems should accept multiple ways of communicating and not marginalize students when they use a variety of English that is not accepted in academic contexts (Zamel & Spack, 1998).

However, one very important fact remains. In order to be successful in a school, all students need to become proficient in academic literacy.

Another view is one that sees academic literacy as a dynamic interrelated process (Scarcella, 2003), one in which cultural, social, and psychological factors play equally important roles. Scarcella provides a description of academic English that includes a phonological, lexical (vocabulary), grammatical (syntax, morphology), sociolinguistic, and discourse (rhetorical) component.

Regardless of how one defines academic literacy, many have criticized teacher education programs for failing to train content-area teachers to recognize the language specificity of their own discipline and thus being unable to help their students recognize it and adequately acquire proficiency in it (Bailey *et al.*, 2002; Kern, 2000).

Ragan (2005) provides a simple framework to help teachers better understand the academic language of their content area. He proposes that teachers ask themselves three questions:

- What do you expect ELLs to know after reading a text?
- What language in the text may be difficult for ELLs to understand?
- What specific academic language should be taught?

Another very useful instructional heuristic to consider when creating materials to help ELLs acquire academic literacy was developed by Cummins and is called Cummins' Quadrants. In the Quadrants, Cummins (2001) successfully aligns the pedagogical imperative with an ELL's linguistic requirements. The four quadrants represent a sequence of instructional choices that teachers can make based on the degree of contextual support given to an ELL and the degree of cognitive demand placed on an ELL during any given instructional activity. The resulting quadrants are illustrated in Table 1.3.

TABLE 1.3 Cummins' Quadrants

Quadrant I High context embeddedness Low cognitive demand (easiest) *Examples*: Copying from the board Selecting food in lunchroom Face-to-face conversation with friend	Quadrant III High context embeddedness High cognitive demand *Examples*: Following a class schedule Chatting on the phone with friend Oral presentation
Quadrant II Low context embeddedness Low cognitive demand *Examples*: Analyzing a photo Reading a map Interpreting a chart Demonstrations Object-based learning	Quadrant IV Low context embeddedness High cognitive demand (most difficult) *Examples*: Standardized test Listening to a lecture Phone conversation with a government agency Reading class textbook

Quadrant I corresponds to pedagogic activities that require an ELL to use language that is easy to acquire. This may involve everyday social English and strategies that have a high degree of contextual support (i.e., lots of scaffolding, visual clues and manipulatives to aid understanding, language redundancies, repetitions, and reinforcements) or this may include experiential learning techniques, task-based learning, and already familiarized computer programs. Activities in this quadrant also have a low degree of cognitive demand (i.e., are context-embedded). In other words, they are centered on topics that are familiar to the ELL or that the ELL has already mastered and do not require abstract thought in and of themselves.

Quadrant IV corresponds to pedagogic activities that require the ELL to use language that is highly decontextualized, abstract, subject-specific, and/or technical/specialized. Examples of these include lectures, subject-specific texts, and how-to manuals. The topics within this quadrant may be unfamiliar to the ELL and impose a greater cognitive demand on the ELL. Academic language associated with Quadrant IV is difficult for ELLs to internalize because it is usually supported by a very low ratio of context-embedded clues to meaning (low contextual support). At the same time, it is often centered on difficult topics that require abstract thought (high cognitive demand). It is important for the teacher to elaborate language, as well as provide opportunities for the ELL to reflect on, talk through, discuss, and engage with decontextualized oral or written texts. By doing this the teacher provides linguistic scaffolds for the ELL to grasp academically.

Quadrants II and III are pedagogic "go-between" categories. In Quadrant II, the amount of context embeddedness is lessened, and so related development increases the complexity of the language while maintaining a focus on topics that are easy and familiar for the ELL. In Quadrant III, language is again made easier through the escalation of the level of context embeddedness to support and facilitate comprehension. However, Quadrant III instruction allows the teacher to introduce more difficult content-area topics.

When a teacher develops lesson plans and activities that are situated within the framework of Quadrant I and II, the ELL engages in work that is not usually overwhelming. In low-anxiety classrooms, ELLs feel more comfortable to experiment with the language to learn more content. As an ELL moves from level 1 of English language development (preproduction) to level 3 (speech emergence), a teacher may feel that the time is right to progress to creating lesson plans and activities that fit pedagogically into Quadrants III and IV. A gradual progression to Quadrant III reinforces language learning and promotes comprehension of academic content. According to Collier (1995, p. 35):

> A major problem arising from the failure of educators to understand the implications of these continuums is that ELLs are frequently moved from ESOL classrooms and activities represented by Quadrant I to classrooms represented by Quadrant IV, with little opportunity for transitional language experiences characterized by Quadrants II and III. Such a move may well set the stage for school failure. By attending to both language dimensions (level of contextual support and degree of cognitive demand) and planning accordingly, schools and teachers can provide more effective instruction and sounder assistance to second-language learners.

Further, the degree of cognitive demand for any given activity will differ for each ELL, depending on the ELL's prior knowledge of the topic.

1.5
Not All ELLs Are the Same

The United States continues to be enriched by immigrants from countries the world over. Many cities have ethnic enclaves of language minority and immigrant groups and these populations are reflected in school classrooms. This section outlines the background characteristics of ELLs that teachers need to be aware of when planning or delivering instruction. Certainly, ELLs bring their own strengths to the task of learning but they also face many challenges. Equally, these diverse backgrounds impact classroom practices culturally in terms of how ELLs behave in classrooms, how they come to understand curriculum content, and how their interactions with others are affected (Zehler, 1994). The following affords a glimpse of their diversity.

María is seven years old and is a well-adjusted girl in second grade. She was born in Colombia, but came to the United States when she was four. Spanish is the medium of communication at home. When she entered kindergarten, she knew only a smattering of English. By grade 2 she had developed good BICS. These are the language skills needed to get by in social situations. María sounded proficient in English; she had the day-to-day communication skills to interact socially with other people on the playground, in the lunchroom, and on the school bus. Of course, all these situations are very much context-embedded and not cognitively demanding. In the classroom, however, María had problems with her cognitive academic language proficiency (CALP). This included speaking, reading, and writing about subject-area content material. It was obvious to her teacher that Maria needed extra time and support to become proficient in academic areas but, because she had come to the United States as a four-year-old and had already been three years in the school, she was not eligible for direct ESOL support. Collier and Thomas (1997) have shown that, if young ELLs have no prior schooling or have no support in native language development, it may take seven to ten years for them to catch up to their peers.

Ismael Abudullahi Adan is from Somalia. He is 13 and was resettled in Florida as a refugee through the Office of the United Nations High Commissioner for Refugees (UNHCR; see www.unhcr.org). As is the case with all refugees in the USA, Ismael's family was matched with an American resettlement organization (see www.refugees.org). No one in his family knew any English. They were subsistence farmers in Somalia and, because of the civil war in Somalia, Ismael had never attended school. The resettlement organization helped the family find a place to live, but financial aid was forthcoming for only six months. While all members of the family were suffering degrees of war-related trauma, culture shock, and emotional upheaval, as well as the stress and anxiety of forced migration, Ismael had to attend the local school. Everything was foreign to him. He had no idea how to act as a student and all the rules of the school made no sense to him. All Ismael wanted to do was work and help his family financially; he knew that at the end of six months financial aid from the government would stop and he worried about how his family was going to feed itself. He is currently placed in a sheltered English instruction class at school.

José came to the United States from Honduras with his parents two years ago. He is now 14. His parents work as farm laborers and throughout the year move interstate depending where crops are being harvested. This usually involves spending the beginning of the calendar year in Florida for strawberry picking, late spring in Georgia for the peach harvest, early fall in North Carolina for the cotton harvest, and then late fall in Illinois for the pumpkin harvest. When the family first came to the United States from Honduras as undocumented immigrants, José followed his parents around the country. His itinerancy did not afford him any consistency with schooling. Last year, his parents decided to leave José with his uncle and aunt in North Carolina so that he would have more chances at school. Now he doesn't see his parents for eight months out of the year. He misses them very much. At school José has low grades and has been retained in grade 8 because he did not pass the North Carolina High School Comprehensive Test. He goes to an ESOL pull-out class once a day at his school.

Andrzej is 17 years old. He arrived with his father, mother, and 12-year-old sister from Poland. They live in Baltimore where his father is a civil engineer. The family immigrated the year before so that Andrzej's mother could be closer to her sister (who had married an American and had been living in the United States for the past ten years). Andrzej always wanted to be an engineer like his father, but now he isn't sure what he wants to do. His grades at school have slipped since leaving Poland. He suspects that this is because of his English. Even though he studied English at school in Poland, he never became proficient at writing. Because he has been in the United States for more than a year, he no longer receives ESOL support at school.

The above cases reflect the very wide differences in the ELL population in schools today. The ELL population in a school may include permanent residents, naturalized citizens, legal immigrants, undocumented immigrants, refugees, and asylees. Of this foreign-born population, 4.8 million originate from Europe, 11.2 million from Asia, 21 million from Latin America, 1.6 million from Africa, and 1 million from other areas, including Oceania and the Caribbean (U.S. Census Bureau, 2010c).

Stages of Cultural Adjustment

What the above cases of María, Ismael, José, and Andrzej also identify is that, since the nation's founding, immigrants have come to the United States for a wide variety of reasons. These may include one or any combination of economic, political, religious, and family reunification reasons. Depending on the reason for coming to the United States, ELLs might be very eager to learn English since they might regard English proficiency as the single best means to "get ahead" economically in their new life, or they might resist learning English because they see this as an erosion of their cultural and linguistic identity. A teacher may find ELLs swaying between these two extremes simply because they are displaying the characteristics and stages of *cultural adjustment.*

The notion of cultural adjustment or, as it is sometimes called, "culture shock" was first introduced by anthropologist Kalvero Oberg in 1954. The emotional and behavioral symptoms of each stage of this process can manifest themselves consistently or only appear at disparate times (Figure 1.4).

Honeymoon Stage

The first stage is called the "honeymoon" stage and is marked by enthusiasm and excitement by the ELL. At this stage, ELLs may be very positive about the culture but may express being overwhelmed with their impressions, particularly because they find American culture exotic and are fascinated by it. Conversely, an ELL may be largely passive and not confront the culture even though he or she finds everything in the new culture wonderful, exciting, and novel. After a few days, weeks, or months, ELLs typically enter the second stage.

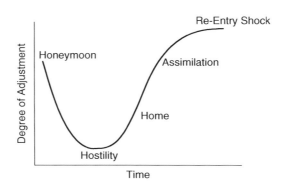

FIGURE 1.4. Stages of adjustment.

Hostility Stage

At this stage, differences between the ELL's old and new cultures become aggravatingly stark. An ELL may begin to find some things or everything in the new culture annoying/or tiresome or both. ELLs will most likely find the behavior of those around them unusual and unpredictable and thus begin to dislike American culture as well as Americans. They may begin to stereotype Americans and idealize their own culture. They may experience cultural confusion and often have communication difficulties. At this stage, feelings of boredom, lethargy, restlessness, irritation, antagonism, depression, and ineptitude are very common. This especially occurs when an ELL is trying to acclimatize to the new culture, which may be very dissimilar to the culture of origin. Shifting between former cultural discourse practices and those of the new country is a problematic process and can take a very long time to overcome. If it is prolonged, an ELL may withdraw because of feelings of loneliness and anxiety.

Home Stage

The third stage is typified by the ELL achieving a sense of understanding of the new culture. ELLs may feel more comfortable living in the new country and experiencing the new culture. They may regain their sense of humor. In psychological terms, ELLs may start to feel a certain emotional balance. Although feelings of isolation may persist, ELLs may stop feeling lost and even begin to have feelings of direction. ELLs re-emerge more culturally stable, being more familiar with the environment and wanting to belong. For the ELL, this period of new adjustment could initiate an evaluation of old cultural practices versus new ones.

Assimilation Stage

In the fourth stage, the ELL realizes that the new culture has positives as well as negatives to offer. Integration patterns and practices displayed by the ELL become apparent. It is accompanied by a more solid feeling of belonging. The ELL enjoys being in the new culture, functions easily in the new environment (even though he or she might already have been in the new culture for a few years) and may even adopt cultural practices of the new culture. This stage may be seen as one of amalgamation and assimilation.

Re-Entry Shock Stage

This happens when ELLs return to the old culture for a visit and notice how many things have changed in the country as well as how they themselves have changed. Upon returning from the home country, an ELL will have developed a new sense of appreciation and of belonging to the new culture.

It is noteworthy that the length of time an ELL spends in each of these stages varies considerably. The stages are neither discrete nor sequential and some ELLs may completely skip stages. They may even exhibit affective behaviors characteristic of more than one stage.

Cultural Practices at School

Whenever an ELL steps into a new school environment, the ELL will be sure to go through a process of cultural adjustment. For an ELL, the countless arrays of unspoken rules acquired in his or her culture of origin may not be suitable in the new school and a new set of practices needs to be discovered and internalized. These include, but are of course not limited to, school rules, what it means to be a "good" student, how to interact with fellow students and teachers, eating practices, bathroom practices, and even ways of learning. It would be fairly easy to learn new rules for living if such were made explicit and one was provided with lists of things to learn. However, most cultural rules operate at a level below conscious awareness and are not easily relayed to students. Often ELLs find themselves in the position of having to discover these rules on their own. Shared cultural discourse practices can be seen as the oil that lubricates social interaction; however, what a community's cultural practices are, as well as the meanings that group members attach to their shared repertoire of cultural practices, are not always made explicit. Unfamiliarity with these cultural rules on the part of an ELL can cause a great deal of stress.

Definitions of what culture is or is not abound. Diaz-Rico and Weed (2006) provide a helpful overview of the characteristics of culture. For them, culture is an adaptive mechanism, culture is learned, cultures change, culture is universal, culture provides a set of rules for living and a range of permissible behavior patterns, culture is a process of deep conditioning, culture is demonstrated in values, people usually are not aware of their culture, people do not know all of their own culture, culture is expressed verbally and non-verbally, culture no longer exists in isolation, and, last but very significant, culture affects people's attitudes toward schooling and it governs the way they learn. It can affect how they come to understand curriculum content and how they interact with fellow students.

Diaz-Rico and Weed (2006) offer a number of strategies to promote cultural pluralism and assuage potential exclusionary practices such as stereotyping, prejudice, and racism in the classroom. Ways to acknowledge different values, beliefs, and practices include accommodating different concepts of time and work rhythms, as well as different concepts of work space. Openness to culturally sensitive dress codes and inclusion of culture in school rituals are effective ways of promoting cultural pluralism. Considering different notions about work and play and maintaining an inclusive understanding of different health and hygiene practices as well as being tolerant of different religious practices and food and eating practices are critical in teaching acceptance. Most important to remember in relation to your ELL students are culturally based educational expectations (roles, status, gender), different discourse patterns, and your need to foster cultural pride and home–school communication.

One way to ease your ELLs' cultural adjustment while demonstrating inclusiveness is to get to know where your ELLs come from and then incorporate aspects of their culture into your lessons. Courses in World Geography, World History, and Sociology provide natural opportunities to make these connections. You could overtly ask your ELLs about their home country, but this tactic may not provide you with the type of information you want since your ELLs may not have the language proficiency in English to express abstract cultural concepts. Therefore, you should observe your ELLs and how they behave, interview people from the same country, conduct a home visit, or visit the community in which the ELL lives. Of course, teachers are often constrained by time, so an alternative is to conduct Internet research or obtain appropriate books and articles.

1.6
Culturally Responsive Pedagogy

As more and more students from diverse backgrounds populate 21st century classrooms, and efforts mount to identify effective methods to teach these students, the need for pedagogical approaches that are culturally responsive intensifies. Today's classrooms require teachers to educate students varying in culture, language, abilities, and many other characteristics.

(Gollnick & Chinn, 2002, p. 21)

The question is: How does a teacher adequately respond to and support the multicultural classroom?

Gay (2000) wrote that culturally responsive pedagogy is validating, comprehensive, multidimensional, empowering, transformative, and emancipatory. In other words, culturally responsive pedagogy often necessitates that teachers tread outside their comfort circles. It is only natural for humans to see, understand, judge, make sense of, and canonize the world around them through their own discursive norms of practice. What this means in the context of education is that teachers make choices every day about what they will and will not teach. More importantly, teachers make choices as to how they will present and frame their curriculum choices. Of course this sends a subtle message to students: What subject matter is taught and how it is framed tends to legitimize, validate, and endorse it over other potential curricular perspectives, which by default are marginalized.

Thus, teachers instruct in ways and about things that are familiar to them. They usually adopt and transmit the dominant voice in society, namely that of white, middle-class America. The problem is, if a student is an ELL, he or she is usually not white, middle-class, or American. This is where the practice of culturally responsive pedagogy can help. Look at the reflection vignette below. It shows how the media can tend to reinforce dominant societal perspectives, perspectives that are reinforced and repeated in school curricula and textbooks across the country.

Reflection Vignette

I was driving my 12-year-old son to school in the fall of 2003 when over the radio we heard a commercial for the movie *Alamo*. Coincidentally, the previous day we had been to the movies and one of the trailers was for the same movie. Kevin Costner was one of the Texan heroes in the movie, and every time the movie trailer showed the Texans, the screen was bright and full of smiling people. The music was light and they were obviously the "good guys." However, when the screen shot showed the Mexican antagonists, the screen was dark, with hues of blue and red, the background images were full of cannon sounds, and the faces were "mean-looking."

Back in the car, I asked my son, who at the time was focused on playing his Gameboy, "You're doing American history now in your social studies class, right?" My son, recognizing that another of dad's teachable moments was upon him, just rolled his eyes and disgruntledly put down his Gameboy. "Yes, why?" he said.

"What aspect of U.S. history are you learning about now?" I asked. "We're learning about the westward colonization of North America." "Did you hear that ad?" I asked.

"Sure."

"Let me ask you something. What do you think would happen if a bunch of Cubans came into the middle of Florida, bought up a cluster of farms, and then told the government they were not going to pay taxes?"

"I suppose the government would fine them," he said.

"Well, what would happen if those same Cubans then told the government that they were going to create their own country?"

"The government would send in the army and kick 'em all out and probably send them back to Cuba."

At that point, I could see a flash of realization cross my son's face. "Oh, I get it," he said, "the Cubans are the Texans."

Tony Erben, University of Tampa

In the United States the Alamo is usually constructed as part of a righteous war of independence against an autocratic foreign government, namely Mexico. Yet in Mexican schools the war surrounding the Alamo is constructed as an aggressive grab for land by non-Spanish-speaking settlers. Who is right? Perhaps the question should be: Am I teaching curriculum matter in a way that alienates and inadvertently marginalizes my students? How would a Mexican ELL feel in your classroom if you taught a unit on the Alamo, or on the westward European settlement of North America, and Mexico and the Mexicans were portrayed as the "bad guys"? At the very least, it marginalizes an ELL's voice in the classroom and indirectly discredits his/her potential contribution of another perspective for the class to think about.

Using Gay's (2000) principles of culturally responsive pedagogy, how does a teacher make the curriculum more validating, comprehensive, multidimensional, empowering, transformative, and emancipatory? A first step is to be conscious of our choice of language. Language is never neutral. What and how we say things in the classroom affects the way our students perceive curriculum matter. A second step is to be conscious of the images we present to students. A third step is to engage in critical and reflexive thinking and writing tasks. By getting teachers to reflect critically on the language, images, and content of their teaching, we begin to open the door on *other* ways to think about teaching that are less ethnocentric. A fourth step is to learn the history and culture of the ELL groups in your classroom. A fifth step is to try and visit teachers who are successful at implementing culturally responsive pedagogy and, last, become an advocate in your own educational institution to reform ethnocentric discursive practices so that it becomes more inclusive. Richards *et al.* (2004) suggest the following activities to become more culturally responsive:

1. acknowledge students' differences as well as their commonalities;
2. validate students' cultural identity in classroom practices and instructional materials;
3. educate students about the diversity of the world around them;
4. promote equity and mutual respect among students;
5. assess students' ability and achievement validly;
6. foster a positive interrelationship among students, their families, the community, and school;
7. motivate students to become active participants in their learning;
8. encourage students to think critically;
9. challenge students to strive for excellence as defined by their potential;
10. assist students in becoming socially and politically conscious.

1.7
Not All Parents Are the Same
Home–School Communication

Any school administrator and teacher will readily admit that a key to a school's success and indeed a key to a child's learning success is the active involvement of parents in the learning process. In the case of ELLs, parents are often at a loss because of barriers that prevent them from fully participating in the school community. Parents' hesitancy to involve themselves in their child's school arises from barriers such as the frustration they feel because of their own limited knowledge of English, their own possible lack of schooling, perceptions about power and status roles, or the anxiety they have because of different cultural norms such that they do not readily understand American school cultures or the cultural expectations, rights, roles, and responsibilities of teachers, parents, and students.

Schools can greatly enhance the effectiveness of ELL home–school communication and involvement by taking active steps to reduce these barriers. Careful planning is required to meet these challenges, though it can be done.

1. *Knowledge is king!* Get as much background information as is possible. Information useful to schools and teachers includes home language, home cultural/ethnic values, parental attitudes towards education, work schedules of parents, English proficiency, and the circumstances under which they have come to be in the United States (e.g., are they refugees, itinerant migrants, political asylees, second- or third-generation heritage speakers?). Depending on the information a school receives, a classroom teacher may make informed decisions about bilingual aide support, translation support, and changing school cultural practices that raise rather than bring down barriers to ELL home–school communication and parental involvement.

2. *Communicate as if it is going out of style!* The importance of fostering ELL parental involvement centers foremost on fostering and maintaining good lines of communication between the school/teacher and the home/parents. An important facet that frames parents' participation in schools is their perceptions of school personnel. Is the school inviting and

welcoming? Are teachers and the administration approachable? Are teachers empathetic to ELL parental concerns, wishes, contributions, values, and cultural practices? How often are they invited to attend school functions? Do teachers follow through on their communications? Do teachers make an effort to talk directly and in person with parents? Are parents allowed to visit often and learn what goes on in the classroom? Do teachers take the time to explain the what, why, and how of their teaching and the ELL child's learning?

3. *It's not just about educating the ELL!* If schools want to enlist the support and help of ELL parents, then both the administration of a school and its teachers need to be prepared to extend their instruction beyond the ELL student to the ELL parent—beyond the classroom and into the ELL home. In other words, in order to break down the types of barriers that inhibit ELL parents from school involvement, steps need to be taken to educate the parents in matters concerning English language, as well as U.S. school customs. What would such steps look like? In an article published in *Essential Teacher,* Bassoff (2004) says it centers solely on *access, approachability,* and *follow-through.*

Ideas: On Fostering Access

- Create, endorse, and implement an ELL parent–school participation program/policy.
- Have an ELL parent representative on school committees.
- Make the school a place to foster ELL community events.
- Provide access to the school library to aid ELL parents' learning of English.
- Translate all school communications into the home language.
- Make sure all written communication reaches the ELL parent.
- Foster in-school support groups for ELL parents.
- Advocate that your school district establish an "Intake Center" for new arrivals that will help ELL newcomers with school registrations, placement, testing, and information services.
- Allow ELL parents to come to school professional development opportunities.
- Provide ELL parent education workshops and orientation opportunities.
- Advertise the contact information of bilingual school staff.

Ideas: On Fostering Approachability

- Use ELL parents as sources of information.
- Invite ELL parents to school.
- Use parents to raise multicultural awareness in the school and classroom; multiculturalism is a two-way street—foster inclusion through the provision of multicultural workshops, presentations, and events to mainstream monolingual school personnel and students.
- Multicultural appreciation events could include ethnic music and dance performances, art displays, drama shows, science fairs, and festival evenings, all accompanied by talks from ELL parents or ELL community leaders.
- Be amenable and open to different ways of thinking about education—show this through inclusive classroom practices, activities, realia, and visuals.
- Embed multicultural routines in everything and all the time.
- Foster ELL literacy family evenings.
- Establish native language parent groups.

Ideas: On Achieving Good Follow-Through

- Give mainstream students service-learning opportunities to help ELL students/parents/ families adjust to U.S. life.
- Foster ELL parent network circles.
- Provide classes that help ELL parents to meet their children's education needs.
- Have the school library purchase a wide range of fiction and non-fiction bilingual books.
- Take the time to learn about the culture, language, and education system of the ELLs' home countries and apply what you learn in your classroom.
- Create virtual spaces to post ongoing information for ELL parents as well as WWW links to useful websites.[1]

1.8
English Language Learners with Special Needs

We want to highlight an important subset of the ELL population that is often disadvantaged because its members fall simultaneously into two special needs groups: exceptional students and ELLs. They are underprivileged because many teachers within these separate discipline areas have not been trained to work with this population of students—ESOL teachers with exceptional education students, or exceptional education teachers with ELLs.

In 1984 the National Office for Educational Statistics reported that 500,000 students in the United States were ELLs with exceptionalities. Today, more than 25 years later, it is projected that there are more than 1 million ELLs with special needs in the United States (Baca & Cervantes, 2004).

Despite an abundance of legislative initiatives (*Civil Rights Act—Title VI* in 1963, *Title VII of the Elementary and Secondary Education Act* (ESEA) reauthorized in 1974, 1978, 1984, and 1998, *Lau v. Nichols* in 1974, and the *Equal Educational Opportunity Act*, extending the Lau decision to all schools, *President's Committee on Mental Retardation* in 1970, the *Education for All Handicapped Children Act* in 1975, the *Bilingual Education Act* in 1984, reauthorization of the ESEA in 1994 coupled with a Presidential Executive Order in 2000, the *Individuals with Disability Education Act* of 1997 and *Title II of the No Child Left Behind Act* 2001), inappropriate referrals, assessments, and the institutionalization of inappropriate instructional processes remain crucial issues in the education of ELL special needs children.

A colleague of ours once told the story of when he first came to the United States. His son was seven years old and at the end of the summer in 2005 was ready to be placed in grade 2. In Florida, the parents of every newly enrolled student are obliged to fill out a home language survey form. Our colleague was raising his children bilingually and both his children were equally fluent in English and German. When asked on the form what languages were spoken at home, he wrote German and English. A week later, his son innocuously said at the dinner table that he enjoyed being pulled out of the classroom, whereupon both parents asked the son what he meant. "Why, I love being in the ESOL class with all the kids who speak other languages." Little did our colleague know that, because he had written German on the home language survey, the school was legally bound to place his son in ESOL classes. The upshot of the story was that our colleague went to the school and explained to the administration that his son was a balanced bilingual speaker and having him in ESOL classes was unnecessary. The administration told him that there was nothing they could do because the home survey was filled out as it was. Ultimately, my colleague had to disenroll his son from school, re-enroll him in the same school, and fill out the home survey again (this time putting just English as the home language) to finally have him pulled from the ESOL classes. The reason this story is related is because parents and teachers are all too familiar with the fact that, within education environments, rule-driven practices, acronyms, and terminologies abound that more often than not pigeon-hole students into predetermined roles and assign these students to inevitable and predictable expectations. Unfortunately, ELLs with special needs have fallen prey to this stereotyping. There is, however, an ever-increasing but incomplete body of research that highlights instructional strategies for ELLs with special needs that teachers may draw upon to help them in their efforts to identify, instruct, and assess. The following section summarizes some of the more important aspects of this research. The following two points may act as instructional guides:

- Students with mild to severe disability levels benefit from native language instruction (de Valenzuela & Niccolai, 2004).
- Instruction needs to be enriching and not remedial, empower language learners, recognize learners' culture and background, provide learners with authentic and meaningful activities, connect students to real-life experiences, begin with context-embedded material that leads to the use of context-reduced material, and provide a literacy/language-rich environment (Echeverria & McDonough, 1993).

But how can we translate the above into effective classroom practice?

There are various pedagogic models that have been developed based on theoretical frameworks, research findings, and recommended practices appropriate for ELLs with special needs (Ruiz, 1995a, b). Ortiz (1984) describes four basic types of pedagogic models that offer structured institutional support for ELLs with special needs to achieve more accomplished social and academic skill levels. These models are:

1. *Coordinated services model*—assists the ELL with special needs with a monolingual English-speaking special education teacher and a bilingual educator.
2. *Bilingual support model*—bilingual paraprofessionals are teamed with monolingual English-speaking special educators and assist with the individualized education plans of ELLs with special needs. Wherever noted on the individualized education program, the bilingual para-professional provides home language instruction concurrently with the teacher providing content expertise.
3. *Integrated bilingual special education model*—consists of one teacher who is certified in both bilingual education and special education, where the teacher is able to assist with level-appropriate English language instruction as the learner develops in proficiency.
4. *Bilingual special education model*—in this model all professionals interacting with the ELL special needs student have received bilingual special education training and are qualified to provide services that meet the goals outlined in any individualized education program.

Another model, the Optimal Learning Environment Project (Ruiz, 1989), is based on a constructivist philosophy and works within a holistic–constructivist paradigm, focusing on the extensive use of interactive journals, writers' workshops, shared reading practices, literature conversations, response journals, patterned writing, as well as the provision of extended assessment time. The aim of the strategies is to build on a student's schema and interest. The benefits of such models highlight the individualized and diverse needs of language learning students with special needs. As yet, guaranteeing unambiguous benefits across the board is not possible precisely because of the dearth of empirical research on instructional planning and curriculum design in this area. A consequence of this situation is the paucity of curricular materials available specifically geared to bilingual special education. Both fields of education have independently developed methods on preparing either ELLs or special needs students. The main point to be internalized here is that materials must be integrated and specifically designed for ELLs with special needs. It is not enough that they receive "half of each curriculum" (Collier, 1995). Lack of curricular materials and trained personnel is still cited as the greatest barrier to providing services to ELLs with special needs.

So, what can teachers do to facilitate language learning for ELL students with a special need?

Of course, implementing well-informed instructional practices is one thing, but awareness raising, understanding of difficulties, and knowledge of differences and disorders are also an integral part of assisting the ELL with disabilities.

In conclusion, we offer Hoover and Collier's (1989, p. 253) recommendations as a point of departure to think about teaching ELLs with special needs:

1. Know the specific language abilities of each student.
2. Include appropriate cultural experiences in material adapted or developed.
3. Ensure that material progresses at a rate commensurate with student needs and abilities.
4. Document the success of selected materials.
5. Adapt only specific materials requiring modifications, and do not attempt to change too much at one time.
6. Try out different materials and adaptations until an appropriate education for each student is achieved.
7. Strategically implement materials adaptations to ensure smooth transitions into the new materials.
8. Follow some consistent format or guide when evaluating materials.
9. Be knowledgeable about particular cultures and heritages and their compatibility with selected materials.
10. Follow a well-developed process for evaluating the success of adapted or developed materials as the individual language and cultural needs of students are addressed.

Gifted ELL Students

It is no surprise that ELLs are underrepresented in gifted education programs. Elhoweris and colleagues (2005) found that Hispanic and African-American students are less frequently identified for gifted and talented programs. Identifying gifted ELLs may be difficult, but there are some behaviors typical of advanced learners, not all of which are tied to language. Granada (2002) urges teachers to look for characteristics of the gifted in students who speak more than one language, given that giftedness is often masked by limited English. Aguirre (2003) identifies the characteristics of gifted ELL students, many of which are tied to their native language and culture. These characteristics include a strong desire to teach peers words from their native language as well as a well-developed sense of cultural heritage and ethnic background. In addition, gifted ELL students may possess cross-cultural flexibility, understand jokes and puns related to cultural differences, learn a second/third language at an accelerated pace, be creative, and demonstrate leadership abilities.

Developing a social studies program that both incorporates appropriate methods and provides for accelerated English learning and practice can be a challenge. To meet the challenging needs of gifted ELLs in your classroom, we suggest you employ the following strategies, as set forth by Udall (1989):

- Use concrete materials to teach abstract concepts.
- Incorporate instructional examples relevant to culture and experience.
- Encourage community involvement.
- Integrate a leadership component.
- Utilize mentors.
- Focus on creativity and problem-solving strengths.
- Concentrate on affective needs.

Conclusion

Understanding your ELLs can be daunting. They probably come from very different home environments from you, their teachers. Some of your students may be third-generation American and yet others may be newly arrived undocumented immigrants.

After reading Part 1, we don't expect you to now know everything there is to know about ELLs. We did not set out to provide you in these few short pages with an all-inclusive research-informed, all-encompassing treatise on ELLs in education. We have been cautious, to be sure, in trying to introduce you to ELLs. There are plenty of ELL-specific books for that. It *was* our intent, however, to raise your awareness about the educational implications of having ELLs in your classroom. Our goal with this is to start drawing a picture of who an ELL is and from this position help you think about the educational possibilities for your class.

Parts 2 and 3 of this book are devoted exclusively to completing this picture. Not in a global sense, but finely etched within the parameters of your own social studies courses.

What will be introduced to you in the pages to come will undoubtedly refer back to some of the points raised in Part 1. We have no intention of offering you static teaching recipes; instead we offer something akin to ideas, understandings, and skills that you can transfer to your own classrooms. Last, we refer you to the Resources chapter of this book, which offers you avenues for future professional development.

Part 2
Principles of Social Studies Teaching and Learning

2.1
Principles of Social Studies Teaching and Learning

In this chapter we attempt to present what often takes up entire books: what sound social studies programs look like. Clearly, we can't be comprehensive, but we will try to sketch some key elements of desirable programs with the hope that these illustrations can be extended to other areas of instruction we don't treat. Even readers who are already well informed about standard social studies programs may profit from this chapter as the instructional recommendations we make in subsequent chapters presuppose a conception of social studies akin to what is here.

Elements of an Instructional Program

Subject Matter

Social studies is a school program concerned with how people, past and present, live together. Program objectives can include not only content about people living together but also classroom activities that involve living together, such as small group work. That is, the social studies have both content and process objectives, as the activities in Part 3 demonstrate. Individual programs often incorporate three main elements: (1) traditional academic subjects (e.g., geography, economics); (2) branches of learning developed for instructional purposes (e.g., civics, global studies); and (3) current events and problems. Teachers, whether they recognize it or not, serve as curricular-instructional gatekeepers. Sound instructional planning requires that they thoughtfully decide beforehand what topics they will discuss and how they can effectively use each topic to realize learning objectives. Although states and school districts normally determine what courses and main topics will be offered at a given grade level, the teacher still has significant input (Thornton, 2005). Abdication of this responsibility is the chief cause of information- and skill-laden, yet thematically unrelated, social studies programs such as the history course over-reliant on chronology or the geography course that consists of lots of facts and figures to remember accompanied by disconnected skills exercises. As a teacher you need to determine the subject matter that is important for students to know, and you have to teach it effectively (Brooks *et al.*, 2007).

Conceptual Planning and Learning

Wise planning is systematic. Creating lesson plans can be overwhelming, but remember that, by taking one step at a time and keeping the following in mind, you can confidently build your own curriculum for all types of learners.

First, we believe that effective social studies instruction emphasizes concepts over facts (Harmon & Hedrick, 2000). We may think of facts as unchanging but facts may change over time, such as the shifting boundaries of Germany over hundreds of years or the twentieth century's appearance and disappearance of Yugoslavia. In addition, new facts, say South Sudan gaining its independence in 2011, are constantly appearing. In history, the primary sources once mined for facts to build accounts of antebellum slavery have more recently been recognized as biased since they were created by whites. Few of the enslaved had opportunities to become literate. The resultant picture of slavery was relatively benign. In this sense, the turn to non-documentary sources of the African-American experience decisively altered the facts about slavery.

Hilda Taba (1967) emphasized, as there are simply too many facts to teach, that facts fail to provide the soundest organizing principle for constructing an instructional program. As well, too many facts get in the way of effective teaching and learning. The alternative, Taba pointed out, is to build a program around selected concepts (see Fraenkel, 1992). Out of the countless facts that could be taught to develop a particular concept, educators should select those facts that meet some significant criterion. A criterion could be, for instance, proximity to where students live. By this criterion, for example, the best facts to use in a study of sea ports would be different in a Los Angeles classroom from a classroom in Honolulu or New Orleans.

Facts also lack transfer value to other learning situations since by definition facts apply only to a single case. Concepts, on the other hand, are words or phrases that are used to express larger ideas. Concepts work to label groups of similar people and to name things, events, actions, or ideas regardless of context (Harvey *et al.*, 1997). Examples are, respectively, serfs, sea ports, the attack on Fort Sumter, ethnic cleansing, and liberty. Conceptual learning generalizes more than factual learning since concepts, unlike facts, transfer to other contexts. The benefit of teaching students concepts is that knowing the characteristics of serfs in medieval western Europe, for instance, provides some sense of the characteristics of serfs in nineteenth-century Russia. As noted, planning based on concepts is a useful antidote to getting weighed down in factual information. Instead of starting with facts, start with concepts and then ask what facts would be useful to illustrate this concept. In sum, concepts are more memorable and more cognitively useful than facts. The *quality* of learning activities usually trumps the *quantity* of what could be learned (National Council for the Social Studies, 2008).

Second, we believe that effective social studies instruction emphasizes the *relationships* among concepts. For instance, in a study of the Russian Revolution relationships exist among concepts such as revolution, soviet, absolutism, famine, and strike. As a teacher, you need to effectively demonstrate the dynamics of these relationships to your students so they can organize this information appropriately. One way to do this is by identifying cause–effect relationships. In this manner, the concept of a famine could be identified as a cause of revolution. Alternately, compare–contrast relationships look for similarities and differences between conditions: How was the revolution in Russia similar to and different from revolution in France, for instance (Brinton, 1965)?

In addition to knowledge objectives such as facts, concepts, and relationships, skills are important in social studies. As with concepts, skills once learned can be applied and transferred to new contexts. For example, reading directions on one map is a skill that can be applied to other maps. Some of the most useful skills in social studies education are discussed later in this chapter.

Interdisciplinary Connections

The proper relationship of social studies (or *the* social studies) to the academic disciplines sometimes causes confusion. The way out of this confusion is recognition that social studies is not a discipline, although it includes disciplines such as history, economics, and geography. Sometimes social studies courses combine the disciplines for pedagogical purposes. Sometimes the disciplines are taught separately.

Thus calls for "interdisciplinary" teaching are neither compatible nor incompatible with social studies as a form of curricular organization. Whether taught in courses where more than one discipline is combined, such as World Cultures or Global Studies, or in discipline-specific courses such as Economics, it is important for students to learn about the disciplines themselves. For example, students should be acquainted with some of the key concepts, principles, and skills of a given discipline.

By the same token, interdisciplinary study is not just a hodgepodge of information from various fields of study; it requires working with the concepts, principles, and skills associated with one or more disciplines (Mansilla & Gardner, 2008). While studies by geographers and historians of the Great Plains will surely overlap, the disciplinary lens they bring will slant their inquiries. Employing different methods and concepts results in different findings about the "same" region and time period (Webb, 1960).

The National Council for the Social Studies recognizes that social studies programs are neither inherently disciplinary nor non-disciplinary. Thus its National Curriculum Standards for Social Studies (National Council for the Social Studies, 2010) are designed to provide a set of principles from which content can be selected for social studies courses, whether they be disciplinary courses or cross-disciplinary. The ten themes that the National Council for the Social Studies identify to guide constructing sound social studies programs are broader and deeper than content specific to a particular discipline. Thus, while one of those themes, "Time, Continuity, and Change," is most associated with the discipline of history, it might also appear in a course on the discipline of geography or a course that combines history and geography.

Social Studies and the Common Core Standards

Under the auspices of the Council of Chief State School Officers, the Common Core Standards (CCS) were developed for English language arts and mathematics. Almost all states are involved with the CCS.

An offshoot of the CCS project was the development of literacy standards as they relate to social studies. At the time of this writing, around 20 of the 50 states, stretching from Hawaii to Maine, had participated in developing social studies standards at any given time (Gewertz, 2011). The social studies literacy standards do not identify a particular body of content such as names, dates, and events for a U.S. history course. Rather, these standards are skills that can be integrated into the existing programs of study of any state. For instance, one standard for grades 6–8 asks students to "cite specific textual evidence to support analysis of primary and secondary sources" (Common Core State Standards Initiative, 2012).

The social studies literacy standards emphasize English language arts skills in instruction in history, geography, civics, and economics. A potential danger in this approach is that social studies instruction may become too exclusively concerned with language skills. For instance, focus on the rhetorical devices Lincoln used in the Gettysburg Address may result in short shrift for the historical context. This approach also implies limited attention to forms of literacy other than written text, such as map interpretation and analysis of historical photographs. For English language learners (ELLs), the net effect of the approach embodied in the social studies standards is reinforced emphasis on language skills as the means of learning social studies.

Study Skills

Study skills are a prerequisite to independent thinking in social studies since, lacking those skills, students must rely on other authorities or sources for their information. Activities that encourage study skills should form part of a balanced social studies program. Typically, students learn to identify relationships through creating or interpreting graphic organizers, summarizing text, identifying cause–effect connections, or extracting information from maps and primary sources. Sometimes it is mistakenly assumed that students will pick up study skills without dedicated instruction, but often study skills do not emerge as byproducts of other learning experiences. Students must be explicitly taught to become independent learners and given frequent opportunities to do so.

Study skills include students' ability to gather information from books, the Internet, maps, and primary sources (visual, three-dimensional, and written), just to name a few. These skills are important in social studies as learning is dependent on being able to obtain and organize information relevant to class work. An example of this would be a teacher assigning homework requiring students to locate an article on a specific current event. Then, after they have familiarized themselves with the topic, instruct them to form an opinion on the issue and debate it. Require your students to conduct research on their own, to read and understand various complex relationships, and to form and articulate opinions in their own words. Doing so will challenge their higher thought processes and further develop their intellectual skills and cognitive/academic language proficiency (CALP).

Intellectual Skills

Intellectual skills are characterized by students' ability to identify a problematic situation, analyze the problem (note this will invariably draw on study skills), and propose possible solutions; that is, they will develop their ability to construct "original" knowledge. You can teach intellectual skills in a carefully guided way or approach it in a more open-ended fashion. Start by asking students to resolve a problem they have experience with, such as how to prioritize multiple homework assignments with varying deadlines. Regardless of the activity, the goal is that the learner plays a significantly independent role in the problem-solving exercise instead of merely learning the outcome by someone else's completed act of thought.

Twenty-first Century Skills

Increasingly, social studies educators are being called on to prepare their students for citizenship in an interdependent world. Globalization has led to an interconnected global economy, cultural diffusion, and the movement of people that has resulted in both challenges and promising prospects. Students need to understand these processes and prepare themselves to live and work in a world very different from the one in which their grandparents, and even their parents, grew up. Organizations such as the Partnership for 21st Century Skills (2012) advocate helping students develop skills such as critical thinking, problem solving, communication, collaboration, and creativity. The National Council for the Social Studies (2001) also supports preparing citizens for a global community. In its position statement, the National Council for the Social Studies asserts that an effective social studies program, by necessity, must include global studies. Fortunately, twenty-first-century skills can be easily integrated into the existing social studies curriculum—but teachers must make an effort to do so.

Genesee (2011) points out that, in comparison with immigrants in earlier generations, today's students need literacy skills for even unskilled labor. Further, he points out that U.S. workers are competing with those in the developing world, many of whose citizens are bilingual or multilingual and know English. These factors add greater urgency to ELLs succeeding in school.

2.2
How Instruction Unfolds

Students (even in the early grades) can learn complex material in subjects such as history, although success depends heavily on the methods used (Barton & Levstik, 2004). Bruner (1960) asserted that "any subject can be taught effectively in some intellectually honest form to any child at any stage of development" (p. 33). Experience confirms that even uninspiring-looking subject matter can be made comprehensible and enlivened through imaginative, engaging instruction.

Much of the subject matter students encounter in the social studies, though, fails to engage them in meaningful learning (Selwyn, 2009). This is not because adolescents lack interest in social matters; in fact, interest in topics covered in social studies usually peaks during adolescence, as it is a time of dealing with issues of identity formation and understanding how people relate to one another (Goodlad, 1984). Forging connections between student interests and curricular-instructional arrangements should be goals of yours. One example of an engaging and relevant topic in a Government or Law Studies class is the downloading and sharing of music and movies, and its relationship to copyright protection versus ownership. Hoose (2001) makes a convincing case that including the activities and contributions of young people in history can lend relevance and increase interest in the subject. Remember that although the larger standards and mandates such as *No Child Left Behind* and CCS are established by outside authorities, you have the responsibility and freedom to create a curriculum that engages and enriches your students' understanding of society.

Even when teachers are held accountable for covering a lot of content, this does not dictate that instructional arrangements must consist of no more than teacher talk and questioning. To ensure you do not overemphasize this approach, we encourage you to develop your own approach that requires thinking instead of recall. Remember that teacher-centered instruction often results in instructing all students with the same subject matter at the same pace but seldom prompts much thinking by students. In contrast, group work can broaden and deepen lesson content compared with teacher talk to the entire class (Yell *et al.*, 2004). At the same time, group work increases the level of student participation and interaction related to academic work (Stahl *et al.*, 2009).

You should also endeavor to make whole-class activities less concerned with recall and more focused on thinking. For example, Taba's (1967) "list–group–label" strategy asks students to look at data sources such as photographs or artifacts. The teacher elicits the words the sources evoke and lists them on the board. Then the words are grouped and generalizations formed. This method is an excellent introduction to a new topic and, simultaneously, promotes concept development, higher-level thinking, and vocabulary knowledge (Irvin *et al.*, 1995). An even simpler way to bolster whole-class questioning is to implement longer wait times for student responses, which generally yields more and richer student responses than the teacher quickly supplying the answer (Brophy, 2001).

As the use of the "list–group–label" method to begin a unit implies, effectiveness of instruction can depend on when a method is used. At the outset of a unit, for instance, advance organizers help order students' thinking about the big ideas they'll encounter and can also access their prior knowledge; advance organizers can also be an efficient and even creative way to summarize and synthesize information at the end of a unit. Similarly, Brophy (2001) suggests that in the early stages of a unit more time might profitably be devoted to interactive lessons in which the teacher scaffolds the topic for students whereas, later, students might work more independently as their confidence in the subject deepens.

Although there is an established body of social studies literature on what and how to teach, a body of work on English language learning in the social studies classroom is only now beginning to appear. In the next chapter, we will discuss social studies-focused research as it relates to English language learning to provide you with additional teaching tools.

2.3
Social Studies-Focused ELL Research

This chapter reviews social studies-focused research for ELLs. As noted, ELL research has dwelled more on language learning than the content areas of the school curriculum. Social studies teachers have, to a significant extent, been left to fathom for themselves what this research might mean to them as practitioners or to their students of social studies. We construe "research" broadly and include work that is subject-specific or seems readily applicable to social studies.

Classroom Environment

The setting in which students learn becomes part of what and how they learn. Before students set foot in a classroom, the teacher already begins to create a classroom environment and establish the tone for the teaching and learning to come. At first, there is no clear-cut atmosphere; it develops gradually, in response to things such as the teacher's communication of expectations, the teacher's approach to classroom management, and the physical make-up of the room. Over time, the classroom environment has an important impact on students' academic achievement and their behavior in class.

The instructional strategies used go a long way toward setting the tone in a classroom. Because ELLs come to U.S. schools with a wide variety of school experiences and cultural backgrounds, teachers cannot make assumptions about students' comfort with various pedagogical strategies. For example, discussion and participation are prized in the U.S. secondary social studies classroom; indeed, some of the most popular teacher evaluation systems today specifically look for student discussion, participation, and engagement (see, for example, Danielson, 1996; Marzano *et al.*, 2011). But this is not necessarily the case in other nations' systems of schooling. Similarly, although timelines are considered *de rigueur* in most social studies classes, teachers cannot assume that all ELLs know how to create or interpret them. This is an elementary task in the United States, but may not be in other countries (Short, 2002). Further, students whose cultural norms do not encourage mixed-gender groups may feel a conflict between conforming to expectations and following the practices they have learned at home (Jones *et al.*, 2001). Also the co-construction of knowledge, shared responsibility for content delivery, and interaction between and among students and teachers are practices that may be unknown or uncomfortable for some ELLs (Short, 2002). Building a classroom community is culturally bound and defined. Before you begin to enact the curriculum, take into account the various groups of students in your class and consider some of the special circumstances and backgrounds they will invariably bring to lessons. These instances can provide opportunities for dialogue as well as growth and enrich the quality of discussion and education of all.

Pedagogical Orientation, Practice, and Reflection

Although good instructional technique has been associated with higher academic achievement, Lindholm-Leavy and Borsato (2006) report an absence of research directly linking instructional strategy and teaching particular content. Nonetheless, there have been a few studies that are instructive for our purposes here. For instance, Short (1997) suggests that effective content instruction for ELLs draws on three knowledge bases: knowledge of the content; knowledge of English; and knowledge of how tasks are to be achieved. She further notes that social studies teachers must include all three components in their instruction to ensure that ELLs achieve academically (Short, 1998).

Consider a map exercise on the Amazon rainforest in which students are asked to locate ports and rivers. Students can be given a copy of a newspaper article on the topic (content) and a list of key terms necessary for understanding the article (language). But teachers need also to make sure students know how to accomplish the required *task* of locating the places mentioned in the article by consulting their atlases.

Another way to engage ELLs (as well as other students) is to include topics relevant to their lives in your lessons. For example, in an economics lesson on how exchange rates generally function among world currencies, ELLs may be particularly interested in how the rates are determined between their heritage countries and the United States. It is also wise for history teachers to, whenever possible, include their ELLs' home cultures in the larger historical narrative of U.S. and world history.

But no matter what pedagogical orientation teachers embrace and practice in their classrooms, they should ideally aim at becoming reflective practitioners (Schön, 1983). Teachers must continually and consistently think about what they do and why they do it, and determine if it works. Teachers of ELLs, we contend, must especially endeavor to explore their own practices, core values, and underlying beliefs to better serve their students. This reflection can be facilitated by keeping a journal, having a respected peer observe you teach, recording yourself teach and then viewing the recording, and soliciting student feedback. We encourage you to consider employing one or more of these strategies as you hone your craft.

Culturally Sensitive Pedagogy

Effective teachers of ELLs embrace a culturally sensitive pedagogical orientation. Also known as culturally responsive or culturally relevant pedagogy, this philosophy and approach refers to instruction that recognizes the importance of students' cultures and addresses the needs of a diverse student population. We define this instruction as using a variety of strategies that takes into account differences in learning styles, incorporates multicultural materials, and builds links between the school and home (Gay, 2000). This instructional approach is based on the belief that culture is central to students' lives and, thus, learning (Chartock, 2010). Pang and colleagues (2011) call educators who do this "culturally competent teachers [who] know how to tap into the diverse cultures of their students to make learning meaningful and comprehensible" (p. 560). They identify basic competencies that teachers who work with ELLs must develop in order to be successful, including affirming home language and ethnic identity, connecting the school curriculum and pedagogy with students' backgrounds, and taking into consideration the differences between schools in other countries and the educational system of the United States.

One approach, called "bicultural affirmation" (Sleeter, 1995), enables students who belong to two cultural groups to appreciate both groups knowing that they are a distinct part of each. Connections between and among cultures can also result in growth and understanding. For example, it is common for a middle school study of ancient cultures to focus on how writing, laws, and societies developed. These developments are often studied for Mesopotamia, Egypt, Greece, and Rome. With Latino students, the same concepts could be learned by studying the pre-Hispanic cultures of Mesoamerica and incorporating the legends, myths, and origins of cultural traditions (Jones *et al.*, 2001).

Another approach focuses on immigration and comparing cultures, assuming this holds considerable interest for ELLs. Students can consider demographic information, explore population studies, and debate immigration policy. Middle school children can construct, compare and contrast graphic organizers or create murals illustrating life in the heritage country and life in the United States. Secondary students can delve into the concept of identity and write short essays concerning how one's sense of self is affected by moving to a new environment where one's language is not that of the native inhabitants and where one's ethnicity and heritage may not be valued (Danker, 2006).

General Approaches for Teaching Social Studies to ELLs

The social studies may present special challenges for ELLs that teachers should be aware of and plan for accordingly. Haynes (2005) explains that the biggest problem for ELLs can be the limited background knowledge from which they can draw. Haynes lists particular challenges that ELL students may face in the social studies (some of which may apply to other content areas as well):

- use of higher-level thinking skills for reading and writing;
- lack of familiarity with historical terms, government processes, and vocabulary;
- social studies texts typically containing complex sentences, passive voice, and extensive use of pronouns;
- amount of text covered and the ELLs' inability to tell what is important in the text and what is not important;
- difficulty with understanding what is said by the teacher and being able to take notes;
- differences in educational systems (e.g., use in our schools of "timeline" teaching vs. learning history by "dynasty" or "period");
- ELLs' lack of experience in expressing their personal opinions, especially in class;
- the often-found nationalistic and culture-centric focus of maps;
- concepts that do not exist in all cultures and may be difficult for some ELLs to grasp (e.g., privacy, democratic processes, rights of citizens, and free will).

To confront these challenges, Crandall (1994) suggests using content-centered language learning or authentic text. That is, as one of us experienced teaching native Japanese speakers in a TESOL program in Tokyo, students will learn both language and content by studying the content of, say, a global studies textbook rather than only engaging in learning language as an abstraction (i.e., not authentically). Crandall asserts that such content-centered language learning is not only desirable, but essential for the overall educational development of the student. She further reports that instructional strategies such as cooperative learning, task-based or experiential learning, "whole language" approach, and graphic organizers are also central for content learning.

It's probably not surprising that much of the "best practice" ESOL research conducted in the social studies corresponds with good teaching practice in the social studies as a whole. But it does not follow that effective teaching for ELLs is interchangeable with effective teaching generally (Au, 2010). In a report prepared for the U.S. Department of Education, Anstrom (1999) identified additional characteristics of effective social studies instruction that should be emphasized for ELLs, namely:

- making social studies content accessible to ELLs;
- adopting a flexible, thematic-based curriculum;
- giving students adequate amount of time to learn social studies content;
- linking social studies concepts to prior knowledge;
- accommodating a variety of learning styles;
- using cooperative learning strategies;
- linking instruction to assessment.

Language Use

In a study of ELLs in social studies classrooms, Short (2002) found that teachers place stronger emphasis on covering content than on language development. Although opportunities for language use are key for ELLs' developing English language proficiency, in the typical classroom they receive few opportunities to engage in extended language use (Truscott & Watts-Taffe, 1998). Yet it is clear that ELLs can and should be actively involved in verbal interaction with peers, as the interactions improve both basic interpersonal communication skills (BICS) and CALP (Barnes, 1995; Simich-Dudgeon, 1998; Egbert & Simich-Dudgeon, 2001). Larsen-Freeman and Anderson (2011) argue that "teaching through communication rather than for it" allows students to acquire and develop language (p. 131). We suggest that all social studies lessons have language objectives in addition to academic content objectives. For instance, in a lesson on ancient history, students could learn how the Greek *graphia* means "description" and is part of many English words.

In addition to encouraging academic talk among peers (Truscott & Watts-Taffe, 2000), content learning by ELLs is fostered through the use of a variety of graphics, objects, and demonstrations including role playing, realia, and exploratory talk (Barnes, 1992). The utilization of historical photographs seems particularly effective in developing ELLs' historical thinking (Salinas *et al.*, 2006). Even ELLs at the very early levels of language production can be guided to point to items in a picture, use simple adjectives to describe what they see, or form short sentences to express what they think about the image (Cruz & Thornton, 2012).

Another strategy that can prove helpful for ELLs is establishing listening centers in your classroom. This method involves recording class discussions and lessons and making them available to students. It can also involve making use of professionally prepared audio tracks that are provided with many contemporary textbooks and picture dictionaries, especially those produced with special needs populations in mind. This makes the lesson content accessible to both students who want to review, expand vocabulary, and clarify information at a later date and students unable to read the text (Egbert & Simich-Dudgeon, 2001). Audio books, recitation programs, and other forms of auditory stimulus help students develop both receptive and expressive communication skills. You can also adapt this technique to the old "task card" method in which each card contains, at varying reading levels, learning activities on a topic that ELL students could work on independently or in groups (Berger & Winters, 1973). Another tried and true strategy is the use of news broadcasts in the classroom (Brinton & Gaskill, 1978). With guided listening to two-minute radio or television news clips, students can get important exposure to the spoken language as well as a better understanding of contemporary issues. TeacherTube (http://www.teachertube.com) has many school-appropriate clips that are free to download and use in class.

Incorporating students' personal stories into social studies is an effective way of both validating ELLs' backgrounds and helping them develop language skills (Short, 1998; Egbert & Simich-Dudgeon, 2001). This approach helps them integrate BICS with academics. Moreover, research suggests that personal narratives can be instrumental in the acquisition of content knowledge (Ballenger, 1997). Exercises in which ELLs research the cultures of students represented in the class activate students' prior knowledge and skills and contribute to creating a culturally responsive classroom and school (Henze and Hauser, 2000). This approach can be extended to members of the community (Olmedo, 1997).

The effectiveness of storytelling is based on it being a universal practice and teaching method. Storytelling can be used to bring historical characters to life, dramatize conflicts and resolutions, and generally stimulate student interest in historical events (Short, 1998). History courses in particular offer many opportunities to tell about events, time periods, and people in an intrinsically interesting narrative fashion.

Teachers often question the practice of allowing ELL students to communicate in their native language. Short (1998) asserts that "encouraging some communication in the native language when they work in pairs or small groups" not only benefits students cognitively, but can also support literacy in English. Mihai (2010) advocates assessing ELLs in the home language as well as English whenever possible. Studies have found that when students are allowed to use their native language in the classroom, they can outperform their English-only counterparts (Ramirez & Yuen, 1991; Oller & Eilers, 2000; Thomas & Collier, 2001). Native English speakers in the class might also be encouraged to learn a few words of the ELLs' home languages which will no doubt foster the kind of classroom environment that will be positive for all students.

Content-Centered Instruction

The most effective English language instruction occurs in social studies classrooms that have both language mastery and content mastery as clear academic goals. This approach integrates language learning with the learning of specific content, encouraging the development of both simultaneously (Larsen-Freeman & Anderson, 2011). Keeping up with grade-appropriate content may be especially important for late-arrival immigrants who are older and often have as good a grasp— if not better—of some social studies content than their English-speaking peers.

Academic content can provide points of interest, relevance, and natural motivation for many students as they learn English. One of the most popular and researched approaches is the Sheltered Instruction Observation Protocol (SIOP). This approach conveys subject area material to students learning another language using strategies that make the content material comprehensible while simultaneously developing students' language skills (Short *et al.*, 2011).

It is often assumed that students must be proficient in a language before they can learn content in that language. This belief first, puts ELLs at an enormous disadvantage academically and, second, is wrong. In fact, proficiency in language develops through the study of subject matter. Hinde and colleagues (2011), for example, found that offering geography education to ELLs not only promotes the discipline but also improves reading comprehension.

Sheltered Instruction

Sheltered instruction is a general approach to teaching that is useful in the social studies (Weisman & Hansen, 2007). Described as specially designed academic instruction in English (Echevarria *et al.*, 2000), the strategy involves making the content accessible to ELLs using comprehensible language and input. SIOP was developed in 1999 based on classroom observations conducted in the United States (Echevarria *et al.*, 2004). It is one of the most useful approaches that content-area teachers can employ in their classrooms because it employs visuals and vocabulary-building activities that can assist both beginning and more advanced language learners. Vocabulary knowledge has been identified as a key indicator of verbal ability (Calderón *et al.*, 2011). SIOP's goal is to provide students with content at the ELL's grade level using scaffolding, which is discussed in Part 1, and other contextual support. One way of providing sheltered instruction is to reduce "cognitive load" for ELLs. Cognitive load refers to the amount of relevant information that learners must keep track of in order to perform the academic tasks at hand (Sweller, 1988). In this approach, the teacher identifies the key elements of a topic and describes the information in the simplest terms possible. Although conceptually the difficulty level of the learning activity should remain unaltered, the language and the form of the presentation change (Szpara & Ahmad, 2007). Part 3 offers many examples of this approach in the learning activities presented.

Individualized and Differentiated Instruction

All students, ELLs included, appreciate and benefit from individualized instruction, sometimes also called differentiated instruction. Individualizing instruction addresses the diverse learning needs of students while teaching essential content in ways that maximize the possibilities of each learner. Tomlinson and Imbeau (2010) describe differentiation in the classroom as the balance created by the teacher between academic content and students' individual needs. They advise modifying four curricular elements:

- content: the information and skills students need to learn in a given subject matter;
- process: how students make sense of the content presented;
- product: how students evidence what they have learned;
- affect: the feelings and attitudes that affect students' learning.

Since students' interests, aptitudes, and language abilities vary, teachers need to develop multiple points of access for students to reach the goals of an instructional sequence. For instance, incorporating multiple techniques into your instruction can accommodate different learning styles. One simple strategy is to present new information using one style and, when reviewing, using a different approach. For instance, the teacher might begin a unit with a film that presents an overview of the main topics to be treated and at the end of the unit conduct a review via a graphic organizer. Another strategy is to vary the forms of assessment used—differentiated home-work, portfolio assessments, project-based evaluations—all of which should be employed to better gauge students' learning.

Just as with English-speaking students, teachers need to remember that the learning styles of ELLs differ. In addition to the many special needs students who may be mainstreamed into the social studies classroom, much has been written about multiple intelligences and the need for varied instruction. Varying instruction so that different styles and modalities are accommodated is sound teaching practice in social studies. The works of Howard Gardner (2006) and Elliot Eisner (2002) underscore the importance of stimulus variation and taking into account students' learning styles. The Teachers' Curriculum Institute has produced a number of curriculum guides that illustrate the importance of using a variety of stimulating methods that accommodate students' learning styles.

As with any student, tailoring instruction to an ELL student is beneficial as it increases the number of opportunities for capitalizing on individual strengths. In a review of research studies that investigated academic achievement among ELLs, Lindholm-Leavy and Borsato (2006) report that ELLs who receive some individualized instruction achieve at higher rates and are less likely to drop out of school than ELLs in a mainstream English language classroom with no individualized instruction.

Individualization generally also enhances student–teacher relations. In order to differentiate instruction, you will need to get to know each of your students as individuals. Students sense that teachers care about them as individual learners when they differentiate instruction. When cross-cultural communication is involved, as it normally is with ELLs and their teachers, even more time must be given to the establishment of trusting relations between the individual student and the teacher (Noddings, 2005). Valenzuela (1999) found that the Mexican American students she studied failed to engage with subject matter until they felt the teacher cared for them as individuals. Although it is challenging to find the time to work on an individualized level with all your students, it is especially important for ELLs. Prior planning can often free up extra time to spend with them.

Technology-Based Instruction and Learning

Today's students are more technologically savvy than previous generations of learners. They communicate through a variety of digital media. For example, over half (54 percent) send text messages daily, whereas only 33 percent talk face to face daily (Pew Internet & American Life Project, 2010). Authorities say that social media is here to stay; educators need to make accommodations with technology and use it for worthwhile ends (Williamson & Johnston, 2012).

Technology-based instructional tools include those that the teacher uses to present information as well as resources students use to enhance their learning. This approach can range from PowerPoint-type presentations to independent Internet research to virtual field trips.

For teachers, the Internet can be extremely useful in obtaining images that can illustrate content and language concepts. Presentation software helps organize content and display information in ways that are both visually pleasing and more easily comprehended. Language labs, audio recordings, and interactive CDs can enable teachers to provide differentiated instruction to the various proficiency levels in their classrooms. Construction of wikis and podcasts can be an effective method for students to work collaboratively in defining a problem, researching it, organizing what they find out, and presenting it to others. In general, web-based, technology-enhanced instruction can help develop language, content, and digital knowledge at the same time (see, e.g., Shand *et al.*, 2012).

For students, word processing can give immediate feedback on spelling and grammar. In the social studies, technology can provide simulated experiences of virtual museum visits and field trips to other countries. There are also a number of websites that allow students to acquire vocabulary, listen to authentic speech, and practice specific language skills. Sanchez Terrell (2011) found that online tools can improve the listening and speaking skills of language learners in large part because they are motivated to practice English outside the classroom.

Discussion and Questioning

Teacher wait time after posing a question is typically only a few seconds, with the questioning often focused on recall rather than critical thinking. Just waiting several seconds longer, however, can increase the number and thoughtfulness of student answers. In the case of ELLs, it is particularly important to provide ample time for students to think about the question and formulate a response. Another way to increase participation and thoughtfulness is to invite students to elaborate upon, rephrase, and generate further examples of the concept being discussed. Many teaching methods books suggest additional means of drawing in more students and building on the discussion rather than quickly moving toward closure (e.g. Hess, 2004; Duplass, 2008).

Some years ago White (1990) provided guidelines for conducting classroom discussions involving different social and cultural groups, which also, she observed, work for mainstream students. Teachers should note that White's recommendations can be implemented at speeds suitable for students' varying abilities. In this spirit, consider what White (1990) recommended for effective conduct of discussions:

- sharing the responsibility and authority for discussions between students and teacher;
- having the teacher speak less;
- using longer wait times;
- selecting meaningful topics from the community;
- modeling desired behaviors such as cause-and-effect reasoning;
- talking about the talk used;
- assisting the students to build on each other's answers.

Working at collaborative tasks fosters discussion among ELLs and their native English-speaking peers. Discussion is crucial to ELL students' comprehension of social studies concepts (Simich-Dudgeon, 1998). Moreover, opportunities to ponder a question, formulate an answer, and articulate a response are beneficial for both BICS and CALP. Sometimes, too, peer discussions can be an opportunity for ELLs to contribute alternative views that reflect conditions in other countries (Haynes, 2005), which allows them to make constructive contributions and at the same time possibly broaden the horizons of the other students, all the while affording ELLs important opportunities for language development.

Generally, studies show that, when ELL students are called upon to answer questions, the interchanges are too brief to qualify as substantive instructional exchanges. Their participation in extended discussion should be encouraged in both whole-class and small-group discussions. Some small yet significant ways to do this are to modify your questioning strategies for the ELLs in your classrooms, avoid idioms, slow down your speech speed, and pay attention to the clarity of your pronunciation. You can also let your ELL students know in advance which questions they will be responsible for answering in class so they have ample time to prepare (Brown, 2007).

To formulate your questioning strategies, consider using a bottom-up approach to create comprehensible questions for ELL students. Haynes (2004) provides a useful model:

- Start with asking ELLs to point to a picture or word to demonstrate basic knowledge.
  Example: "Point to the United States."
- Use visual cues if necessary and ask simple yes/no questions.
  Example: "Is that Napoleon Bonaparte?"
- Ask either/or questions in which the answer is embedded.
  Example: "Which is longer: the Mississippi or the Illinois River?"
- Then break complex questions into several steps.
  Example: "Look at this map of the United States. Find the Allegheny Mountains. To the west of the Allegheny Mountains, how do the rivers reach the sea?"
- Ask simple "how" and "where" questions that can be answered with a phrase or a short sentence.
  Example: "How is the Lewis and Clark expedition like space exploration today?"

ELLs, especially those at the beginning levels of language proficiency, cannot be expected to answer broad, open-ended questions such as, "How did Lewis and Clark manage to map such a vast, uncharted territory?" But do not take this to mean that questions low in language complexity can be dismissed, as they, too, can provide valuable prompts for critical thinking and language development, including BICS and CALP. For instance, valuable learning can result from asking, "Name one river that Lewis and Clark saw on their journey that flows east toward the Mississippi and one river that flows west toward the Pacific." ELLs may not be able to provide answers appropriate for abstract questions, but this is not necessarily because they failed to understand the question.

Discovery and Exploration

Discovery and its cousin, exploration, are significant intellectual processes that should not be ignored in teaching ELLs. Much of what was said above about discussion applies to discovery. Discovery involves students hypothesizing and investigating for themselves instead of relying on authorities (e.g., teachers, textbooks, encyclopedias, and authoritative websites) to tell them the right answer. Students are normally more interested in their own discoveries than in what they are told. Capitalize on this by incorporating discovery exercises as frequently as you can in your class. For example, select a topic that encourages students to develop their own theories. One example is to ask students to name ways in which geography affects where civilizations develop. To help, some of the best sources for ideas and inspiration on discovery are old, but worth consulting (e.g., Bruner, 1960; Koenigsberg, 1966; White, 1986). When planning, remember that the act of discovery requires more class time to reason through to solutions than exercises where there is a direct path from the question to a definite answer.

Exploratory talk, like discovery learning, rests on both hunches and prior knowledge, as well as the occasional need to find more information. In the case of history, this involves students engaging in a story-like account of a specific topic. By applying their prior knowledge and informed estimations, they are able to creatively construct a best approximation of a real historical event. Although students' knowledge may be limited, this does not mean their thinking is entirely uninformed. As Barnes (1992) explains, a student may already possess the requisite background from former history lessons or from outside school. Exploration facilitates organizing this prior knowledge and identifying relationships in it. Talking makes this old knowledge conscious knowledge to be applied to the new task. So for instance, you can engage your students in an exploratory conversation about what it might have been like to be on board during Christopher Columbus's first voyage to America or to be one of the first settlers at Jamestown.

Cooperative Learning Skills

Effective teachers of ELL students recognize the value of cooperative learning (Calderón *et al.*, 2011). As noted, cooperative learning can both facilitate learning subject matter and simultaneously serve as an exercise in learning to work collaboratively with others. Researchers have shown that cooperative learning is an important component of successful bilingual education programs (Cohen, 1994; Montecel & Cortez, 2002). Cooperative learning skills are the kinds of skills that are used during group work, which includes the skills to communicate, listen, and articulate thoughts, and the ability to listen to and respect different opinions. Collaborative verbal interaction is a means for ELLs to develop thinking skills and clarify their own thinking about new concepts (Simich-Dudgeon, 1999, as cited in Egbert & Simich-Dudgeon, 2001). Cooperative learning in small or large groups encourages interaction and requires, to varying degrees, both BICS and CALP, depending on the topic of discussion. Engaging students in cooperative learning is generally beneficial; however, it is most effective if tasks are carefully structured and role responsibilities clearly articulated (Cohen, 1994). Cooperative learning does most to help ELLs acquire academic English when it is aligned with instructional goals (Jacobs *et al.*, 1996). Steps teachers might take include:

- Have well-established management procedures in place.
- State early on what the academic and social instructional goals are for the activity.
- Describe the teacher's role as an observer or facilitator.
- Know students' work habits, capabilities, and special needs.
- For the first few activities in particular, select tasks that are well defined and can be accomplished successfully.
- Organize each group in the optimal size and composition for the assigned task.
- Arrange the room and/or spaces and seating to promote group sharing and noise mitigation.
- Supervise the work of each group as needed; be available to answer questions, clarify, and redirect efforts if necessary.
- Closely monitor the behavior and work of students who are not as self-directed (offer extra help, redirect attention, move to another group if necessary—but do not remove from the activity altogether).
- Have each group share its progress and achievements with the rest of the class.

2.4
Enacting the Social Studies Curriculum

Textbooks and Trade Books

Typically the course textbook is the dominant instructional material; however, trade books, Internet resources, atlases, historical fiction, newspapers, and videos should also be used to add to instruction. The traditional reliance of social studies teaching on teacher talk and the textbook (Thornton, 1994) poses a particular challenge for ELLs because social studies vocabulary can be complex and abstract. Some social studies textbooks, even those written for an elementary audience, use "long sentences with multiple embedded clauses" (Chamot & O'Malley, 1994, p. 260). ELL students may have a difficult time understanding the text if they do not receive the language and academic support needed to understand complex reading assignments. Stopping to discuss a few key terms highlighted in the text and defined in the glossary, for instance, can make understanding the text easier for ELLs. We have found that showing images that represent key terms is especially effective (Cruz & Thornton, 2012). Conducting a simple image search on the Internet can yield visual representations that can help increase comprehension.

Students may also have problems with complex verb forms used in social studies print materials, particularly the past tense, the subjunctive, and the past perfect (Egbert & Simich-Dudgeon, 2001). But teachers can help by showing how to say more or less the same thing in different ways. If the text said, for instance, "Should Ben Franklin have been wiser when . . . ?" one could paraphrase by asking "Was Ben Franklin wise when . . . ?" There are a number of strategies that greatly aid in reading texts typically used in schools. Short (1998) suggests, for example:

- *prereading discussions* that connect a topic with students' knowledge and experiences;
- *vocabulary overviews* that explain new words and terms in the reading;
- *prediction guides* that help students predict what a chapter will be about by using clues such as pictures and headings;
- *sectioned readings* that separate the chapter into manageable sections; these can be assigned to groups of students who read their section and then peer-teach it;

- *graphic organizers* that present information visually;
- *note-taking practice* that allows students to take notes while reading.

Fortunately, the situation is improving as publishers respond to ELLs' needs (see, for example, Cengage/National Geographic's *Gateway to Social Studies,* 2013 and *Longman Social Studies,* 2006). In a review of six annotated teachers' editions of high school history textbooks, for example, Case and Obenchain (2006) found that nearly all the texts included teaching suggestions and modifications to accommodate ELL students. It is important to mention that simplified language has long been used as a strategy by content-area teachers to express meaning to ELLs; however, Yano *et al.* (1994) questioned whether this was in fact the most beneficial way to communicate meaning. In their study, three groups of second language learners each had a text to read: the language in one was simplified, the language in the other was "normal," i.e. unadjusted, and the language in the third was what was called "elaborated." The researchers wanted to see which group of second language learners best comprehended the text. They reported that the group reading the elaborated text outperformed the other two groups and concluded that it was precisely because the language was not simplified but elaborated, and had more vocabulary and used circumlocutions, redundancies, and repetitions so that the second language learners were better able to facilitate their learning because the text provided them with linguistic scaffolds.

Along similar lines, Montecel and Cortez (2002) found that using a wide variety of books and materials was important in the success of ELLs in bilingual education programs. An elaborated curriculum provides conceptual scaffolding and can encourage the application of prior knowledge as it provides ELLs more issues to relate to. Doing so helps ELLs as they often "need access to specialized materials that make the curriculum comprehensible to them" (Lindholm-Leavy & Borsato, 2006, p. 192). Short (1998) recommends supplementing the class textbook with social studies resources developed by language specialists. Supplemental materials are helpful for ELLs because they include pre-reading activities, graphics of social studies content, modified reading passages, listening and speaking activities, and critical thinking and study skill tasks.

Graphic Organizers and Realia

Short (2002) found in her study that, whereas social studies teachers do use some visual aids to help students understand the content, demonstrations and hands-on materials such as realia are rarely used. Visual aids such as diagrams, maps, tables, and charts have been shown to help ELLs understand and organize information (Moline, 1995). As already noted, Brown (2007) also outlines specific strategies for making social studies texts more comprehensible for ELLs, including outlines, content maps (which show how parts of text are connected), and using guiding questions. Larsen-Freeman and Anderson (2011) effectively argue for the integration of visuals into all language instruction, including realia and graphic organizers, especially those that are content-based. Harmon and Hedrick (2000) show how conceptual learning can be enhanced through visual representations of social studies vocabulary.

Because language can be a barrier for ELLs, graphic organizers, realia, and physical demonstrations that do not rely on speech should be used to express academic concepts. They can be especially useful as a comprehension check for non-verbal students (Tannenbaum, 1996). Incorporating the use of objects to support your lecture and class discussion will engage students and help them organize and comprehend information.

Graphic organizers organize and show information visually, often presenting concepts in a way that is more comprehensible for ELLs. Because only the most essential information is included, content is more manageable for students. Examples of graphic organizers include timelines, cause-and-effect graphs, and Venn diagrams. These can be used to introduce a topic, during instruction, or in closing activities. Students can also organize their notes, make sense of academic texts, and demonstrate comprehension of content matter by creating their own graphic organizers. Specific examples of graphic organizers are presented in learning activities throughout Part 3.

Another particularly useful strategy is the K–W–L or K–W–L–Q–H approach. Originally developed by Donna Ogle (1986) and subsequently modified (cited in www.readingquest.org/strat/kwl.html), the K–W–L strategy is essentially a mechanism for having students reflect on the process of learning. Using a five-column chart, ask your students to respond to:

K—What do I already *know* about this topic?
W—What do I *want* to know about this topic?
L—What have I *learned* about this topic?
Q—What other *questions* do I still have about this topic?
H—*How* can we learn more?

Complete the "K" and "W" portions at the beginning of a unit of instruction and the "L," "Q," and "H" at the conclusion of the lesson or unit.

Although many teachers use this strategy as a whole-class exercise, it can also prove to be valuable as a daily exercise for ELL students. Simple and more detailed K–W–L–Q–H charts can be downloaded at www.readingquest.org/strat/kwl.html; they can also be easily constructed with a word processing program (Insert→Table).

Realia, too, can be helpful in making content more comprehensible for students as well as invite critical thinking (Tishman, 2008). For example, you can locate an item or object that directly relates to the topic of your discussion. After the connection between the object and the larger concept is made, clearly and slowly restate the main idea of the discussion for your mainstream students and ELLs. The realia could be authentic, such as a manual kitchen appliance that has now been replaced by an automated version. Reproductions also suffice. For example, it is unlikely you will have a vase with painted images from ancient Greece; a reproduction that includes the images works well enough.

Demonstrations and Total Physical Response

To aid comprehension, teachers of ELLs find that physically demonstrating verbs can go a long way in helping students understand directions, in storytelling, and in class discussions. Keep in mind that the oral directions that usually accompany an assignment may be ineffective with ELLs. You may need to model the task and written directions that are needed so students can see what you are referring to (Short, 2002).

In addition to graphic organizers, teacher gestures, and physical demonstration, having students interact through movement has also been shown to be effective in language development. Total physical response or TPR (Asher, 1982) integrates both verbal and physical communication so that students can internalize and eventually "code break" a new language. It is especially effective with beginning language students, for vocabulary building, and with those students who are primarily kinesthetic learners. TPR is based on the belief that comprehension precedes language production and can be demonstrated by bodily movements (Cantoni-Harvey, 1987). Just as in first language learning, when children typically go through a "silent," receptive period and rely on facial expressions, gestures, and the like, the TPR approach encourages language learners to develop listening and comprehension of oral language before speaking tasks are assigned to them. For the more advanced levels of language acquisition, TPR can still be an invaluable aid in the classroom. Articles for further reading on this topic can be found at www.tpr-world.com and www.tprsource.com.

Role Playing and Simulations

Along the line of visual representations are role playing and simulations, which are strategies that actively engage students in their own learning. The general format of role plays are often enactments or re-enactments of a situation or event in which the players assume certain roles, are confronted with a problem involving a moral or value dilemma, and in conclusion are required to make a decision. It is possible that more than one outcome occurs, as consequences are not always predictable, but this too is part of the learning process for students. Role playing is an inclusive method in which students of all types and ability levels can participate; it is useful not only for academic learning and language development but also for learning social behaviors (Shaftel & Shaftel, 1967; Smith & Smith, 1990).

You can assign roles spontaneously in class or provide a more structured experience by creating role sheets, assigning roles, and having specific directives and learning objectives. Generally, ELLs will do better if given advance notice of procedures. The purpose of these simulations is to encourage students to gain information, clarify values and positions, understand other cultures, and to develop skills. Be sure to inform the class of the rules that must be followed and tell them beforehand that in the case of simulations, there are usually winners and losers. The applications for role playing and simulation are countless, but a few examples are model United Nations, mock societies, or students role playing different perspectives in the American Revolution, including the perspective of a Native American, an African American, a woman, a British loyalist, and an American rebel.

A valuable component of role playing and simulations is that they often blend instruction and assessment. Although tests serve important and valid purposes, they can be overused as assessment devices. Teachers can assess student learning by looking at how students can use knowledge in new applications. In this sense, ELLs can demonstrate knowledge through role playing or simulations instead of on a test written in English.

Visual Resources

Another way of engaging students is through the use of visual materials. Although field trips can be invaluable, in many schools these days they are hard to arrange. But social studies has very many substitutes. There are plenty of other opportunities to incorporate visual images in your social studies curriculum. Some examples are maps, photographs, old postcards, portrait and landscape paintings, virtual tours of museums and sites of historical or cultural or geographical interest, and, finally, educational video.

Not only do visual sources readily draw students in, but they engage students in ways that traditional materials simply don't. Another reason they should be included as a method of teaching is because we live in a more visually stimulating society and young people need to be taught how to evaluate these stimuli. For example, postcards are a form of advertising; when they are used in class, students can consider what is being "sold" and how it is accomplished. The common misconception that pictures are objective representations of reality should be thoroughly critiqued through exercises showing, for instance, how Leni Riefenstahl represented the 1934 Nazi party rally at Nuremberg and to what effects.

Pictorial products and projects, such as posters and dioramas, have long been used in the social studies classroom. For students in the early stages of English language acquisition, they can be an effective mechanism for demonstrating their grasp of content knowledge (Tannenbaum, 1996). The cognitive load of photographs can be low, yet the interpretive skills entailed complex (Werner, 2006).

Picture dictionaries have increasingly come to the fore. They are important materials that present vocabulary both in oral and written contexts (Cardoso, 2006). They can be useful in both classroom instruction (Fregeau & Leier, 2008) and for assessment purposes (Kopriva *et al.*, 2007). Picture dictionaries' combination of basic yet important words and their visual representations are plainly useful for beginning speakers of English. In recent years, a growing number of picture dictionaries have become available that are about particular school subjects. These dictionaries help scaffold what is in the textbook for ELLs. This is a boon for content-area instruction, especially in its potential to allow conceptual learning with a reduced cognitive load.

Creating dioramas has also been shown to be an effective tool for meeting the challenge of teaching social studies to ELL students (Short, 1994). Identifying and then creating replicas of physical features helps students internalize concepts. This activity provides students with the opportunity to create their own biosphere that contains several important geographic features. Although all students will be engaged learners, ELL students will particularly benefit from the concrete nature of the learning experience. Learners who prefer kinesthetic activities will appreciate the hands-on project as well. Also, this project more fairly assesses knowledge because it communicates non-verbally.

Assessment

Perhaps the biggest challenge in assessing student learning in the social studies classroom is separating language from content, especially if a student is not achieving at grade level. If an ELL is not succeeding in a course, you need "to determine if the cause of the failure is that the content has not been mastered or if the language of the subject is interfering with the student's learning of the content" (Short, 1991, p. 51). Mihai (2010) offers three things content-area teachers should consider when assessing ELLs in their classrooms:

- Be sure you understand the process and stages of language acquisition.
- Assess ELLs in their home language as well as in English whenever possible.
- Include parents and other family members in assessment since they can provide valuable information about the student's language development.

When traditional writing assessments such as essays and term papers are assigned, some students may require additional assistance not only in writing the paper itself, but also in prewriting. Teaching them about RAFT (role, audience, format, topic), outlining, and developing persuasive thinking will help them prepare for this task. Easy-to-understand instructions, examples, and downloadable handouts for RAFT, Opinion-Proof, and Thesis-Proof can be found at www.readingquest.org/strat. Traditional assessments can be made more accessible with accommodations such as allowing more time for test taking, developing ELL-specific test preparation support, and including graphic and visual support in the assessment (Fox & Fairbairn, 2011). But even with these helpful resources for using traditional assessment strategies, we recommend utilizing a wide variety of evaluation strategies, including alternative assessment methods.

Alternative assessments include strategies that offer unconventional options for students to demonstrate their understanding and growth. These forms of assessment usually have a higher rate of completion and student involvement. Strategies that fall under this umbrella include authentic, performance-based, and portfolio assessments. Of critical importance in these types of assessment is the feedback provided by the teacher and the reflection engaged in by students at the completion of the assignment (Mihai, 2010).

Product-based assessment requires a concrete end result. Some examples include having students present knowledge or skills through projects such as posters, art, music, poetry, videos, scripts, and exhibits. Many topics in social studies curricula naturally lend themselves to being represented in multiple media. In fact, for years teachers have been assigning projects like these that give students the opportunity to demonstrate their comprehension of core concepts and key events. These product-based activities can help you determine your students' successful acquisition of content, especially by ELLs and students with different learning styles.

Another tool you can use in your classroom is portfolios and journals. An integral part of portfolios and journals is that they require self-assessment and reflection. Since these approaches do not require racing against the clock, portfolios and journals are well suited to ELLs. Both portfolios and journals can include traditional evaluations, alternative assessments, and electronic or audio-visual products as well. Portfolios are a meaningful collection of student work over a period of time, showing growth and development. Students take responsibility and ownership of the project, careful to document their effort and progress. As students become familiar with these formats, their understanding of content and growth in class will be documented and easy for you to see.

Learning logs, response logs, and dialogue journals allow students to reflect on learning and record their impressions, reactions, and comprehension of concepts and events. Journals afford teachers with an excellent means to track students' progress over time.

An additional way to use journals is, Short (1991) suggests, as a simple, standard format for responding to readings (Figure 2.1). In this manner, students log what was comprehensible and record what was not understood, giving you the chance to provide additional assistance. In this way, you can use journals as an interactive, two-way mechanism for communication. Students will communicate what they did and did not learn, and after reading their journals you can provide feedback, which they'll appreciate. This private dialogue can serve you and your students with a way to communicate in supportive and positive ways.

Authentic assessments are methods of assessing student achievement or performance that are as close to real-life situations as possible. Some social studies examples are:

- history—conducting an oral history project by interviewing individuals who have first-hand knowledge of an event;
- government—tracking and researching an issue, taking a stand, and writing a letter to a government or business leader;
- economics—creating an advertisement that will combine the study of propaganda, audience analysis, and research;
- geography—plotting the course of a hurricane on a map using longitude and latitude;
- sociology—students studying the use of surveys and questionnaires in sociology actually construct a survey, use it to gather data, and analyze the information collected.

Reading Title:	
What I understood	What I didn't understand
What I learned	

FIGURE 2.1. Standard format for responding to readings.

In an overview of social studies literature, Case and Obenchain (2006) conclude that authentic assessment is "considered a highly effective body of practices and philosophy" (p. 42).

Performance-based assessments are, as the term implies, forms of evaluation that require students to show what they know and what they can do. Role playing, surveying, and presenting oral reports are all examples of ways to conduct performance-based assessments. As an alternative to a perspective essay assignment (where students write from a particular viewpoint), students could role play instead. By taking on roles of characters, students can explore the multiplicity of perspectives in any given time period. You should create tasks and assignments that allow students to practice and apply language *and* content knowledge and skills. In addition to utilizing traditional oral and written assignments, Short (1998) advocates incorporating a hands-on, performance-based approach in assessing ELLs. Because some of these forms of assessments may rely heavily on the spoken word and are better suited for students at one of the higher levels of language production, be sure to include in the assessment strategies appropriate for ELLs at lower levels (speech emergence and intermediate fluency) that rely more on acting out, displaying or creating visuals such as collages, mime, and other less word-dependent ways of communicating.

In general, remember that effective assessments should be similar to tasks that, when the material was first introduced, teachers had explained or students had engaged with (Anstrom, 1999). By putting in place a high-quality assessment plan, both students' content knowledge and language proficiency will be enhanced.

Conclusion

In addition to all of the specialized strategies described above, Short (1991) points out that remembering basic principles and presenting information clearly are especially important for ELLs. She suggests:

- presenting the lesson's objectives and activities;
- writing legibly and listing instructions individually;
- developing classroom routines;
- using multiple media in presenting information;

- paraphrasing and summarizing main points often throughout the lesson;
- reducing teacher talk and allowing more student talk;
- increasing the number of higher-order thinking questions asked;
- developing a student-centered approach to teaching and learning (pp. 9–11).

In sum, the instructional strategies that have been proven to be effective in the social studies classroom primarily include scaffolded lecture techniques, the infusion of reading strategies, active learning, cooperative learning techniques, and modified questioning and discussion. Emphasis should be placed on what Krashen (1985) calls "comprehensible input," that is, creating structured learning environments in which material is presented and supported by contextual clues along with language and curricular modifications (e.g., using shorter sentences, simplified language when appropriate, preselected topics). These strategies will be utilized in the discipline-based chapters in Part 3 to concretize them in content-rich contexts.

Part 3
Teaching Social Studies

3.1
Introduction

Victor Marino, a history major in college, began teaching high school social studies over 20 years ago. All that time he has taught in the same suburban school district. His passion is European history and he has taught courses mainly in it and world history. Mr. Marino has always taught both general track and college preparatory track students and differentiated course contents according to the district curriculum guide.

Almost from the outset of his teaching career Mr. Marino recognized that a number of students in both tracks had problems "seeing the wood for the trees" when they delved into their textbooks. Initially, especially since this ability had always come easily to someone so deeply interested as himself, he engaged in what has been called "assumptive teaching." That is, he assumed that his task was to "teach history" with only the occasional distraction to demonstrate to students how to study and how to develop and use concepts (Herber, 1970, p. vii).

After discussion with his department chairperson about the problems many students had with reading the course textbook, Mr. Marino enrolled in a graduate course on "reading in the content areas" at the local college. Although the purpose and logic of this course made sense to Mr. Marino, he was skeptical that he could possibly individualize his courses, units, and lessons to the extent the course instructor seemed to be recommending. Eventually, however, he realized that he could incrementally build a collection of instructional materials and methods to serve students with different reading needs. Although it is impossible to meet the needs of every single individual in every classroom every day, it is possible to come much closer to this ideal than has often been the case (Herber, 1970, p. 46). For example, he created graphic organizers to illustrate complex cause–effect relationships and audio-taped sections of the textbook that some students consistently couldn't comprehend. Although once he got started these new approaches proved easy enough to do with his regularly taught courses, he also developed ways to adapt materials for other classes he occasionally taught such as U.S. history. More recently, Mr. Marino encountered a new teaching challenge: the growing number of English language learner (ELL) students in his courses. Again he sought further information. In some ways many of the changes he incrementally added to his courses for ELL students paralleled changes to reading in the content areas years before. This time he adjusted discussion techniques, organized small group work in a variety of ways to capitalize on student strengths, and provided a wider variety of ways students could present their work. He also found, given that most of his ELLs were Spanish speakers of Latin American heritage, that a number of English language instructional materials—such as videos and books he already used—were available in Spanish versions.

Thus, in his unit on the Reformation, he now utilized textbooks with different reading levels that covered the same conceptual content. He also used far more maps and pictures than in the past. For example, students pored over maps showing where Protestantism spread and different groups researched the course of the Reformation in different regions. Students examined pictures of St. Peter's in Rome and contrasted it with a stark Calvinist church in Geneva. He added, too, new content to the unit such as how the Reformation was contemporaneous with Spanish conquests in the Americas and the Caribbean and their efforts to spread the Catholic faith there, which Mr. Marino hoped might make connections with ELL students' knowledge and interests, as well as place the Reformation in a global context for all of his students. He also turned to the school English to speakers of other languages (ESOL) specialist and community members for ongoing assistance.

"Mr. Marino" is not a real person but in a sense he does exist: he is a composite of experiences we have had or have witnessed. The important point is that he illustrates how teachers of the social studies or of other content areas do not want to compromise the content they rightly feel they are employed to teach. But at the same time they have students whose effective learning of that material requires new ways of approaching the curriculum and instruction. The two goals do not have to be in conflict.

In Part 3 (Chapters 3.2–3.8), we describe learning activities for middle and high schools. The activities are intended to apply the principles explored in the first two parts of the book. We chose topics for the activities that are adaptable to more than one grade level and span the range of subjects (e.g., geography) and courses (e.g., U.S. history) included under the umbrella of "social studies." It also seemed sensible to select commonly taught topics, as their familiarity may prevent the reader from being distracted by the necessity of absorbing new material. Moreover, if the ideas we are advancing in this book are to prove useful, looking at familiar material through a fresh lens may most convincingly show this.

Most of the learning activities are accompanied by questions that we have endeavored to align with the process of second language acquisition (see Part 1). The four levels are preproduction, early production, speech emergence, and intermediate fluency. Although there is overlap in the teaching strategies used at each level, we will largely employ these levels in the learning exercises as follows (for a list, see Table 3.1). As Cruz *et al.* (2003) explain, this approach "equips teachers to deal effectively with ELL students and to select appropriate teaching strategies" (p. 15).

At all of these levels social studies instruction can be meaningful. Plainly, the greater challenges come at the lower levels. Yet even questions for preproduction students can be made meaningful. Reliance on looking at maps and pictures, pointing, gesturing, and the like may be labor-intensive but it need not be uninteresting or intellectually empty. As we have been at pains to point out, even seemingly cognitively undemanding or context-embedded activities such as pointing to the location of San Francisco on a map of the western United States can be made into a thinking exercise (see Chapter 3.2).

As we created and modified learning activities we kept in mind that social studies classrooms generally contain students with varying needs, interests, and aptitudes. We were cognizant, for example, that linguistically diverse gifted students require the same academic rigor as English-speaking gifted students. To that end, many of the exercises are designed to challenge and engage gifted students whether or not their native language is English.

We do not regard the exercises and activities that follow as complete lesson plans but, rather, points of departure. We encourage you to plan for instruction by using an ELL-sensitive lesson plan format. At our university, we utilize a template developed by Dr. Joyce Nutta that takes into

TABLE 3.1 Four levels of speech emergence

	Preproduction	Early production	Speech emergence	Intermediate fluency
ELL linguistic ability	Teaching strategies "Silent" period Pointing Responding with movement Following commands Receptive vocabulary up to 500 words	One- or two-word responses Labeling Listing Receptive vocabulary up to 1,000 words Expressive vocabulary 100–500 words	Short phrases and sentences Comparing and contrasting Descriptions Receptive vocabulary up to 7,000 words Expressive vocabulary 2,000 words	Dialogue Reading academic texts Writing Receptive vocabulary up to 12,000 words Expressive vocabulary 4,000 words
Teaching strategies	Yes/no questions Simplified speech Gestures Visuals Picture books Word walls K–W–L charts Simple cloze activities Realia TPR	Questions that require: yes/no; either/or; two-word response; lists of words; definitions; describing Reader's theater Drama Graphic organizers	How and why questions Modeling Demonstrating Cooperative learning Comprehension checks Alternative assessments Simulations	Brainstorming Journal writing Literary analysis Problem solving Role playing Monologues Storytelling Oral reports Interviewing and applications

ELL, English language learner; TPR, total physical response.

account students' varying levels of language proficiency (Table 3.2). The important thing to remember is that all lesson plans need to have language objectives as well as social studies objectives. With some subjects, you may need to begin with language instruction before the lesson can be taught (for example, teaching preproduction students about interrogative words or explaining conditional tenses to students at the speech-emergent level).

TABLE 3.2 Lesson plan with English language learner (ELL) modifications

Lesson plan	Preproduction	Early production	Speech emergence	Intermediate fluency
Content objective Should be valid for all language levels				
Language objective The goal should be one level above students' present level				
Preparation What materials can you identify to provide comprehensible input for each level?				
Procedures How are you going to provide comprehensible input in your delivery? What strategies will you use?				
Assessment How are you going to assess at each of the language levels?				
Home–school connection What activity can you use to connect with all learners' home cultures?				

Modified by B. Cruz and S. Thornton from a grid created by Dr. Joyce Nutta, University of South Florida.

If you've not read Part 1, we encourage you to do so now, so that you have a solid understanding and frame of reference for the different levels of language acquisition. Another excellent overview of second language acquisition theory can be found on the website of the Northwest Regional Educational Laboratory (www.nwrel.org/request/2003may/overview.html). You can also view and hear the four different stages of English language development by accessing the University of South Florida's online database of video samples. These video clips feature students representing each of the language levels and include annotated audio that further assists users in understanding second language acquisition theory. The online database also includes speaking, reading, and writing samples of ELLs from different backgrounds, ages, and grade levels along with a number of case studies for further study. The online databases for elementary, middle, and high school levels can be found at http://esol.coedu.usf.edu/elementary/index.htm, http://esol.coedu.usf.edu/middleschool/index.htm, and http://esol.coedu.usf.edu/highschool/index.htm.

Teaching Tip

 - The webcasts at www.colorincolorado.org/webcasts offer an exciting new way to learn about teaching ELLs. Each webcast features a 45-minute video program, which includes recommended readings and suggested discussion questions, and is accompanied by a PowerPoint presentation.

To facilitate your usage of the book and easily locate learning activities that correlate to levels of language ability, we have indicated at the top of each lesson which levels of language acquisition can be met by each lesson or exercise. In some cases, all four levels are included because modifications have been made for all levels of language acquisition. In other cases, fewer levels are included because the exercise was developed with only certain levels of language ability in mind. That is not to say, however, that the lesson couldn't be modified for other levels; we leave that to the discretion of the teacher and, in fact, invite readers to take this opportunity to adapt the learning activities for the specific needs of their students. Similarly, we also specify the main instructional strategies highlighted in each lesson or learning activity. In addition, all of the National Council for the Social Studies curricular themes are represented in the activities and can easily be cross-referenced with most state and local curriculum standards.

You will also find "Teaching Tips" sprinkled throughout each of the content chapters. These tips are additional teaching ideas to consider or ELL modifications to keep in mind as you implement the learning activities in your classroom.

Finally, we hope that the activities and strategies described hereafter succeed in making tangible what we have been talking about in this book so far. Even though we apply these techniques in specific examples, we have done so in a general way to demonstrate how the techniques would be implemented. Some of the exercises we have used successfully for many years in various ways; others have been created more recently and piloted with our teacher education students. In all cases, we think it is worth repeating the already cited sentiment expressed by Noddings (2006): "try things out, reflect, hypothesize, test, play with things" (p. 284). Creating and modifying these activities was a humbling experience as it constantly reminded us that not all topics can be easily transfigured and, therefore, of the challenge social studies teachers of ELLs face every day.

3.2
Geography

As with most other academic subjects, the first thing that may come to mind when thinking of geographic study is written text (Hardwick & Davis, 2009). But valuable, some might say better, geographic learning can result from observing the features of Earth as well. This can be accomplished through field trips, certainly, but in classrooms visual information can also provide a basis for geographic study. Still and moving pictures, maps, graphs, and charts are wonderful sources in geography (Cruz & Thornton, 2012). Exercises based on visuals have been shown to be highly effective with ELLs (Salinas *et al.,* 2008).

Take photographs. Textbooks today are normally full of useful photographs. On a growing number of topics, too, relevant photographs can be found on the Internet. These sources of photographs, however, may be insufficiently specific for in-depth study. In a case study of Switzerland, say, in a unit on the geography of Europe, trade books can fill the gap. Such a book (e.g., Levy, 1994) offers dozens of photographs that illustrate the topography, trade routes, and economic activities likely to be emphasized in a study of Switzerland. Photographs make meaningful, even sophisticated study possible even if ELLs are at early stages of mastering written English (Wilkins *et al.,* 2008). The breadth of trade books, moreover, means that a variety of potentially relevant pathways to understanding the geography of Switzerland are available in one book or a collection of books teachers may build up over time.

No subject in the social studies is broader in scope than geography. The distinguished educator Lucy Sprague Mitchell (1991) went so far as to say that perhaps "modern geography should not be regarded as a separate subject but as a point of view which can color many subjects" (p. 20). Thus, it should not be surprising that geography can take the form of separate courses such as "World Geography" or be integrated with other social studies such as history and anthropology in courses such as "World Cultures."

In either case, the subject matter of geography in general education, John Dewey (1916/1966) underscored, is "the cultural or humane aspects of the subject . . . needed to help appreciate the significance of human activities and relations" (pp. 212–213). Geographic study basically concerns why features on the face of Earth are located where they are. It encompasses study of particular features or places on Earth such as the Grand Canyon or Greater Los Angeles. In addition to the character of particular places, however, geographic study aims to identify patterns of features on Earth and the processes that account for how and where they are placed (Schmidt, 2011). A geographic inquiry might explore, for instance, where cattle ranching takes place in Texas and what physical and human processes account for this placement. More than the physical aspects of the subject, most American school geography programs concentrate on spatial relationships between the natural world and human activity (Hardwick & Holtgrieve, 1996).

Geographic study should, then, be aimed at more than examining isolated geographic phenomena. Rather, it should be conceptual and thematic—the purpose is to generalize, to learn about classes of phenomena and the relationships among them. Thus, recognizing that "the Mississippi" is a river is a first step towards understanding the concept of "river" and distinguishing it from other concepts. As Dewey (1910/1991) put it, "The river-meaning (or character) must serve to designate the Rhone, the Rhine, the Mississippi, the Hudson, the Wabash, in spite of their varieties of place, length, quality of water, and must be such as not to suggest ocean current, ponds, or brooks" (p. 130).

Concepts are chosen for study based on their usefulness for illuminating relationships. For instance, a study of the Rhone Valley might entail relationships among the meltwater, types of agriculture, and settlement patterns. Embedded here is understanding of concepts such as "alpine" and "river" as well as factual material.

Although teaching is ideally conceptual, in practice it sometimes isn't. Rather, it assumes the form of emphasizing "where" questions (e.g., Where is the Rhone? How long is it?) and neglecting the other "wh-" questions (e.g., When is the Rhone's flow greatest? What is its significance for a region with a Mediterranean climate?). In ELL settings particularly, the temptation to pose "where" questions and ignore other "wh-" questions may be great, as the former appear to place fewer language demands on the learner. But, if ELLs (or other students for that matter) experience geography mainly as facts, they have missed most of the point of the exercise.

The same admonition holds for map skills. For example, noting the absolute location of San Francisco on a map of the western United States, by itself, is unlikely to stimulate conceptual thinking. But the same map exercise could be recast into an exercise in relative location (i.e., where the geographic feature is in relation to other features). Students could, using a map, hypothesize what seems significant about the relative location of San Francisco. For example, they might note that it lies at the mouth of a large bay or it appears to have easy water access to the California interior via the Sacramento River.

As the prototypical geographic skill, it is too bad that it is so often assumed map skills are effectively taught discretely or will simply develop as an automatic product of maturation (and thus don't need to be taught at all). In the case of the latter assumption, there is a considerable body of research suggesting that "reading" maps is a complex form of "literacy" that does not necessarily develop in tandem with reading text (Wiegand, 2006). Although there is no time here to explore map reading fully, some activities later in this chapter suggest a few approaches to it.

To maximize learning, equipping classrooms with geographic materials is highly desirable. Having a decent-sized globe is one of the best ways to foster spatial thinking. While globes (and atlases and wall maps for that matter) appear to be less common in classrooms than they once were, many times globes remain a superior way to learn about Earth to flat maps. For example, students who cannot understand why flying from New York to Tokyo crosses into the polar region will readily grasp it by looking at a globe. This is a case where hands on a three-dimensional model are superior to learning from a book or computer screen.

A considerable impediment to conceptual teaching and learning is the widespread belief that geography courses should emphasize facts and broad coverage (rather than a significant amount of in-depth learning as implied by a conceptual approach). We have met plenty of teachers, administrators, parents, and children who deem facts to be the proper focus of study. Sometimes this belief reflects an ignorance of geography as a field of study and sometimes an overdeveloped fear that, without emphasis, geographic facts will fail to be learned. The effects of an overemphasis on facts, however, are not really in dispute: student boredom and rapid "forgetting." Although no one questions that facts are needed in conceptual thinking—you can't think with what you don't know—their acquisition is to scant avail if that's where geography instruction ends.

A final obstacle to conceptual teaching in geography to be raised here is no obstacle in principle but often turns out to be so in practice: integration of geography with history. Consider New York state's requirement of two years of "world history and geography" in high school. Perhaps because history is a far more common background among social studies teachers than geography, what sounds on the surface like a blended treatment of the two subjects turns out to be mostly history: geography becomes an enabling subject providing a more or less passive backdrop for the unfolding of historical developments. In the same manner, curriculum guides tout teaching geography in American history courses. But both textbooks and teachers typically relegate geography to opening chapters on map skills and noting locations thereafter. Geographic relationships—and what they might add to historical meanings—tend to go unexplored (Thornton, 2007).

Thus far a number of obstacles to conceptual teaching in geography have been identified. Normally, these obstacles can be overcome with forethought and planning. As with any curricular planning, which geographic relationships and concepts are going to be taught in a given instructional unit should be determined ahead of time. (Of course, unforeseen ideas can arise spontaneously during instruction—this can be considered a bonus.) Once the relationships have been identified, then decide which facts, concepts, and skills are likely to be useful in learning those relationships.

In the remainder of this chapter we look at activities that hold potential for conceptual teaching. We will begin with a basic concept in map work—scale—and illustrate some ways it can be approached with ELLs at different levels. We also explore how human settlement is related to physical features. Whereas the first two activities are pitched at relatively abstract levels, the next two are designed to look in more detail at human activities and the intricacies of their relationships with the physical environments in which they occur. In this sense they underscore how human interaction with the natural environment is far more complex than mere human adaptation to or alteration of physical conditions. Indeed, the environment itself is at least in part a human creation as we respond to it according to our own cultural patterns (Gillespie, 2010).

Kinesthetic Learning and Stratified Questioning: The Concept of Scale (Levels 1–4)

The concept of scale is fundamental to the study of geography. Although most secondary students understand that a map is a representation of what actually exists, they sometimes have difficulty with the variety of scales that exist and how they change from map to map. In this lesson, students will consider different types of maps, investigate the concept of scale, measure the dimensions of their classroom, and create a map of the room that is drawn to scale.

You will need the following materials: several maps (each using a different scale), drawing paper, pencils, rulers, and tape measures to measure the dimensions of both the classroom and the items in the classroom.

Start the lesson by leading students in a discussion using the questioning strategies in Activity 3.1 as a guide, modified for each level of language development in your classroom. In addition to asking the appropriate level of questions for your ELL students, remember that, although all students benefit from additional wait time after being asked a question, ELLs typically need even more as they meet the linguistic challenges of a question as well as the embedded content-specific vocabulary and concepts.

ACTIVITY 3.1. Map questioning strategy

Stage	Map questioning strategy
Preproduction	Open your textbooks and point to a map. Point to the legend or key on the map. Can you find the scale used in this map? Find a physical or topographical map (that shows mountains, rivers, lakes, etc.). Find a political map (that shows borders of countries, states, cities, etc.). Find a weather map (that shows temperatures, wind patterns, etc.).
Early production	How are maps helpful? How are maps used? Find a map in your textbook that would be helpful in predicting rainfall for an area. Find a map in your textbook that would be useful in locating the capitals of Europe. Find a map in your textbook that shows landforms in Africa.
Speech emergence	Why do we use maps? For what purposes? Describe the main function of a physical or topographical map. Why are physical maps more stable (less likely to change) than political maps? What kinds of features are you likely to find on a weather map?
Intermediate fluency	What do all maps have in common? Why do different maps have different scales? Why do some maps show things that other maps do not?

Adapted with permission from the National Council for the Social Studies.

After the introductory discussion on maps, show several examples of maps and show that different maps are drawn at different scales. Explain the concept of scale. Use modeling and concrete examples, paraphrasing and restating.

Tell the class that they will be creating a map (floor plan) of the classroom. Students will use a scale of 1/4 inch = 1 foot. Draw a rough example on the board to illustrate.

Allow students sufficient time to measure the dimensions of the outer walls of the room, the dimensions of the desks, other furniture, and any other significant features in the room. Remind students that they also need to measure how far items are from the walls so that they can place them in the correct relative location on their maps.

Using a piece of drawing paper, the students will then begin to draw an overhead view of the classroom. Encourage students to create a map key that labels each item so that others may read and interpret their maps accurately.

After the students have created their maps of the classroom, have them compare theirs with others' and ask them to compare the students' representations to the actual physical space of the class. Lead students in a reflective discussion by asking the following closing questions:

1. What are some of the mistakes that people made when creating their classroom maps? (Write answers on board.) Do you think cartographers (map makers) make similar mistakes?
2. Why is it important to draw everything on a map using the same scale? What would happen if we changed scale during the creation of our maps?
3. Explain to the students that no map shows everything for a given space. Why is some information always necessarily lost when creating a map?

Teaching Tip

■ Have students create another map of a space they frequent (e.g., their bedroom, home, a park).

Selected Internet Resources for Teaching about Maps

ESRI GIS Lessons (http://gis2.esri.com/industries/education/arclessons/arclessons.cfm)

National Geographic Map Machine (http://plasma.nationalgeographic.com/mapmachine/index.html)

Social Studies for Kids: Are You Map Savvy? (www.socialstudiesforkids.com/articles/geography/mapsavvy1.htm)

Xpeditions Atlas (www.nationalgeographic.com/xpeditions/atlas)

Kinesthetic Learning and Visual Aids: Africa: Physical Geography and Population Distribution (Levels 3 and 4)

For many students, Africa is a vast but uniform continent. Students seem to envision either dense tropical jungles or dry, open savannahs and deserts—with few populated areas. Misconceptions about Africa have proven hard to change. Decades ago researchers uncovered much the same faulty notions that persist today (Beyer, 1969). In this lesson, students are able to compare their mental maps of Africa with the physical reality of the African continent. They will also analyze the relationship between physical geographical characteristics and population distribution.

Mental Map Activity

Start by removing or covering up any wall maps that you may have in your classroom. Provide students with a blank piece of paper, telling them that they are to conjure up a map of Africa in their minds. You can have them close their eyes to assist with the visualization. In the case of preproduction ELLs, it would be appropriate to briefly show them a map of Africa first and motion that they are to draw the region from memory. Instruct everyone to envision the outline of the continent, any rivers and lakes, vegetation areas, countries and cities, and mountainous regions. They are then to draw their mental maps on the blank sheets of paper, labeling as much as possible.

After allowing the students a sufficient amount of time to complete the activity, distribute a map of Africa showing the features you asked them to envision and draw. Some websites that offer useful printable maps of the continent include:

■ CIA World Factbook (https://www.cia.gov/library/publications/the-world-factbook);
■ Infoplease (www.infoplease.com/atlas/africa.html);
■ WorldAtlas (www.worldatlas.com/webimage/countrys/af.htm);
■ Xpeditions (www.nationalgeographic.com/xpeditions).

Direct students to note the differences between the two maps. An alternative activity would be to have students compare their maps with other students', noting differences and similarities (see Mental Cartography activity in Chapter 3.7). This cooperative learning approach can afford ELL students the opportunity to develop their expressive language skills with peers. The visual supports of maps will aid in comprehension of the subject matter.

Stimulate class discussion by asking:

■ How accurate do you think your maps are?
■ Which places and features were accurately included and depicted? Which places and features were omitted from your map? Why might that be?
■ What observations or generalizations can you make about your map and this exercise?

At this point, you may wish to lead the class in a teacher-directed discussion of Africa's principal features, focusing on principal rivers and lakes, natural vegetation, average rainfall, and population density. A helpful map for pointing out how large Africa is, especially in relation to Europe and the United States, can be found at www.bu.edu/africa/outreach (Figure 3.1).

Next, have students consider a physical map of Africa made before circa 1880 (several excellent ones are available at http://etc.usf.edu/maps/galleries/africa/complete/index.php). You might have students discuss what makes the map look old. Then relate that accurate knowledge of the interior of Africa was then new to Westerners.

Ask students to locate where Africans live in relation to some of the continent's salient physical features. A beginning might be made with major rivers, such as the Niger, and possibly the great lakes of East Africa. If necessary, the teacher might offer prompts such as "Why do people so often live by bodies of water?" Most likely, accounting for the role of remaining features such as the Atlas Mountains will prove more difficult and prompting may be essential.

Now, using the stages and questioning strategies on scale as a guide, construct the same sort of table for this activity on population distribution in Africa.

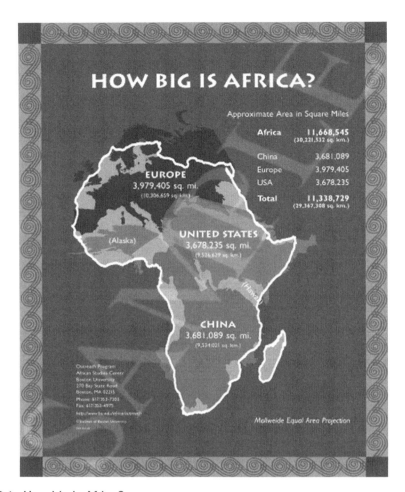

FIGURE 3.1. How big is Africa?

Reprinted with permission from the African Studies Center, Boston University.

Selected Internet Resources for Teaching about the Geography of Africa

African Studies Center (Boston University) (www.bu.edu/africa/outreach)

Africa-Related Links WorldWide (University of Wisconsin–Madison) (http://africa.wisc.edu/?
   page_id=939)

African Studies Internet Resources (Columbia University Libraries) (www.columbia.edu/cu/lweb/
   indiv/africa/cuvl/index.html)

GlobaLink-Africa Curriculum Project (UCLA) (www.globalization-africa.org/projects.php?project=
   curriculum)

K–12 Electronic Guide for African Resources on the Internet (www.africa.upenn.edu/Home_
   Page/AFR_GIDE.html)

K–W–L–Q–H, Visual Aids, Guided Imagery, and Stratified Questioning: Women's Work in Southern India (Levels 2–4)

Scholarship of the last generation or two has highlighted what has always been true: human experience is gendered. Let's explore this notion in southern India.

When measured in terms of the number of duties performed and the amount of time spent in agriculture, women's contributions are greater than men's (Coonrod, 1998). Further, because men's agricultural work usually employs machinery and draft animals, women's farm work is more arduous, tending to consist of just their own energy and manual labor (Mies, 1986, cited in Coonrod, 1998). Of all agricultural work, perhaps the most laborious is rice cultivation, done almost completely by women, without the use of labor-saving tools.

Rice is a staple component of the daily diet in southern India. Because the region has abundant rainfall, it is especially well suited for the planting of rice, a crop that is cultivated almost solely by women. In this case study of women and rice cultivation in southern India, students will consider how seasonal and technological factors affect women in rural, traditional societies.

Have students consider a climate map of India (such as the one found on www.maps ofindia.com) and complete a modified K–W–L–Q–H chart (Activity 3.2; note that the last three columns have been transposed to better suit this lesson). For this exercise, you will have students fill in the first two columns (K and W) while they also consider what remaining questions they have (Q) and types of resources they would need to access to learn more (H). Finally, they will summarize the central concepts learned (L) from the lesson.

ACTIVITY 3.2. K–W–L–Q–H chart

K: What do I already know about this topic?	W: What do I want to know about this topic?	Q: What other questions do I still have?	H: How can we learn more?	L: What have I learned about this topic?

Create a whole-class chart by asking for volunteers to share their ideas with the entire group and noting them on the board.

Guided Imagery Exercise

Ask students to clear their desks and get comfortable in their seats. Dim the lights and decrease any external stimuli by shutting doors and windows. Tell the students that they will be going on a trip to India. Read the following passage,[1] providing ELLs with a print copy to follow along. ELLs can also be given the print copy the night before so they can translate it at home and be better prepared for what they will experience in class.

> Your name is Jaya and you are a young woman living in southwest India. It is rice-growing season now. You start work at 4 a.m. and don't stop until 8 p.m., with a one-hour rest in between. You use no tools or work animals, only your own hands and energy. After 15 hours of work in the rice fields, you are exhausted.
>
> You feel a bit of resentment because your husband, whom you married last year, works about seven to eight hours per day. He gets up about 5 a.m., takes a one- or two-hour break in the middle of the day, and then works again from 3 p.m. to 5 p.m.
>
> Even still, you are grateful for the work since one of your cousins in a wheat-growing part of India recently lost her job. Your cousin had been a grain thresher but, with the increased use of mechanized grain threshers, she lost an important source of income for her family.
>
> You worry about the same fate for you and your family.

Ask students to slowly come back to the present and open their eyes. Have them consider what life was like for them as Jaya. Direct them to take out a sheet of paper and a pen or pencil. Tell them that they are going to respond to the story you have just read to them by doing a timed writing exercise. The object of the exercise is to try to write as much as possible in the time allotted. Allow a five- to ten-minute writing period. Tell students that their stories should convey a sense of what a day might be like for Jaya. ELLs at levels 1 and 2 should be encouraged to use their bilingual dictionaries as they craft their responses. They can also be allowed to write their responses in their home language first and then translate them into English.

> It is [today's date]. It is 4 a.m. and I must get to the fields . . .

When the writing period is over, ask students to stop. Assure them that it is not necessary to complete their stories and ask for volunteers to share their stories with the rest of the class. After sufficient stories have been read, ask students to summarize their feelings and ideas about Jaya's life. Inform the class that the work conditions described in the story actually describe a common situation for many women agricultural workers in India.

Teaching Tip

- Because guided imagery exercises tend to have a high cognitive demand but are low-context, allow ELLs to follow along with a print copy or give it to them a day earlier for them to review. ELLs in the early stage of language production can also be allowed to draw their stories and simply list pertinent words that have textual meaning.

Maps and Discussion

Distribute (or project) two maps of India (one depicting annual rainfall and the other showing main food crops cultivated). If your class textbook does not have suitable maps, the website Maps of India has several appropriate ones (e.g., www.mapsofindia.com/maps/india/annualrainfall.htm and www.mapsofindia.com/indiaagriculture/foodcrops.htm).

Engage students in a discussion by using Activity 3.3 as a guide, modified for each level of language development in your classroom.

ACTIVITY 3.3. Women in India questioning strategy

Stage	Strategy
Preproduction	Point to the areas that get the most rain. Find the Bay of Bengal. Where is the Arabian Sea? Where is wheat grown? Where is rice grown?
Early production	List all the countries shown on the map. What are the most important coastal cities? According to the map, does New Delhi get a lot of or a little rainfall? Where are the driest parts of India located? Where might Jaya (hint: rice cultivating) live? Where might her cousin (hint: wheat cultivating) live?
Speech emergence	How might people's diets in India be influenced by rainfall received? What rainfall levels are needed for successful rice cultivation? How might women's lives in large cities such as New Delhi differ from Jaya's life?
Intermediate fluency	Why is rice cultivation primarily women's work? Would it benefit women if a rice-cultivating machine was introduced to the region? Which parts of India would you predict to be least populated?

Research Activity

Direct students' attention to their K–W–Q–H–L charts, focusing on "H—How can we learn more?" Have students share their ideas with the rest of the class, noting others' ideas they had not thought of.

Provide them with the resources and time to research something they would like to learn more about. After allowing sufficient time to complete the research, have students share their findings with the rest of the class.

> **Teaching Tip**
> - Know your students' capabilities and needs before assigning them to dyads and small groups.

Closure: Ask students to reflect on their K–W–Q–H–L charts once again, focusing on "L—What have I learned about this topic?" Allow students to share their reflections with one another.

Resources for Teaching about Women in India

Centre for Social Research (www.csrindia.org)

Coonrod, C. S. (1998). Chronic hunger and the status of women in India. Retrieved from www.thp.org/reports/indiawom.htm.

Cruz, B., and Prorok, C. (1997). "Women at work": A sample lesson for incorporating gender into geography. *Social Education*, 61 (7): 385–389.

Maps of India (www.mapsofindia.com/geography)

Patel, V., and Crocco, M. S. (2003). Teaching about South Asian women: Getting beyond the stereotypes. *Social Education*, 67 (1): 22–26.

Reese, L. (2001). *Women in India: Lessons from the ancient Aryans through the early modern Mughals.* Berkeley, CA: Women in World History Curriculum.

South Asian Women's Studies Bibliography (www.lib.berkeley.edu/SSEAL/SouthAsia/sawomen.html).

Status of Women in India (www.unodc.org/pdf/india/publications/women_Book-6-5-03/09_statusofwomeninindia.pdf).

Discovery Exercise Using Visual Aids and Stratified Questioning: Adaptation of the Environment: Place Where Native Americans Lived (Levels 1–4)

Geographers are very interested in questions of how the natural environment influences where human beings settle and how they move about the surface of Earth. They study these questions about the past as well as the present. This exercise asks students to inquire into differences and similarities between places in which two groups of Native Americans once lived. Emphasis in this activity is upon how the types of natural environments in which the groups lived led to differences between them. But some attention is also devoted to similarities—how humans must meet basic needs such as food, water, and shelter wherever they live. ELLs will benefit from the opportunity to develop language skills while examining two illustrations and hypothesizing from them.

Discovery exercises generally ask students to draw information from one or more sources, in this case pictures. However, in the process of drawing information from the pictures, students also use knowledge they have but didn't necessarily realize they possessed. For example, students are aware at some level that all people need water to survive; however, until an exercise such as this, they may not have thought about how the availability of water greatly affects where and how people live.

Direct students to examine the pictures of the pueblo (Figure 3.2) and of the chickee (Figure 3.3).

We will describe two approaches to engage students in the act of discovery. The second approach features more accommodations for beginning-level English learners.

FIGURE 3.2. A pueblo.

Visuals reprinted with permission by National Geographic/Cengage Learning. Cruz, B.C. and Thornton, S.J. (2013). *Gateway to social studies*. Boston, MA: National Geographic/Cengage Learning, p. 126.

Approach 1

Starting with the pueblo, begin a list on the board of what students can see in each picture, noting the structures themselves as well as the surrounding environment. Explain that pueblos were found mostly in the dry American Southwest at high elevations. Chickees were shelters built by Native Americans in the wet Southeast at low elevations.

Classify students' responses into categories such as types of building and building materials, vegetation, and slope or elevation of the ground. Ask students:

FIGURE 3.3. A chickee.

Visuals reprinted with permission by National Geographic/Cengage Learning. Cruz, B.C. and Thornton, S.J. (2013). *Gateway to social studies*. Boston, MA: National Geographic/Cengage Learning, p. 129.

- Using these categories, what can we guess about how people who lived in each type of home got materials for the houses? (In the Southwest, people made homes from adobe, sun-dried bricks made of clay and straw. In the Southeast, people made homes of wood, leaves, and fronds from the trees in the area.)
- Why do you think people in the American Southwest built the types of homes they did? (Guide students to note the small entrances to the homes that were reached by ladders; this protected the people from enemies and animal attacks.)
- Why do you think people in the American Southeast built the types of homes they did? (Guide students to note how the chickee's floor is elevated off the groud, thus protected against flooding and animals.)
- What kind of food do you think people in each setting ate? (Accept all reasonable responses but ask students to back up their guesses.)

To bring closure to the lesson and assess what students have learned, have students complete a Venn diagram with two circles overlapping. One circle should summarize the features of the pueblo that made it different from the chickee setting. The other circle should repeat the process for the chickee. The overlap should include what the two settings have in common.

Approach 2

If you have more students in class who are at the very beginning levels of language production, you could use a stratified questioning strategy for hypothesizing about the natural and human landscapes. After showing students both pictures and giving them a few minutes to study them, proceed as in the table below.

Stage	Questioning strategy
Preproduction	Ask students to point to which picture has trees. Which has water? Which home is high in the mountains?
Early production	Provide students with the words "stone," "wood," "steep," "flat," "high," "low," "dry," and "wet." Ask them to point to which picture shows each word.
Speech emergence	In your own words, describe the two places. In which of the places does it rain more? How can you tell?
Intermediate fluency	What effects does the climate have on how the people live in each place? Which of the places would be easier to live in? Why?

Selected Resources for Teaching about Traditional Native American Environments

Ducksters. (2012). Native American history for kids: homes and dwelling. Technological Solutions, Inc. (TSI). Retrieved from http://www.ducksters.com/history/native_american_homes.php.

Giese, P. (1996). Pre-contact housing types. Retrieved from http://www.kstrom.net/isk/maps/houses/housingmap.html.

Harvey, K.D., Harjo, L.D., and Jackson, J.K. (1997). *Teaching about Native Americans*, 2nd edn. Washington, DC: National Council for the Social Studies.

Kidport Reference Library. Adapting to a changing environment. Retrieved from http://www.kidport.com/reflib/socialstudies/nativeamericans/Environment.htm.

Native Languages of the Americas. (2011). Native American houses. Retrieved from http://www.native-languages.org/houses.htm.

Nystrom. (2009) *Nystrom atlas of U.S. history*. Indianapolis, IN: Nystrom.

Selected Internet Sites for Teaching Geography

About.com—Geography (http://geography.about.com/od/blankmaps/Blank_and_Outline_Maps.htm)

American Geographical Society (www.amergeog.org)

Blank Outline Maps of the World, Continents, Countries, and the U.S. (http://geography.about.com/science/geography/cs/blankoutlinemaps/index.htm)

CIA Factbook (https://www.cia.gov/library/publications/the-world-factbook)

Cool Planet: Mapping our World (http://www.oxfam.org.uk/education/resources/mapping_our_world)

Explore the Globe Program (http://www.globe.gov)

Geographic Learning Site (http://future.state.gov/educators/online/geography)

Geography Action! (www.nationalgeographic.com/geographyaction)

Google Earth (http://earth.google.com/#utm_campaign=en)

The Great Globe Gallery (www.staff.amu.edu.pl/~zbzw/glob/glob1.htm)

Historical Maps at the University of Texas Library (http://www.lib.utexas.edu/maps/historical/index.html)

National Council for Geographic Education (www.ncge.org)
National Geographic (www.nationalgeographic.com)
National Geographic Education (www.natgeoed.org)
National Geographic Maps and Geography (www.nationalgeographic.com/maps/index.html)
United States Geological Survey (http://www.usgs.gov)
50 States and Capitals (www.50states.com)

3.3
U.S. History

The most widely taught social studies course is U.S. (or American) history. Generally, students take this course three times during their K–12 education: once in elementary school, once in middle school or junior high, and once in high school. It is arguably the single most important course ELL students take as it can serve as an introduction to American culture. Authorities attach so much importance to this course that many states require its teaching by law (Thornton, 2006). Successful completion of a high school course in U.S. history is also a common requirement for admission to college. Candidates for naturalization as citizens are tested on U.S. history (United States Citizenship and Immigration Services, 2011). And, because ELLs are often liaisons between home and school, they can be teachers for their family members. Yet U.S. history may be among the least familiar subjects to many ELL students as they or their parents may be immigrants.

Native-born students absorb a great deal of U.S. history simply growing up in the culture and interacting with popular media, as well as from acquaintances and families. This cultural knowledge, in addition to English language skills that native U.S. English speakers take for granted, is often very difficult for non-natives to learn. Nevertheless, they encounter the demands of U.S. history across the social studies curriculum as well as in other school subjects. Geography courses, for instance, assume students bring appropriate associations to differences in ways of life in "the North" and "the South." In English language arts courses, much of the meaning of *The Great Gatsby* or *The Grapes of Wrath* or *To Kill a Mockingbird* resides in knowledge of American history. In daily life outside of school, too, references to U.S. history are common; for example, Abraham Lincoln can be a metaphor for honesty and integrity. Homilies on "being born in a log cabin" speak to the myth of the "self-made man." Other factors may also be at work. For example, a standard topic in U.S. history is equal rights for women in the workplace. Although most Americans these days adhere to the principle that men and women should enjoy equal employment rights, this principle may be absent in the cultures from which some ELLs come.

In addition to academic mastery of the subject matter of U.S. history, the aims of instruction extend to everyday life. For example, Hillsborough County Public Schools in Florida are characteristic of most places when they ask eighth graders to use historical knowledge of "the Exploration period through Reconstruction" to solve problems in "civic, social, and employment settings" in the present. In this way, learning U.S. history is a key school experience for ELLs. They use the knowledge acquired in the workplace, the community, and the home (Short, 1998).

The nature of historical subject matter is a further stumbling block for ELLs. By definition, of course, events in the past are removed from present-day experience. Political and military history, which dominate the curriculum, are strikingly removed from the present. These topics are remote from most ELLs' (and most other young adolescents') experiences. Some educators have risen to this challenge. Kobrin (1996), for example, taught a unit called "The United States Fights Wars" to classes with a high proportion of immigrants and ELLs. He told students it was about them by posing existential questions all people might confront: "What it is you would be willing to die for, and what it is you would be willing to kill for?" (p. 53; see also Noddings, 2004). He then used concrete instances from students' lives to illustrate how information is used in decision making. With student interest aroused, he brought in carefully selected primary sources about wars in U.S. history. Students then worked collaboratively with a partner or small group with primary sources—about how information was used in decision making about wars—to make their own inquiries.

Social and economic history, especially the history of the activities of ordinary people, bears a more direct relationship to students' daily experiences. Since the 1960s, this kind of history has been a growing part of what schools are expected to teach in American history courses, although it has by no means displaced the political and military history traditionally presented (Drake & Nelson, 2005).

In general, American history teachers must marshal subject matter to stimulate active student involvement if the material is to be effective in relating the American past to the demands of living now. The simple delivery of historical information won't do it (Grant, 2001). Thus the content and learning activities teachers select for instruction are crucial to effective learning.

Usually teachers have limited or no choice in selecting the general topics or units to be covered in an American history course they are assigned to teach. Rather, they will be expected to treat, for example, units on the westward movement, the Civil War and Reconstruction, the Industrial Revolution, the New Deal, and the U.S. role in twentieth-century world affairs. But what the teacher does with these general topics is crucial. Researchers suggest that the effectiveness of a social studies curriculum for developing students' understanding and ability to apply its content depends less on what general topics are covered than on what content is selected, how that content is organized and presented to students and developed through discourses and activities, and how learning is assessed through assignments and tests (Brophy *et al.*, 1991).

One major element of subject matter selection should be choosing important concepts and relationships rather than mere historical information such as names and dates. Most often, learning of the latter should arise from students grappling with the former. That is, for example, a unit on the Industrial Revolution could emphasize the concept of "trade." Students could trace the growth of trade and how it is related to specialization in industry and economic growth. After you have settled on trade as a key concept to develop in the unit, illustrations could then be selected. For instance, John D. Rockefeller and the rise of the oil industry well illustrate the identified concept and relationships.

Another major element in selecting content should be its continuity with what students have already learned and will be expected to learn later on. For example, instructional units taught before the Industrial Revolution may have dealt with how the growth of trade following the completion of the Erie Canal had stimulated the economic development of New York City and the state of New York. In this fashion, students' understanding of this concept and its relationship to other concepts is refined and developed. They are, in other words, learning more than new information: They are learning to think across time (see Neustadt & May, 1986). Moreover, in a later unit on the New Deal, they would be well positioned to ponder what happens when trade contracts.

U.S. history should also be connected to the other social studies subjects. As the naturalization test for immigrants, mentioned above, suggests, the demands of citizenship make civics and geography part of understanding U.S. history. Civics could contribute through historical investigations in the local community (Wade, 2007). In more classroom-bound instruction, the use of an atlas each day in U.S. history lessons could bring a geographic perspective to the topic under study. Or maps from long ago could be investigated as primary sources (Segall, 2003).

Let us take some general topics and consider how to plan one lesson in some detail. We will be sure to consider conceptual learning and continuity of subject matter; and we will also consider other principles vital to making historical content applicable to living today, such as inclusiveness. Note that many of these strategies can be easily applied to the teaching of other social studies disciplines as well.

Visual Aids, Stratified Questioning: Lewis and Clark Expedition (Levels 1–4)

A standard topic in instructional units on the westward movement is the Lewis and Clark expedition. Soon after the American acquisition of the vast Louisiana territory from France in 1803, President Jefferson sent Lewis and Clark to explore this largely uncharted region. Jefferson had a variety of motives. He wanted to know, for example, what Louisiana contained, including what peoples lived there and the character of the native flora and fauna as well as whatever other resources it might hold. In addition, as Europeans and Americans had tried to discover for centuries, Jefferson wanted to find an easy route across the North American continent to the Pacific Ocean. He hoped that such a route might be found by following the Missouri River west to the Rocky Mountains, which formed the continental divide, and locating a passage through those mountains to rivers that flowed to the Pacific. Facilitating trade was foremost in Jefferson's mind, as a letter to Lewis, dated June 20, 1803, illustrates:

> The object of your mission is to explore the Missouri river, and such principal stream of it as by its course and communication with the waters of the Pacific Ocean whether the Columbia, Oregon, Colorado or any other river may offer the most direct and practicable water communication across this continent for the purposes of commerce.
> (Jefferson's Instructions to Meriwether Lewis, Library of Congress)

But Jefferson, like nearly all people in the United States at the time, knew almost nothing about what was to be found once the expedition started out from the frontier of American settlement. The frontier outpost of St. Louis marked the edge of what Americans knew of the vast West beyond. Lewis and Clark set out from St. Louis to sail up the Missouri into the wilderness.

The following learning activities are designed to engage students after an initial, brief introduction to the Lewis and Clark expedition.

Lewis and Clark Activity 1: Questioning and Discussion

Create a handout of Figure 3.4, "The United States, showing extent of [European] settlement in 1790." This map can also be directly accessed by downloading it from http://etc.usf.edu/maps/pages/3600/3674/3674.htm.

Lead students in a discussion by using Activity 3.4 as a guide, modified for each level of ELL language development in your classroom.

Teaching Tip

■   PBS Teachers has a wealth of both content and pedagogical resources for teaching a number of historical topics (www.pbs.org/teachers).

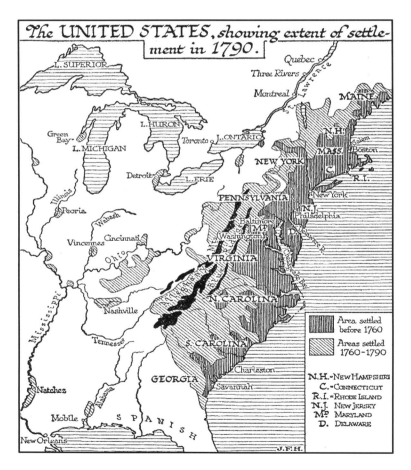

FIGURE 3.4. The United States, showing extent of settlement in 1790.

Reprinted with permission of Dr. Roy Winkelman, Florida Center for Instructional Technology, University of South Florida.

ACTIVITY 3.4. Lewis and Clark map questioning strategy

Stage	Strategy
Preproduction	Point to the states shown in this map. Find the Allegheny Mountains. Where is the Mississippi River? Which areas were settled before 1760? Which areas were settled between 1760 and 1790? Point to the Atlantic Ocean.
Early production	Do you think Lewis and Clark will complete their trip safely? Which is longer: the Mississippi or the Illinois River? List all the states shown on the map. What are the most important coastal cities? If you were Lewis or Clark, would you go on the expedition?
Speech emergence	Describe the main pattern of settlement (where people lived) in 1760. Where did settlement extend furthest from the Atlantic Ocean coastline? (Hint: look at South Carolina or New York.) Why did President Jefferson want the West explored? What kind of people would Lewis and Clark likely find on their expedition west? To the west of the Allegheny Mountains, how do the rivers reach the sea? Why does it say "Spanish" south of Georgia? If you were on the Lewis and Clark expedition, what would you take? Using an outline map of North America, create your own route for Lewis and Clark to follow. How is the Lewis and Clark expedition like space exploration today?
Intermediate fluency	In 1790, what do the scattered patches of settlement west of the Allegheny Mountains have in common? What provisions/supplies would you suggest that Lewis and Clark take on their trip? How long do you think their trip will take? What do you think Lewis and Clark will find on their journey? Locate New Orleans on the map. Why do you think President Jefferson wanted to buy the port of New Orleans from its powerful owner, France? Do you think it was right for President Jefferson to ask Lewis and Clark to go on such a dangerous journey? Compare the United States in 1790 with today. [Have students create a Venn diagram of the similarities and differences.]

Teaching Tip

- Jackdaw Publications (http://www.jackdaw.com/) offers a large photo collection that is useful for illustrating various historical topics and events.

Visual Aids, Cartography, and Critical Thinking: Lewis and Clark Activity 2: Cartography (Levels 3 and 4)

In 1803, the United States purchased a large parcel of land from France, known as the Louisiana Purchase, for about $15 million. Totaling about a quarter of the territory of the present-day United States, the purchase was highly controversial. Thomas Jefferson, president at the time, wanted to ensure a trade route west, in case the United States lost the use of the port of New Orleans. He and others also wanted an accurate survey of the flora, fauna, terrain, and peoples in the area.

Project a map of the Louisiana Purchase so it is visible to all students in the class (see, for example, the maps available at www.civics-online.org/library/formatted/images/lpurchase.html or http://www.lpb.org/education/tah/lapurchase/Web_quest1/index.cfm).

Distribute an outline map of North America to each student. Ask students to draw the Louisiana Purchase on their outline maps. Using maps with physical information, have them trace the path of the Missouri, along with other physical features (such as mountains and large lakes). Ask students to consider:

- How many modern-day states are part of the Louisiana Purchase?
- What sorts of terrain did Lewis and Clark encounter along the Missouri?
- How was it different from the settled parts of the United States east of the Mississippi River? (Hint: look at natural vegetation and precipitation maps.)
- What natural resources did the Unites States gain from the Louisiana Purchase?

Dioramas, Kinesthetic Learning, and Cooperative Learning: Lewis and Clark Extension Activity: Creating a Diorama (Levels 1–4)

Dioramas have been shown to be an effective tool for ELL students (Short, 1994) because, by creating replicas of physical features, the student can internalize the concepts easily. Although all students will be engaged learners in this project, ELL students will particularly benefit from the concrete nature of the learning experience; learners who prefer kinesthetic activities will appreciate the hands-on project. Working in pairs (ELLs should be paired with English speakers), have students create a diorama of the terrain from the Mississippi to the Pacific. When assigning an activity such as a diorama, you should list several features that must be included in all scenes, as well as optional features that the students may include. Optional features could be such things as animals or additional human-constructed features such as docks on shores or livestock on grassy plains.

After students have created their dioramas, have the students share with the class through a "walking gallery." Divide the students into two groups and instruct the first group to stand by their displays while the other group visits each display and listens to the creator's description. Have students label each feature in the diorama and instruct them to say each feature so the ELLs can hear the pronunciation of each word and then read it for themselves, which will build their vocabulary and reading skills. In this sense, dioramas offer ELLs multiple access points through which they can learn.

Teaching Tip

- Dioramas can also be used to create a "living history" museum, wherein students can role play various characters from the Lewis and Clark expedition. A helpful demonstration on how to make dioramas can be found at: http://www.wikihow.com/Make-a-Diorama. For a description on conducting a living history museum, see Cruz and Murthy's (2006) article, "Breathing life into history: Using role-playing to engage students," in *Social Studies and the Young Learner*, 19 (1): 4–8.

Cooperative Learning, Peer Teaching, and Primary Documents: Lewis and Clark Activity 3: Primary Documents Using Cooperative Learning (Levels 3 and 4)

Collaborative discussion with peers has been shown to support ELL students' comprehension of social studies concepts (Simich-Dudgeon, 1998). In this activity, students engage in small group discussions while utilizing historical documents. It is an excellent language-building opportunity for ELLs because of the cooperative learning strategies used, the opportunity to speak and hear English spoken, and the chance to discuss content in English with native English-speaking peers.

Teaching Tip

- As a vocabulary-building and comprehension-aiding exercise, have students write down unfamiliar vocabulary encountered in the documents. Monolingual students can help explain what the listed vocabulary means, a good exercise in language awareness-raising for native English speakers.

Make sufficient numbers of copies of the following primary source documents:

- Group 1: Jefferson's Instructions for Meriwether Lewis (www.loc.gov/exhibits/lewisandclark/transcript57.html)
- Group 2: Memorandum of Articles of Readiness, 1803 (www.pbs.org/lewisandclark/inside/idx_equ.html)
- Group 3: Journal Entries of the Corps of Discovery (http://www.pbs.org/lewisandclark/archive/idx_jou.html)
- Group 4: The Native Americans (PBS web page) (www.pbs.org/lewisandclark/native/index.html)
- Group 5: Curing the Corps (www.loc.gov/exhibits/lewisandclark/lewis-landc.html)
- Group 6: First Published Map of Expedition's Track (www.loc.gov/exhibits/lewisandclark/lewis-landc.html)

Divide your class into six heterogeneous groups. Ensure that each group has an English dictionary (mainstream students might also need assistance with antiquated verbiage or stilted language) and a bilingual dictionary (for the ELLs present in your class). Make sure that non-ELLs understand what it means to be communicatively engaged to avoid situations where a monolingual student dominates the group conversation because an ELL communicates at a slower pace. You can also give non-ELLs some specific strategies to use, such as assistance with vocabulary, with their ELL peers.

After describing your role as a facilitator, allow students to work through the assignments' challenges. Constantly monitor groups for comprehension and on-task behavior, clarifying and redirecting as necessary. Before assigning students to groups, review the six documents and consider which might be more appropriate for your ELLs.

In this jigsaw activity, students will investigate the following questions, using the documents assigned to their groups:

- Group 1: What did President Jefferson ask Lewis and Clark to find out?
- Group 2: What items did Lewis and Clark take on their expedition into the unknown wilderness? (Hints: What did they need to survive? What did they take to trade with Native Americans? What might they have taken with them to stay healthy?)
- Group 3: How did Lewis and Clark document what they found? What kinds of things did they note?
- Group 4: What Native American groups did Lewis and Clark meet as they traveled? How did they communicate? What did they say and do upon meeting them? How was their progress advanced by Sacajawea?
- Group 5: How were diseases and injuries dealt with on the trip? What kinds of medicines and implements were used?
- Group 6: What territory did they claim for the United States? What did they take to Jefferson that increased knowledge of Louisiana and beyond?

Selected Websites on the Lewis and Clark Expedition and the Louisiana Purchase

American Originals: The Louisiana Purchase (http://www.archives.gov/exhibits/american_originals/loupurch.html)

Lewis and Clark (PBS site) (www.pbs.org/lewisandclark)

Lewis and Clark: Inside the Corps of Discovery (http://www.pbs.org/lewisandclark/inside/index.html)

Library of Congress: The Louisiana Purchase (www.loc.gov/rr/program/bib/ourdocs/Louisiana.html)

Louisiana State Museum Map Database (http://www.crt.state.la.us/museum/lsmmaps.aspx)

Bar Graphs and Historical Photograph Analysis: City Life 1860–1920s (Levels 2 and 3)

In the period from the Civil War until the 1920s, the United States changed from a predominantly rural nation to a predominantly urban one. One of the main reasons the population of cities grew was people moving there from rural areas. With machines developed during the Industrial Revolution, fewer workers were needed on farms. While cities were growing, city life was also changing because of the Industrial Revolution. One of the main causes of this change was the use of the new energy source of electricity.

Earlier industrial cities were dirty and dark places. If cities were lighted at all during the night, they depended on gas lights, which were fire hazards and not as bright as electric lights. Thus, darkness curtailed most night-time outdoor life. Now electric street lights brightly illuminate city streets. Stores and theaters could easily function at night. There was a huge growth at night in sports and other forms of outdoor entertainment such as amusement parks. Horse-drawn streetcars were replaced by electric streetcars which were quieter, cleaner, quicker, and roomier. Suburbs distant from the city center developed.

In this activity, two forms of visual aids—a bar graph and a historical photograph—help students understand the major changes that the United States underwent during this time.

Start by displaying the bar graph (Figure 3.5) of America becoming urbanized.

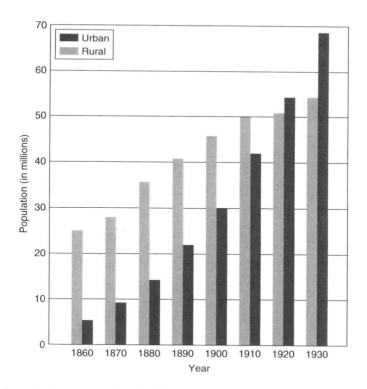

FIGURE 3.5. America becomes urbanized.

Bar graph reprinted and text adapted with permission by National Geographic/Cengage Learning. Cruz, B.C. and Thornton, S.J. (2013). *Gateway to social studies*. Boston, MA: National Geographic/Cengage Learning, p. 172.

Explain that a bar graph uses bars of different lengths to show things such as changes over time. Point out how this bar graph shows how the number of people in rural and urban areas in America changed between 1860 and 1930 (explain that "rural" refers to areas of land that are sparsely populated; "urban" refers to cities). Help students analyze the data presented in the graph by asking:

- What does the horizontal part of the graph refer to? (It shows the years between 1860 and 1930 in ten-year increments.)
- What does the vertical part of the graph refer to? (It shows the population in millions who lived in rural and urban areas.)
- About how many people lived in rural areas in 1910? (50 million)
- In which year did more people begin to live in urban areas than in rural areas in the United States for the first time? (1920)

Ask students to look at the photograph of city life (Figure 3.6). Have them work in pairs to answer the following questions:

- Look at the photo. When do you think it was taken?
- Look at the buildings. In what country or city do you think this was taken?
- What forms of transportation are being used in this city?
- Does this city have electricity? How do you know?
- How is this city different from ours today? How is it similar?

FIGURE 3.6. A photograph of city life.

Reprinted with permission of Dr. Roy Winkelman, Florida Center for Instructional Technology, University of South Florida.

Timelines and Stratified Questioning Strategy: Woodrow Wilson (Levels 1–4)

Woodrow Wilson is a major figure in most history textbooks. However, as with the lives of most other historical figures students encounter, Wilson's biography is likely restricted to little more than the period when he was involved in events of great historical significance—in Wilson's case, peaking around the time of his Fourteen Points. Yet, students may also benefit from and be interested in a sense of Wilson as a person in the broader context of times he lived through.

In this learning activity, students interpret a timeline which is a type of graphic organizer particularly suited to understanding chronology and placing life and historical events the stream of time. Timelines are deservedly a commonplace in history courses as they serve not only as efficient summaries of events but also show the length of time between events as well as their chronological sequence. These affordances are important in themselves; however, they can also be important for realizing other objectives such as identifying cause-and-effect relationships.

Project the timeline shown (Figure 3.7) or create your own (see Teaching Tip).

Teaching Tip

- There are several free timeline-making sites on the Internet that enable you to select the number of events and enter the information in easy-to-understand terms. Simply enter "free timeline maker" in any search engine and you can create timelines that meet your students' needs. (You should also check your word processing programs, many of which come with timeline makers built in.) Several also allow you to insert images, further facilitating comprehension.

Teaching Tip

- In order to benefit ELL language growth and comprehension, effective interaction needs to occur. In other words, all students need to learn about what it means to be communicatively engaged to avoid situations where a monolingual student dominates the group conversation because an ELL communicates at a slower pace.

Lead students through an analysis of Wilson's political biography as reflected in the timeline by asking the questions in Activity 3.5.

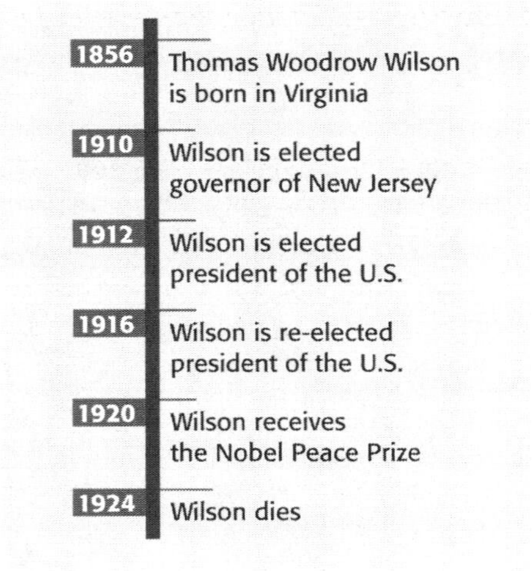

FIGURE 3.7. Woodrow Wilson's political biography.

Visuals reprinted with permission by National Geographic/Cengage Learning. Cruz, B.C. and Thornton, S.J. (2013). *Gateway to social studies*. Boston, MA: National Geographic/Cengage Learning, p. 184.

ACTIVITY 3.5. Woodrow Wilson political biography timeline questioning strategy

Stage	Strategy
Preproduction	Who is this timeline about? Point to the beginning of the timeline. When was Wilson born? Where? What prize did Wilson receive in 1920? Where does the timeline end? How old was Wilson when he died?
Early production	Wilson was governor of which state before he was president? In what year was he elected president of the United States? How many years between Wilson presenting his Fourteen Points and receiving the Nobel Peace Prize?
Speech emergence	In your own words, tell the life story of Wilson by using the information on the timeline. How long did it take the United States to enter World War I? Why do you think it took that long?
Intermediate fluency	Why do you think Wilson left the presidency of a university to become a state governor? Do you think Wilson's earlier jobs were good preparation for becoming president of the United States?

Selected Internet Sites to Teach about Woodrow Wilson

Woodrow Wilson, Official Web Site of the Nobel Prize (http://www.nobelprize.org/nobel_prizes/peace/laureates/1919/wilson-bio.html)

Woodrow Wilson: The Film and More, PBS (http://www.pbs.org/wgbh/amex/wilson/timeline/timeline1.html; graphic view: http://www.pbs.org/wgbh/amex/wilson/timeline/index.html)

Woodrow Wilson, Timeline (http://www.xtimeline.com/timeline/Woodrow-Wilson)
Woodrow Wilson, Total History (http://totallyhistory.com/woodrow-wilson)

Modified Text, Visual Aids, Picture Books, Stratified Questioning, and Music: Women in WWII (Levels 1–4)

In 1941, following the attack on the American naval base at Pearl Harbor in the Hawaiian Islands, the United States entered World War II (WWII). The largest armed forces in the nation's history were raised. Mostly these people in the armed forces were men. But President Roosevelt knew that, if the war was to be won, the United States had to become what he called "the arsenal of democracy," to make the guns, ships, and planes to fight the war. With so many men in the armed forces, however, there was a shortage of workers for these war industries.

Women took jobs in war industries to replace men. Sometimes in history texts these women are referred to as "Rosie the Riveter"; they took jobs that in the United States had traditionally been done by men. By the end of the war, women made up about 35 percent of the civilian labor force. By using historical photographs, graphics, and music, students can develop an appreciation of the enormous social paradigm shift that occurred.

These activities about women in WWII should be preceded by an introduction to the topic by the teacher that provides an overview of the changes in response to the wartime situation.

Women in WWII Activity 1: War Industries

Using their textbooks, have students find places across the United States where many people moved to work in war industries. Alternatively, if your class text does not provide a suitable map, tell students to check the locations of the following cities in their atlases: New York, Los Angeles, San Francisco, Detroit, and New Orleans. Point out that these cities were central in the WWII industry, providing a natural connection to the topic at hand. Ask them to consider:

- Nearly all of these places were located close to what?
- What are some of the jobs that women took on during the war?
- In your opinion, how do you think the lives of these women changed during the war?
- Do you think they wanted to go back to their "old lives" once the war was over?

Teaching Tip

- Create a modified text of the classroom textbook passage on this topic. Working through the text highlights the concepts you are trying to address and engages the ELL in language.

Women in WWII Activity 2: Historical Poster Analysis

Create and project the three images to the class (Figures 3.8–3.10). Compare and contrast the three posters by engaging students in a discussion, using the stratified questioning strategy in Activity 3.6.

FIGURE 3.8. "I'm proud . . . my husband wants me to do my part: see your U.S. Employment Service War Manpower Commission." John Newton Howitt, 1944.

Prints and Photographs Division, Library of Congress. www.loc.gov/rr/print/list/126_rosi.html; http://history.sandiego.edu/gen/WW2Pics7/worldwar46w.JPEG; http://history.sandiego.edu/gen/WW2 Timeline/WMC.html. Credit: National Women's History Museum.

FIGURE 3.9. "Women in the war—We can't win without them." 1942.

Prints and Photographs Division, Library of Congress. http://www.loc.gov/pictures/item/94511046.

FIGURE 3.10. The poster of "Rosie" was created for Westinghouse by J. Howard Miller in 1942. Its official title is "We Can Do It!"

Credit: National Archives (NARA) Still Picture Branch. http://library.umkc.edu/spec-col/ww2/warnews/rosie.htm. Produced by Westinghouse for the War Production Co-Ordinating Committee NARA Still Picture Branch (NWDNS-179-WP-1563).

ACTIVITY 3.6. Women in WWII Activity 2: Historical poster analysis

Stage	Questioning strategy
Preproduction	"I'm Proud" poster: Point to the U.S. flag. "We Can't Win Without Them" poster: Point to the woman in the poster. "Rosie the Riveter" poster: Point to what Rosie is saying.
Early production	"I'm Proud" poster: What is the woman wearing? What is the man wearing? "We Can't Win Without Them" poster: What is the woman doing? "Rosie the Riveter" poster: What is she wearing? What does "We Can Do It" mean?
Speech emergence	"I'm Proud" poster: How does the woman feel? What is the man thinking? "We Can't Win Without Them" poster: What is the woman working on? "Rosie the Riveter" poster: How is Rosie depicted (shown)? Would this poster convince you to sign up for duty?
Intermediate fluency	"I'm Proud" poster: What is the purpose of the poster? Who is the intended audience? "We Can't Win Without Them" poster: What is the purpose of the poster? Who is the intended audience? "Rosie the Riveter" poster: What is the purpose of the poster? Who is the intended audience? Closure What kinds of work did women do during the war? What kinds of service industries likely grew as a result of women working outside the home? Which poster do you think is most effective?

Teaching Tip

- Have ELLs practice listening and writing skills by writing down each student's contribution to the class discussion prompted by the questioning strategy. Writing the answers on the board also affords the ELL the written backup, in the event that the oral response was not understood.

Women in WWII Activity 3: Historical Photo Analysis

In this exercise, students will have the opportunity to examine historical photos using a guided analysis worksheet. The National Archives and Records Administration has developed excellent worksheets for analyzing a wide variety of primary source documents, including photographs. Download the one for photographs by visiting their website (www.archives.gov/education/lessons) and making the appropriate number of copies for your class. Project the images (or distribute photocopies) to show the class Figures 3.11 and 3.12.

Teaching Tips

- Have students locate images of women in other countries during WWII.
- After students have had sufficient time to complete their photo analysis worksheets, bring closure to the lesson by asking: How do you think women's lives in the United States have changed since WWII?

FIGURE 3.11. "Women Learn 'War Work'." This black-and-white photo, taken in April 1942, shows some of the "secretaries, housewives, waitresses, and other women from all over central Florida getting into vocational schools to learn war work. Typical are these in the Daytona Beach branch of the Volusia County vocational school." Florida is one state that many people moved to because of war-related employment.

Photo credit: Still Picture Branch, National Archives at College Park. Image enhancement by Florida Center for Instructional Technology. Source: http://fcit.usf.edu/florida/photos/pics_18/1804.jpg; http://fcit.usf.edu/florida/photos/military/wwii/1804.htm.

FIGURE 3.12. "Long Beach Plant, Douglas Aircraft." Dora Miles and Dorothy Johnson, 1944.
Library of Congress. http://www.nwhm.org/online-exhibits/partners/23.htm.

Women in WWII Activity 4: Using Picture Books to Enhance Comprehension

Although picture books are usually associated with the elementary classroom, these books have been shown to be effective in the secondary classroom (Carr *et al.*, 2001; Billman, 2002). Usually 32 or 48 pages in length and featuring illustrations or photographs on every page, they can be especially effective for ELLs in the social studies because the imagery highlights the content of the book. The concise format and simplified text also assist ELLs in decoding and comprehending the written word. And, whereas traditional textbooks often survey the more well-known personages in history, picture books often include stories of everyday people, providing insightful perspective for students (Wilkins *et al.*, 2008).

For this activity, locate some or all of the titles listed in Activity 3.7. Have students read the books in small groups and then assign each group (or allow them to select) an extension activity from Activity 3.8.

Women in WWII Activity 5: Since You Went Away

Analyzing primary source documents, especially personal ones such as diaries and letters, is an excellent way to give students insight into a particular time period. In the case of women's changing roles during WWII, letters written to and from soldiers' girlfriends and wives provide a fascinating opportunity for analysis and discovery. One useful resource is Judy Barrett Litoff and David C. Smith's (1991) compilation, *Since You Went Away: World War II Letters from American Women on the Home Front* (New York: Oxford University Press). This collection of actual letters written during WWII illuminates women's changing roles in the United States, both personally and professionally.

ACTIVITY 3.7. Picture books to teach about women in WWII

Adler, D. (2003). *Mama played baseball*. San Diego: Harcourt.
While Amy's father is serving in the army during WWII, she helps her mother get a job as a player in the All-American Girls Professional Baseball League.

Anderson, M.K. (1995). *So proudly they served: American military women in World War II*. New York: Franklin Watts.
This book chronicles women's historical struggle for military posts and highlights their military involvement during WWII.

Colman, P. (1995). *Rosie the Riveter: Women working on the home front in World War II*. New York: Crown Publishers.
Based on interviews and original research and illustrated with black and white period photographs, this book explains women's contributions from the home front.

Colman, P. (2002). *Where the action was: Women war correspondents in WWII*. New York: Crown Publishers.
Despite rules prohibiting women from covering combat, there were women who risked their lives as war correspondents and managed to report on some of the biggest stories during WWII.

Langley, W. (2002). *Flying higher: The Women Airforce service pilots of World War II*. North Haven, CT: Linnet Books.
Enhanced with historical photographs, *Flying Higher* chronicles the formation of the Women Airforce Service Pilots' training program, and follows one class of trainees.

Petersen, C. (2005). *Rosie the Riveter*. New York: Children's Press.
This book chronicles the history of the over 18 million women who served in the U.S. labor force during WWII. First-hand accounts, propaganda posters, and archival photographs illustrate the text.

Rappaport, D. (2000). *Dirt on their skirts*. New York: Dial Books for Young Readers.
Recounts the excitement of the 1946 championship game of the All-American Girls Professional Baseball League through the eyes of a young girl.

Sinnott, S. (1995). *Doing our part: American women on the homefront during World War II*. New York: Franklin Watts.
This book examines the changing roles of women during WWII: most of these women had been housewives but entered the work force by assuming jobs in the defense industry.

Williams, B. (2006). *Women at war*. Chicago: Heinemann Library.
This book documents the changes in women's roles and their importance during the war years. Topics covered include: "Why are we at war?," "War work," "Feeding the family," "Women under fire," and "The impact of war."

ACTIVITY 3.8. Picture books teaching ideas

Diary writing
Assuming the perspective of someone in the book, have students write a diary entry for a day in the life of that person.

Role playing
Have students act out the picture book, using dialogue taken directly from the text.

Letter writing
Have students write a letter to a legislator from the time period on an issue of vital concern to the war effort.

Newspaper
Using period information found in the picture book, allow students to create a class newspaper.

Simulation
Have students create and perform a historical re-enactment of an actual event recounted in the book.

Teaching Tip

- Although bilingual dictionaries may not include colloquialisms and common lingo (often found in letters and diaries), there are resources that can help students make sense of common expressions. See the Resources section of this book for suggestions.

In this exercise, students will be placed in small groups of no larger than three students. Each group will be given a short letter to read and analyze, utilizing the letter analysis worksheet provided (Activity 3.9). ELLs can consult their bilingual dictionaries to aid in translation and comprehension. Although you can find many sample letters on the Internet, the chapter entitled "I Took a War Job" in Litoff and Smith's book has many appropriate letters to choose from for this activity. Here is one example:

> Sweetie, I want to make sure I make myself clear about how I've changed. I want you to know now that you are not married to a girl that's interested solely in a home—I shall definitely have to work all my life—I get emotional satisfaction out of working; and I don't doubt that many a night you will cook the supper while I'm at a meeting.
> (Edith, Cleveland, November 9, 1945, p. 157)

Some of the letters underscore the newfound financial freedom many women experienced:

> Opened my little checking account too and it's a grand and a glorious feeling to write a check all your own and not have to ask for one.
> (Polly, Louisville, June 12, 1944, p. 147)

Although women pointed out some of the hardships that came with working outside the home, they also pointed out that they did not always mind the sacrifices:

> Going out into the snow at 7:00 a.m. and catching buses wasn't half bad and I really enjoyed it. I was the only one out on our street . . . I liked the feeling of not depending on someone else to get me to and from work.
> (Polly, Louisville, January 30, 1945, p. 150)

ACTIVITY 3.9. Letter analysis worksheet

Who wrote the letter?

To whom was the letter addressed? What is the person's relationship to the writer?

What is the date of the letter?

What was likely happening in the United States at the time? What is the writer trying to convey in the letter? What is the most significant quote from the letter? What do you think happened when her husband returned?

What would you like to find out about the author? What would you ask her about?

Women in WWII Activity 6: Music

Incorporating music into the social studies classroom can be an effective and enjoyable way of providing historical and social context. For ELLs, music activities can not only be motivating, they can also help to teach pronunciation and intonation patterns (Short, 1991). In this activity, students will learn a bit more about Rosie the Riveter (building on the historical poster analysis activity) through a popular song released in 1943.

Make one copy of the song analysis worksheet (Activity 3.10) for each student. Locate an audio file on the Internet for "Rosie the Riveter" by Redd Evans and John Jacob Loeb (1943) and secure appropriate audio equipment for playing the song. Have the students follow along with the lyrics by making an overhead transparency of (or otherwise projecting) the lyrics to "Rosie the Riveter" (these, too, can easily be found on several websites; just enter the keywords in a search engine to locate). The song begins:

All the day long,
Whether rain or shine,
She's a part of the assembly line.
She's making history,
Working for victory,
Rosie the Riveter.

Teaching Tip

- Making a "cloze" activity out of this is good listening and comprehension practice for the ELL. For example, take out every seventh word (or key words as you deem important) and have the class listen to the song; as they listen, they write down the missing words.

Play the song twice so that students can fill in the song analysis worksheet (Activity 3.10), paying attention to thoughts and feelings that emerge as they listen. Have students complete steps 2 and 3 in small groups. Reassemble the class and discuss as a whole group. Bring closure to the lesson by asking them to consider the enduring quality of Rosie the Riveter as an icon in American society.

Teaching Tip

- Ask students to consider popular, contemporary tunes and compare them with popular music from the WWII era.

ACTIVITY 3.10.   Song analysis worksheet

Song Title: "Rosie the Riveter"	Singer/Lyricist: Redd Evans and John Jacob Loeb (1943)

Step 1. Listen and observe
Listen to the song and follow the lyrics below. As you listen, write down any thoughts or feelings you may have in the space provided.

Lyrics	Thoughts and feelings	Explanation of lyrics
Write lyrics here		

Step 2. Explanation of lyrics
Using your dictionary if needed, explain what the lyrics mean in the column provided.

Step 3. Analysis
Based on what you have written above, list three things the song tells you about life in the United States at the time it was written.

1.
2.
3.

What questions do these lyrics raise in your mind?

Why do you think this song was written?

How might this song be useful to historians?

Adapted from Stevens and Fogel (2007).

Selected Websites on Women Workers in WWII

About.com: Women's History (http://womenshistory.about.com/od/warwwii/Women_and_World_War_II.htm)

American Rosie the Riveter Association (www.rootsweb.com/~usarra)

American Women's History: WWII (http://frank.mtsu.edu/~kmiddlet/history/women/wh-wwii.html)

Beyond Rosie the Riveter (http://www.gilderlehrman.org/history-by-era/world-war-ii/resources/beyond-rosie-riveter-womens-contributions-during-world-war-ii)

Florida during WWII (http://fcit.usf.edu/florida/lessons/ww_ii/ww_ii1.htm)

The Life and Times of Rosie the Riveter (http://wings.buffalo.edu/academic/center/csac/rosie theriveter.pdf)

National Women's History Museum: Partners in Winning the War (http://www.nwhm.org/online-exhibits/partners/exhibitentrance.html)

Rosie the Riveter (www.rosietheriveter.org/painting.htm)

Rosie the Riveter: Real Women Workers in World War II (www.loc.gov/rr/program/journey/rosie-transcript.html)

Scholastic's Women during WWII (http://teacher.scholastic.com/lessonrepro/lessonplans/womww2.htm)

Eisenhower's Military–Industrial Complex Speech, 1961: Simplifying Text and Role Playing (Levels 3 and 4)

At the height of the Cold War on January 17, 1961, as President Eisenhower was leaving office, he delivered a farewell address warning of the growing threat of seeming collusion between the defense industry and the military. Although the term was first used in 1914 (DeGroot, 1996), "military–industrial complex" became part of public discourse after Eisenhower's farewell address. Coming from an unlikely source—a career military officer, a popular war hero, and a political conservative—the address is one of the most remembered features of Eisenhower's presidency. It was, for example, later used by antiwar factions to decry U.S. involvement in Vietnam. The entire speech can be accessed via the Avalon Project at Yale Law School (http://avalon.law.yale.edu/20th_century/eisenhower001.asp).

In this activity, students will have an opportunity to examine excerpts from Eisenhower's famous speech, translate the passages into comprehensible language, and develop critical thinking by answering targeted questions. All students should have access to an English-language dictionary; ELLs should have bilingual dictionaries at hand to assist with translation and aid in comprehension.

Teaching Tip

- Although the more complex linguistic nature of this lesson is better suited for levels 3 and 4, some additional modifications for this activity include:
  - Levels 3 and 4: Put the speech into your own words.
  - Level 2: Have an English-speaking student explain what each section means and have ELLs paraphrase what they just heard.
  - Level 1: Create an adjusted worksheet for ELLs by including visuals on the worksheet and using simple sentences to "unpack" the speech.

Place students in dyads and distribute the military–industrial complex speech worksheet (Activity 3.11). Working together, they are to complete the worksheet by filling in columns two and three.

Another possible activity for examining Eisenhower's farewell address is a role play. Students could investigate the reactions to the address by groups such as defense industry executives, defense industry lobbyists (who are ex-military officers), Congressmen (liberal, conservative, isolationist, etc.), admirals and generals, and President Eisenhower himself reminiscing on the address after he

ACTIVITY 3.11. Military–industrial complex speech worksheet

Military–industrial complex speech Dwight D. Eisenhower, 1961	Translation of key terms and phrases	Questions and answers
My fellow Americans: Three days from now, after half a century in the service of our country, I shall lay down the responsibilities of office as, in traditional and solemn ceremony, the authority of the Presidency is vested in my successor.		To whom is President Eisenhower speaking? When is he delivering this speech? On what occasion?
Throughout America's adventure in free government, our basic purposes have been to keep the peace; to foster progress in human achievement, and to enhance liberty, dignity and integrity among people and among nations.		According to Eisenhower, what had been the United States' main intention up to that point?
Progress toward these noble goals is persistently threatened by the conflict now engulfing the world.		To what "conflict" is Eisenhower referring? Which countries are likely to be at the center of the conflict?
Crises there will continue to be. In meeting them, whether foreign or domestic, great or small, there is a recurring temptation to feel that some spectacular and costly action could become the miraculous solution to all current difficulties.		What does Eisenhower believe about people's efforts to solve crises?
Good judgment seeks balance and progress; lack of it eventually finds imbalance and frustration.		Do you think the contrast Eisenhower draws is valid? Why or why not?
A vital element in keeping the peace is our military establishment. Our arms must be mighty, ready for instant action, so that no potential aggressor may be tempted to risk his own destruction.		What should be the status of the military according to Eisenhower?
Until the latest of our world conflicts, the United States had no armaments industry . . . we have been compelled to create a permanent armaments industry of vast proportions.		To which world conflict is Eisenhower referring? What was a direct result?
This conjunction of an immense military establishment and a large arms industry is new in the American experience.		In what sense is Eisenhower speaking when he says it is "new in the American experience"?

ACTIVITY 3.11. Continued

Military–industrial complex speech Dwight D. Eisenhower, 1961	Translation of key terms and phrases	Questions and answers
We must guard against the acquisition of unwarranted influence . . . by the military–industrial complex. The potential for the disastrous rise of misplaced power exists and will persist.		How is the military dependent on industry? How is the defense industry dependent on the military?
Only an alert and knowledgeable citizenry can compel the proper meshing of the huge industrial and military machinery of defense with our peaceful methods and goals, so that security and liberty may prosper together.		What did Eisenhower mean when he said that an "alert and knowledgeable citizenry" offered the only hope against the "misplaced power" of the military–industrial complex?
Disarmament, with mutual honor and confidence, is a continuing imperative. Together we must learn how to compose differences, not with arms, but with intellect and decent purpose . . .		What is Eisenhower suggesting be the United States' ultimate goal?

leaves office. The teacher should prepare questions for each group or individual that could be asked by a journalist from the nearest metropolitan newspaper or a specific paper with a national readership, such as the *Christian Science Monitor, Washington Post,* or *Wall Street Journal.* Students should script and then perform their answers to the questions at a press conference.

Teaching Tip

- Remember that not all ELLs will be familiar with role playing as a strategy. Teachers might want to review the process and illustrate with possible scenarios.

Closure: Lead the class in a discussion by asking: "How is the situation Eisenhower warns of similar to or different from the situation now?"

Further Reading

Barton, K.C. (2001). A picture's worth: Analyzing historical photographs in the elementary grades. *Social Education*, 65 (10): 278–283.

Cruz, B. C. and Thornton, S. J. (2010). Using visuals to build interest and understanding. National History Education Clearinghouse, TeachingHistory.org. Retrieved from http://teachinghistory. org/teaching-materials/english-language-learners/24143.

Cruz, B. and Thornton, S. J. (2012). Visualizing social studies literacy: Teaching content and skills to English language learners. *Social Studies Research and Practice*, 7 (3), http://www.socstrpr.org.

Griffin, C. (1992). New light on Eisenhower's farewell address. *Presidential Studies Quarterly*, 22 (3): 469–479.

Hartung, W. D. (2001). Eisenhower's warning: The military–industrial complex forty years later. *World Policy Journal*, 18 (1). Retrieved from www.worldpolicy.org/journal/hartung01.html.

Hossein-Zadeh, I. (2006). *The political economy of US militarism*. New York: Palgrave Macmillan.

Keller, W. W. (1995). *Arm in arm: The political economy of the global arms trade*. New York: Basic Books.

Kurth, J. (1999). Military–industrial complex. In J. Whiteclay Chambers II (Ed.), *The Oxford companion to American military history*. Oxford: Oxford University Press, pp. 440–442.

Libresco, A. S., Balantic, J., and Kipling, J. C. (2011). Uncovering immigrants' stories: It all begins with picture books. *Social Studies and the Young Learner*, 23 (4), 1–4.

Singer, P. W. (2003). *Corporate warriors: The rise of the privatized military industry*. Ithaca, NY: Cornell University Press.

Selected Resources for Teaching U.S. History

The Abraham Lincoln Presidential Library and Museum (www.alplm.org/intro.html)

Archiving Early America (http://earlyamerica.com)

African-American History (http://school.discoveryeducation.com/teachers/african_american)

America's Story from America's Library (www.americaslibrary.gov/cgi-bin/page.cgi)

American Memory (Library of Congress) (http://memory.loc.gov/ammem/index.html)

Bailey, J. (1990). *From the Beginning: A First Reader in American History*. McHenry, IL: Delta Publishing Group.

Barton, K.C. (2005). Primary sources in history: Breaking through the myths. *Phi Delta Kappan*, 86: 745–753.

Benjamin Franklin (http://www.ushistory.org/declaration/signers/franklin.htm)

Bernstein, V. (2006). *America's history: Land of liberty*. Mchenry, IL: Delta Publishing Group.

Best of History Websites (http://besthistorysites.net)

Center for History and New Media (http://chnm.gmu.edu/index1.html)

Charles H. Wright of African American History (http://www.thewright.org)

The Civil War (www.pbs.org/civilwar)

The Civil War Home Page (www.civil-war.net)

Colonial Williamsburg (www.history.org)

DiGiacomo, R. *U.S. history activities for English language learners*. Magnifico Publications (www.magnificopublications.com/USELL.htm)

Digital History (www.digitalhistory.uh.edu)

Discovery Channel Social Studies Sites (http://www.discoveryeducation.com/teachers)

Documenting the American South (University of North Carolina at Chapel Hill) (http://doc south.unc.edu)

Exploring Florida (http://fcit.usf.edu/florida/default.htm)

Federal Resources for Educational Excellence: History & Social Studies (http://free.ed.gov/HandSS.cfm)

Gateway to African American History (http://usinfo.state.gov/usa/blackhis)

Historical Text Archive African American History (http://historicaltextarchive.com/sections.php?op=listarticles&secid=8)

Historical Text Archive Women's History (http://historicaltextarchive.com/links.php?op=view link&cid=20)

The History Channel (www.historychannel.com)

The History Place (www.historyplace.com)

History Wired (http://historywired.si.edu)

Independence Hall Association (http://ushistory.org)

In Motion: The African-American Migration Experience (www.inmotionaame.org)

Liberty! The American Revolution (www.pbs.org/ktca/liberty/index.html)

The Library of Congress (www.loc.gov)

The Library of Congress: Today in history (http://lcweb2.loc.gov/ammem/today/today.html)

Mapping History (http://mappinghistory.uoregon.edu)

Mayflowerhistory.com (www.mayflowerhistory.com)

Memorial Hall Museum (http://memorialhall.mass.edu/home.html)

National Archives and Records Administration (www.archives.gov/index.html)

National Center for History in the Schools (1996). *Bring history alive: A sourcebook for teaching U.S. history.* Los Angeles: National Center for History in the Schools.

National Constitution Center (www.constitutioncenter.org)

National Geographic Lewis and Clark (www.nationalgeographic.com/lewisandclark)

The National Park Service (www.nps.gov)

National Standards for U.S. History, Grades 5–12 (www.sscnet.ucla.edu/nchs)

The National Underground Railroad Freedom Center (http://www.freedomcenter.org)

National Women's History Museum (www.nmwh.org)

The New York Times on The Web Learning Network: American History (www.nytimes.com/learning/general/subjects/ushistory_index.html)

Online Resources for Education, History/Social Science (Schools of California) (http://score.rims.k12.ca.us)

Our Documents (www.ourdocuments.gov)

Plimoth Plantation (www.plimoth.org/visit/what/index.asp)

Schur, J. B. (2007). *Eyewitness to the past: Strategies for teaching American history in grades 5–12.* Portland, ME: Stenhouse Publishers.

Short, D. J., Mahrer, C., Elfin, A., Liten-Tejada, R., and Montone, C. (1994). *Protest and the American Revolution.* Berkeley, CA: National Center for Research on Cultural Diversity and Second Language Learning and Center for Applied Linguistics.

The Smithsonian Center for Latino Initiatives (http://latino.si.edu)

Smithsonian Institution National Museum of American History (http://americanhistory.si.edu/index.cfm)

Smithsonian Institution National Museum of the American Indian (www.nmai.si.edu)

Teaching with Historic Places (www.cr.nps.gov/nr/twhp)

The Valley of the Shadow: Two Communities in the American Civil War (http://jefferson.village.virginia.edu/vshadow2)

The Virginia Center for Digital History (http://jefferson.village.virginia.edu/vcdh)

Virtual Jamestown (www.virtualjamestown.org)

Virtual Marching Tour of the American Revolution (www.ushistory.org/march/index.html)

Wilen, W.W. (Ed.) (2000). *Favorite lesson plans: Powerful standards-based activities.* Washington, DC: National Council for the Social Studies.

Wineberg, S., Martin, D., and Monte-Sano, C. (2011). *Reading like a historian: Teaching literacy in middle and high school history classrooms.* New York: Teachers College Press.

Women's History Workshop (www.assumption.edu/whw)

50 States (www.50states.com)

3.4
World History

Like U.S. history programs, world history programs are, in significant ways, expressions of national outlooks. Thus, what ELLs who have recently arrived from Vietnam hear in World History about the war fought in Southeast Asia from the 1950s to the 1980s, for example, will most likely differ significantly from their prior school knowledge. Although many other cases may be less striking, as Danker (2005) points out, the "cultural threads" ELLs carry with them "subtly determine" how they "make sense of and react to the world" (p. 80).

In U.S. education, World History is usually considered a vital part of a general education for all secondary school students. Its goals include providing a background for understanding the contemporary world, introducing students to the diversity of human behavior, passing on Western heritage, and tracing the rise of democratic ways of life (Drake & Nelson, 2005). Much of what we said about teaching U.S. history in Chapter 3.3 also applies to World History. But there are some particular issues that more commonly arise in the latter that warrant separate treatment.

To begin with, the legitimate content and organization of World History programs are disputed (Marino, 2011). Although, to be sure, there is disagreement about the content of U.S. history, there is at least agreement that the primary content is those portions of the globe that eventually became the 50 states and the District of Columbia as well as their relations with other parts of the globe. In the case of World History, one of the main disputes is whether it should emphasize a Western perspective—the United States is part of the West—or represent patterns of human experience in other ways, such as equal treatment of each of the world's major culture realms. Another important dispute, which can overlap with the preceding dispute, concerns whether the course should be organized chronologically or thematically or regionally (see Williams *et al.*, 2001; Merryfield & Wilson, 2005).

In recent years, a radical rethinking of World History has been proposed (Christian, 2008). This is "big history," which is centered on the physical setting and broad patterns of human experience. Although it is yet to influence the school curriculum in most states, big history would redefine the scope of World History courses. For instance, emphasis would be on global leaps such as the Agricultural Revolution, the beginnings of urban life, and the world transformation brought about by the Industrial Revolution.

However the preceding questions are answered, World History courses today are inclusive of more than the Western experience. Educators have rejected a "Eurocentric" approach to world history whereby areas outside the West are considered only from a Western perspective. Thus, for example, the traditional view of Columbus "discovering" unknown America represents only a Western view. It has been superseded by multiple perspectives on the Columbian encounter that include not only, for example, the views of indigenous peoples but also the biological and environmental consequences of the new connections among Europe, the Americas, and Africa. Inclusion is no longer a "negotiable" item but a cornerstone of school programs in world history.

Typically the main problem educators confront in teaching World History is the scope of potential subject matter that could be included. There is far more worthwhile material than time to teach it. This problem is felt acutely in ELL instruction as students' reading abilities limit how much text can profitably be assigned. It is therefore essential to distinguish basic material from material that can be safely omitted. The teacher should make such decisions based on the goals of the world history course in question. The only principled way we know to distinguish basic material from more peripheral subject matter is to first decide what goals the course is supposed to address (which in no way precludes other worthwhile objectives emerging during the course). It's no use saying "we will cover everything," as it is impossible, even with the best native-speaking readers. It would be irresponsible, on the other hand, to include and exclude subject matter arbitrarily. But what are the proper goals?

Goals should provide a basis for selecting what to teach out of the practically unlimited possibilities. For example, a study of the results of WWI could focus on many possibilities. Traditionally, pride of curricular place was given to the Treaty of Versailles with Germany. But a default response of focusing on the West has become questioned more often. Take the case of the demise of the Ottoman Empire, which had united much of southwest Asia under Turkish rule; it unleashed rivalries that are still salient. Thus, of the many possibilities, we might choose this as an outcome of WWI if we have a goal of teaching the background of contemporary world affairs.

As noted in earlier chapters, history places considerable demands on ELLs because it is dense in concepts that carry connotations which might be lost on non-native speakers of English. For example, young people who grow up taking freedom of speech and the press for granted may readily appreciate how Hitler's attacks on these freedoms undermined the bases of democratic life. This may be less evident to ELL students who come from authoritarian nations. Similarly, some ELL students may be unfamiliar with contemporary Western norms concerning gender equity. They may therefore fail to appreciate how their textbook judges subservient roles for women as demeaning or even as violations of human rights.

Conversely, ELL students may already have a good foundation for the study of world history. An immigrant student from Latin America, for example, may know more about that region's history than the typical U.S. student. The same can be said for students from other parts of the world.

Teaching Tip

- While native English speakers may feel comfortable ad-libbing during a role play, for ELLs the teacher would likely have to help them draft possible reactions ahead of time (the writing process or word walls strategies mentioned in the Teaching Tip on page 127 would be effective for all ELL language levels).

Fortunately, there are many sound instructional strategies for teaching World History. In addition to timelines, World History teachers can use graphic organizers, primary sources, role playing, and realia to explore premodern and modern history as well as current international events to explore contemporary history. The learning activities that follow feature a wide assortment of strategies that will provide all students with meaningful learning opportunities, with special accommodations to help ELLs noted. Seven varied topics in World History are presented here: the Agricultural Revolution, inventions and architecture of the Renaissance, cultural encounter and exploration, the Enlightenment, the Industrial Revolution, Japanese Americans during WWII, and the 1985 Mexico City earthquake. Each activity features a strategy that can also be easily modified and implemented in other social studies disciplines. This chapter also incorporates several writing activities, providing students with the opportunity to develop language production and refine language writing skills. To set an inclusive tone and establish the diverse cultural and historical connections already present in the classroom, an introductory lesson will highlight the students' global connections.

Culturally Sensitive Pedagogy, Visual Aids, Stratified Questioning, and Research Skills: World Origins of Our Class[1] (Levels 1–4)

This activity underscores the class's global interconnections, fosters intergenerational communication, develops research skills, and enhances positive self-esteem and appreciation for diversity. By incorporating students' personal stories and their cultural knowledge and experiences, the activity supports the understanding of social studies content (Egbert & Simich-Dudgeon, 2001). It also incorporates an oral history approach, which can be beneficial in developing language skills, learning new concepts, and developing a link between the home and the school (Olmedo, 1996). This activity allows students to gather the data in their home language and then apply it to a communal world map logged by all the students in the class.

Create a "Family Interviews" activity sheet (see below) and distribute one to each student. Explain that they are to interview two older family members and gather the data asked for on the sheet. A family member can be someone they live with, but it can just as easily be someone who does not live with the student ("family" can be construed broadly where necessary). The interview can be completed over the telephone, by mail, or in person. Allow an appropriate amount of time for the collection of the data.

After conducting the interviews with their family members, students bring the data back to class. Make available one bulletin board or wall with a world map on it. Have students construct a composite map noting, with thumbtacks or pushpins, the national origins of students in the class. Using yarn or string, connect all the points on the map to the school's location. Use the questioning strategy in Activity 3.12.

Extension Activity

You may want to use data collected during this activity to introduce and/or reinforce bar graph skills. Origins data can be categorized into world regions or continents (North America, Latin America, the Caribbean, Europe, Africa, Asia, etc.) and students can construct a bar graph showing distributions of their relatives according to world region. If your students are already organized into small learning groups, each group may develop its own bar graph—these may be combined into one graph showing distribution for the entire class.

ACTIVITY 3.12. Questioning strategy for world origins of our class

Stage	Strategy
Preproduction	Find your family's country origins on the map. How many countries on our map have a pin? What are the names of some countries on our map that have a pin? Which cities are closest to our own? Which cities are farthest away?
Early production	How many different countries were identified by classmates' families? What part of the world has the most pins? Is there a region of the world that does not have a pin?
Speech emergence	Why do you think that certain regions have fewer thumbtacks on them? Why do you think certain regions have more thumbtacks on them? How many different languages are spoken in these countries? Can you name some?
Intermediate fluency	What countries or regions would be more represented if our school was located in [another U.S. state or city]?

Family Interviews Worksheet

Family Member #1
Relation to you:
What is your date of birth?
Where were you born? (city, country)
Where were your grandparents born? (city, country)
With what ethnic or cultural group do you identify most?
Do you speak a language other than English? If yes, which one(s)?
Which special holidays, if any, do you observe? How are they celebrated or commemorated?
Do you follow special traditions that come from other countries? If so, which?
Are there any traditional foods or recipes that you make in honor of your background?

Family Member #2
Relation to you:
What is your date of birth?
Where were you born? (city, country)
Where were your grandparents born? (city, country)
With what ethnic or cultural group do you identify most?
Do you speak a language other than English? If yes, which one(s)?
Which special holidays, if any, do you observe? How are they celebrated or commemorated?
Do you follow special traditions that come from other countries? If so, which?
Are there any traditional foods or recipes that you make in honor of your background?

Visual Aids, Guided Observation, Word Wall, and Stratified Questioning: The Agricultural Revolution (Levels 1 and 2)

No revolution in world history was more significant than the transition from nomadic ways of life dependent on hunting and gathering to a more sedentary agricultural life. The first cultures to experience agricultural revolution experienced it more as a slow process from foraging lifestyles to full-blown agriculture (Christian, 2008).

Students often have a difficult time of grasping the significance of an event, really a series of events, as remote in time as the Agricultural Revolution. This activity's main language objective is to develop basic vocabulary in preproduction and early production ELLs. The social studies objectives for this learning activity are to grasp what life was like in a hunting and gathering culture and to contrast it with life in a settled farming culture. Although it is valuable for students to appreciate that there are significant similarities between the two ways of life—by present-day standards, for example, both were vulnerable to famine, even starvation, if food was scarce for some reason beyond their control—this activity mainly concerns the differences.

Start by obtaining images of a hunting and gathering society and one of an agricultural one, such as Figures 3.13 and 3.14: It is important to contrast the two pictures at the outset. That is, lead students through questioning—this might require some hints—to see that the hunting and gathering landscape is varied and probably not arranged by humans. Contrast this with the farming picture where the plants are all of the same type, suggesting humans have planted them in the same place. Students may even deduce that farming is associated with sedentary lifestyles and foraging with nomadic lifestyles, but it is not necessary that they do so in this part of the activity.

FIGURE 3.13. Hunters and gatherers getting food.

Visuals reprinted with permission by National Geographic/Cengage Learning. Cruz, B.C. and Thornton, S.J. (2013). *Gateway to social studies*. Boston, MA: National Geographic/Cengage Learning, p. 52.

FIGURE 3.14. Farmers getting food.

Visuals reprinted with permission by National Geographic/Cengage Learning. Cruz, B.C. and Thornton, S.J. (2013). *Gateway to social studies*. Boston, MA: National Geographic/Cengage Learning, p. 53.

Teaching Tip

▪ A word wall is a specific collection of words displayed on a wall or other large display place in the classroom. Typically, they are high-frequency, academic vocabulary words that are used in a unit of study; for secondary classrooms, brief definitions should accompany accurate spellings. Word walls are especially helpful for ELLs but are of value for all students.

The Agricultural Revolution: Activity 1

Show the image of hunting and gathering. On the classroom's word wall, place the following vocabulary: tree, animal, tool, gathering, hunting, and nomad. Have the students write down the vocabulary words. As you read aloud each vocabulary word, ask for a volunteer to point to each vocabulary word on the projected image. Ask each preproduction student to complete the following sentences:

1. The children are gathering fruit from the _____.
2. The men killed an animal by _____.
3. A person who moves from place to place to find food is a _____.

Ask each early production student to write a sentence about how the nomads got food to eat.

Show the image of the farmer. Ask students, "What is the famer doing?" Summarize these answers on the board so students can see the list. Ask, "How is this way of getting food different from the people in the first picture?" Construct on the board a chart with two columns. Label one column "Hunters and Gatherers" and the other "Farmers." On parallel lines, record the contrasts and comparisons for the same category, such as "food," "movement," and "tools." Ask students questions—pointing at the pictures if necessary—and fill out the chart on the board.

Realia, Word Wall, and Visual Aids: The Renaissance (Levels 1–4)

The Renaissance—that innovative period of time roughly between 1300 and 1600—brought forth changes and inventions that altered how Europeans, and eventually most of the world, lived. In addition to the well-known developments in art, advances in science and technology also contributed to the "rebirth" of knowledge.

Renaissance Inventions

Start by bringing in and displaying several of the following objects in front of the class: a clock, eyeglasses, a book, microscope, telescope, and a book of matches. Hold up each item, while stating the name of each, so that all students can see. Ask: "What do all of these objects have in common?" Probe and prompt so that students conclude that they were all important inventions, conceived during roughly the same time period, the Renaissance.

Using Activity 3.13 as a guide, create and project "Inventions of the Renaissance" without the answers in the cells (have answers available for your reference nearby). Also create an outline worksheet for your students and distribute copies. Have students fill in their worksheets while you fill in the transparency master on the projected image. As you fill in each of the boxes, explain the invention (using gestures and visuals), and direct students to fill in their own worksheets.

Teaching Tip

- Have students research inventions from the Industrial Revolution. In what ways are the Renaissance and the Industrial Revolution similar?

Lead a class discussion by asking the following questions, augmenting with your own and those likely to be asked in class:

- Which invention do you think had the greatest effect on world history?
- Which of these inventions has had the greatest effect on you personally?
- Which do you think has created the most problems for humans?
- What characteristics do you think all the inventors shared?
- What region of the world were most of the inventors from? What was happening in that part of the world during this time?
- Which of these inventions has created the most problems for the natural environment?
- What are some inventions that are likely to be created in the coming years?

Teaching Tip

- Have students research other Renaissance innovations in art, science, medicine, and architecture.

ACTIVITY 3.13. Answer key: Inventions of the Renaissance

Invention	Description	Year	Inventor/country
Eyeglasses	Convex and concave lenses used as vision correctors	1280	Italy
Portable clocks	Spring drives make the clocks portable	1410	Filippo Brunelleschi, Italy
Printing press	Machine that made mass publication less tedious and more affordable	1436	Johann Gutenberg, Germany
Microscope	Enlarges objects and images too small to be seen with the naked eye	1590	Hans Lippershy, Hans Janssen, Zacharias Janssen, Netherlands
Flush toilet	Made it possible to have indoor sanitation by using water to flush waste through a drainpipe	1596	Sir John Harington, Great Britain
Telescope	Enlarges objects and images too far away to be seen with the naked eye	1608	Hans Lippershy, Netherlands
Submarine	Based on da Vinci's sketches, the first sub was a leather-covered rowboat from which oars protruded through watertight seals	1624	Cornelius van Drebbel, Netherlands
Matches	Combination of phosphorus and sulfur made starting a fire much easier	1680	Robert Boyle, Ireland

Selected Internet Sites to Teach about the Renaissance

Biographies of Notable Medieval and Renaissance Women (About.com) (http://womenshistory.about.com/library/bio/blbio_list_medieval.htm)

The Labyrinth: Resources for Medieval Studies (Georgetown University) (www8.georgetown.edu/departments/medieval/labyrinth/)

Looking at the Renaissance (Open University) (www.open.ac.uk/Arts/renaissance2/defining.htm)

History of the Renaissance (History World) (www.historyworld.net/wrldhis/PlainTexthistories.asp?groupid=3093&historyID=ac88)

The Renaissance (PBS) (www.pbs.org/empires/medici/renaissance)

Renaissance Art Map (www.all-art.org/history214_contents_renaissance.html)

Renaissance Connection (www.renaissanceconnection.org/main.cfm)

Renaissance Architecture

With its conscious return to classical Greek and Roman thought and art, the Renaissance marked a period of retrospection and innovation in architecture. In contrast to the Gothic spirals of medieval architecture, structural designs during the Renaissance reflected symmetry, proportion, and human intellect and ability.

Renaissance artists and architects were especially fascinated by the ancients' use of mathematics to bring proportion and beauty to structures. In fact, architects routinely traveled to Rome to study the ancient buildings and ruins as part of their education. There, architects in training would measure the structures, learning about proportion and symmetry that they would later apply to their designs.

In this activity, students will have the opportunity to view famous Renaissance buildings, using critical viewing and analysis skills to discern classic elements of this style of architecture.

Start by showing three images: the exteriors of the Parthenon, Athens (Figure 3.15), Notre Dame Cathedral, Paris (Figure 3.16), and St. Peter's Basilica, Rome (Figure 3.17).

Ask students to consider the buildings, noting the main characteristics of each in a three-column format (Activity 3.14).

Ask for volunteers to share their observations with the rest of the class, creating a whole-class chart on the board. Conclude by disclosing that each of the buildings is an exemplar of three different styles of architecture, in three different time periods:

- the Parthenon, classic Greek style, fifth century BCE;
- Notre Dame Cathedral, Gothic (medieval) style, construction begun in 1163;
- St. Peter's Basilica, Renaissance style, construction begun in 1506.

Have students observe the similarities and differences among the buildings, guiding their viewing by asking them to note features such as symmetry, shape, and use of columns. Ask them: "Which two buildings seem to have more in common?" After they identify the Parthenon and St. Peter's Basilica, segue into a discussion of the influence of classical Greek studies on Renaissance architects, by showing them images of Renaissance buildings such as:

FIGURE 3.15. The Parthenon, Athens.

- Chateau de Fontainebleau, Fontainebleau, France;
- Tempietto di San Pietro in Montorio, Rome, Italy;
- Duomo, Santa Maria del Fiore, Florence, Italy;
- Piazza del Campidoglio, Rome, Italy;
- Teatro Olimpico, Vicenza, Italy;
- The Escorial, near Madrid, Spain.

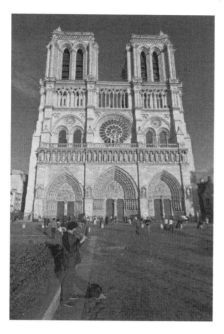

FIGURE 3.16. Notre Dame Cathedral, Paris.

FIGURE 3.17. St. Peter's Basilica, Rome.

ACTIVITY 3.14. Worksheet for Renaissance architecture

The Parthenon, Athens	Notre Dame Cathedral, Paris	St. Peter's Basilica, Rome

As each image is shown, point out (and write the terms on the board) the distinctive Renaissance features of the buildings including:

- geometric proportion;
- symmetry;
- columns;
- arches;
- domes;
- windows (often paired);
- painted ceilings;
- frescoes.

These terms would also be appropriate for the class word wall. Depending on the level of your ELLs, you can ask them to assist you in writing the words, finding the definitions, and attaching identifying visuals to each.

Activity 3.15 is another way of approaching the first three buildings discussed.

Alternative Activity

Design a virtual field trip of the sites and buildings of major import to the Renaissance. For helpful information on creating your own, see Lacina (2004).

Extension Activity

Have students investigate other changes brought about by the Renaissance, such as in health, religion, art, and science. Have students discuss which buildings today reflect Renaissance characteristics. What might today's architecture suggest about our values?

Selected Resources for Teaching about Renaissance Architecture

The Art of Renaissance Europe: Publications for Educators (www.metmuseum.org/explore/publications/renaissance.htm)

Campbell, G. (2004). *Renaissance art and architecture.* New York: Oxford University Press.

ACTIVITY 3.15. Renaissance architecture questioning strategy

Level	Activity	Questions
Preproduction	Matching pictures with words Labeling objects in a picture Using sentence completion	Say "temple" or "church" for each picture. Write the name of each building. The Parthenon is in the city of _____. Notre Dame is in the city of _____. St. Peter's is in the city of _____.
	Finding points on a map from oral directions	Circle Athens on the map. Draw a line from Athens to Paris. Color Italy green.
Early production	Labeling a picture with a short sentence	The Parthenon is ____. Notre Dame is _____. St. Peter's is _____.
	Finding picture differences	Name one thing that makes each building different from the others.
	Using different genre literature	On the Internet, find a picture of each of the cities today.
Speech emergence	Creating a paragraph based on a sequence of paragraphs	Use each of these words one or more times in a paragraph about the pictures: ancient, Greece, Parthenon, temple, church, Rome, Paris, medieval, built, Christian.
	Making a timeline	Make a timeline showing when each temple or church was built and today.
Intermediate fluency	Oral reports	Speak about important temples and churches in European history.
	Brainstorming	List as many words as you can about each building and then put the words in categories.

The Civilization of the Renaissance in Italy (www.idbsu.edu/courses/hy309/docs/burckhardt/burckhardt.html)

Frommel, C. L. (2007). *The architecture of the Italian Renaissance*. New York: Thames & Hudson.

Renaissance (Annenberg) (www.learner.org/exhibits/renaissance/symmetry.html)

Renaissance Architecture: Great Buildings online (www.greatbuildings.com/types/styles/renaissance.html)

Renaissance Art and Architecture (MSn Encarta) (http://encarta.msn.com/encyclopedia_761554529/renaissance_Art_and_Architecture.html)

Renaissance and Baroque Architecture (University of Virginia Library) (www.lib.virginia.edu/dic/colls/arh102)

Renaissance Florence: Time Machine Adventure (www.activehistory.co.uk/Miscellaneous/free_stuff/renaissance/frameset.htm)

Rice, E. F. Jr. and Grafton, A. (1994). *The foundations of early modern Europe*, 2nd edn. New York: Norton.

Virtual Renaissance: A Journey through Time (www.twingroves.district96.k12.il.us/renaissance/Virtualren.html)

Wilkins, D. G. and Wilkins, D. (2006). *History of Italian Renaissance art*. New York: Prentice Hall Art.

Visual Aids and Primary Source Documents: Cultural Encounter and Exploration (Levels 3 and 4)

"Portuguese Discoveries": Activity 1

Have students examine the "Portuguese discoveries" map from the early twentieth century (Figure 3.18). Ask why the title, "Portuguese discoveries in Africa," might today be considered "Eurocentric" (you may need to explain this term, using a modern-day world map to help clarify). After locating the small European nation of Portugal on the map, have students consider the following:

- What is distinctive about Portugal's relative location?
- Looking at the map, mark where early Iberian navigators headed. Why might they have stayed relatively close to known waters and shores?

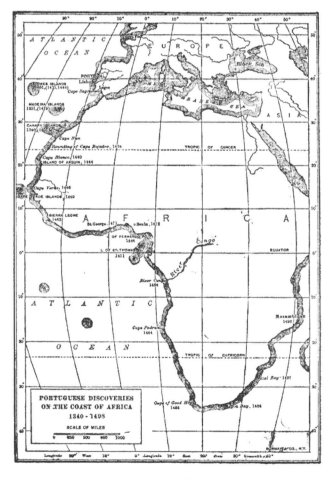

FIGURE 3.18. Portuguese discoveries in Africa, 1340–1498.

Bushnell Hart, A., *The American nation*, vol. 1. New York: Harper and Brothers, 1906. Downloaded from Maps ETC at http://etc.usf.edu/maps (map #02507).

- Have students use their atlases and locate the Sahara Desert on their maps. What might this suggest about why sub-Saharan Africa was a mystery to Europeans? Why might Arab and Indian Muslims have been more familiar with sub-Saharan Africa?
- Vasco da Gama, the first Portuguese navigator to sail to India, arrived there in 1498. Why do you think it took so long to reach the Cape of Good Hope and then only a few years to complete a voyage to India?

To develop and strengthen writing skills, ask students to write a navigator's journal from the perspective of one of the early navigators. Students in the preproduction and early production stages may be asked to trace the routes some of the early navigators took on a contemporary map, giving them a general orientation about the lesson's topic.

Extension Activity

Access visuals from the Smithsonian exhibition, "Encompassing the Globe: Portugal and the World in the 16th and 17th Centuries" (www.asia.si.edu). Artifacts from this collection clearly illustrate the cultural cross-pollination that resulted from Portuguese exploration. Alternately, Zax (2007) provides an excellent overview of the collection as well as images that can be shared with students.

Conquistadors: Activity 2

In this lesson, students will compare and contrast different accounts of the Spanish conquest of Mexico. They will consider conflicting descriptions and formulate their own account of the arrival of Spanish conquerors in the Americas. Key terms to explain and discuss beforehand include: conquistador, Catholic Church, Aztecs, Inca, gunpowder, horse, and gold. These terms would be especially appropriate for the classroom's word wall.

Teaching Tip

- The Quincentenary resulted in curricula appropriate for explaining different perspectives on the Columbian encounter. A simple Internet search using the term "columbian quincentenary" will yield many useful resources.

Start by identifying and reproducing excerpts from various sources on the exploration and conquest of the Americas. Your classroom text may have some, but here are some additional suggested sources.

Christopher Columbus

Christopher Columbus: Extracts from Journal (Medieval Sourcebook) (www.fordham.edu/halsall/source/columbus1.html)

Christopher Columbus's Account of 1492 Voyage (www.loc.gov/exhibits/kislak/kislakexhibit.html)

Hernán Cortés

Cortés, Hernán. (2001). *Letters from Mexico.* Translated by Anthony Pagden. New Haven, CT: Yale University Press.

Motecuhzoma (Montezuma)

Aztec Account of the Conquest of Mexico (Modern History Sourcebook) (www.fordham.edu/ halsall/mod/aztecs1.html)

Bartolomé de las Casas

de las Casas, Bartolomé. (1999). *Short account of the destruction of the Indies* (1542). New York: Penguin Classics. Excerpt also available at http://web.archive.org/web/19980116133031/ and http://pluto.clinch.edu/history/wciv2/civ2ref/casas.htm.

Francisco Pizarro

Capture of an Incan King (www.fll.vt.edu/Culture-Civ/Spanish/texts/spainlatinamerica/ pizarro.html)

Hernando de Soto

Recollections of the Hernando de Soto Expedition: The Testimony of Alonso de Argote (www.as.ua.edu/ant/Mabila/Argote%20Account%201557.pdf)

The Expedition of Hernando de Soto in southeastern North America, 1539–1543, as recounted by a member of the expedition (www.nhc.rtp.nc.us/pds/amerbegin/exploration/text1/desoto. pdf)

Fray Tomás de Berlanga

A letter to His Majesty, from Fray Tomás de Berlanga, describing his voyage from Panamá to Puerto Viejo (www.galapagos.to/texts/berlanga.htm)

Allow students to work in small groups, with each group assigned a different explorer and document. Allow all students to have access to a dictionary and/or thesaurus. Using the document analysis worksheet (Activity 3.16), have students analyze the document assigned to their group.

After allowing sufficient time to complete the document analysis activity, allow each group to present its findings to the rest of the class. After all groups have presented, close the lesson by asking:

Why is it important to know who the intended audience is?

How might the account recorded in a personal journal or diary differ from a letter to a superior?

Why is it important to know what was happening in the world at the time when analyzing a historical document?

Extension Activity

Have students conduct research to find the answers to their questions (generated on the document analysis worksheet).

ACTIVITY 3.16. Document analysis worksheet

Who wrote the document? What was his/her title or position?

What is the date of the document?

For whom was this document written? Who was the intended audience?

What was happening in the world at the time? What is the writer trying to convey? What is the main purpose of the document?

What is the most significant quote from the document?

What would you like to find out about the author?

What questions do you have about the document?

Teaching Tip

- PBS Teachers (www.pbs.org/teachers) provides a plethora of preK–12 educational resources and activities for educators tied to PBS programming and correlated with local and national curriculum standards.

Additional Resources

The Aztec Account of the Spanish Conquest of Mexico (www.ambergriscaye.com/pages/mayan/aztec.html)

Bartolomé de las Casas (http://oregonstate.edu/instruct/phl302/philosophers/las_casas.html)

Conquistadors (www.pbs.org/conquistadors/index.html)

Culture and history of the Americas: Library of Congress (www.loc.gov/exhibits/kislak/kislak exhibit.html)

de las Casas, B. *Devastation of the Indies.* Ed. B. M. Donovan. Trans. H. Briffault. Baltimore, MD: Johns Hopkins University Press, 1992. Can also be accessed through Project Gutenberg at www.gutenberg.org/etext/20321.

European Voyages of Exploration (www.ucalgary.ca/applied_history/tutor/eurvoya/inca.html)

Hernán Cortés and the Conquest (www.latinamericanstudies.org/cortes.htm)

Mexico Connect (www.mexconnect.com/mex_/history.html#1521)

Portilla, M. L. (Ed.) (1962). *The broken spears: The Aztec account of the conquest of Mexico.* Boston, MA: Beacon Press.

Simplified Text and Concept Map: The Enlightenment (Levels 2–4)

The Enlightenment was a time of great change in society. In addition to advances in science, Enlightenment philosophers introduced important new ideas that changed the way people lived, including changes in government. In this activity, students will have an opportunity to understand some of the effects of Enlightenment thinking by reading a simplified text passage and interpreting a concept map.

Begin by distributing copies of the simplified text on the Enlightenment:

Enlightenment Thinking

The Enlightenment was a time of great change in society. Up until this time, emperors and kings ruled in most countries. Enlightenment thinkers believed that people had the right to be in charge of their own lives. They said that all people are created equal and there should be no nobility. This new way of thinking led to revolutions in North America, France, and Haiti.

In North America, people living in the English colonies fought for independence from Great Britain. The colonists won the war and formed the United States of America. In France, the people also wanted changes in their government. They overthrew the monarchy of Louis XVI, the ruler of France, and his wife, Marie Antoinette. Finally, in Haiti, people fought for their independence from France.

Read the passage aloud while students follow on their handouts. Ask them to underline or highlight any words they do not know. After the reading, allow time for students to look up words in their dictionaries and discuss any unknown vocabulary words.

Next, project or distribute copies of the concept map (Figure 3.19).

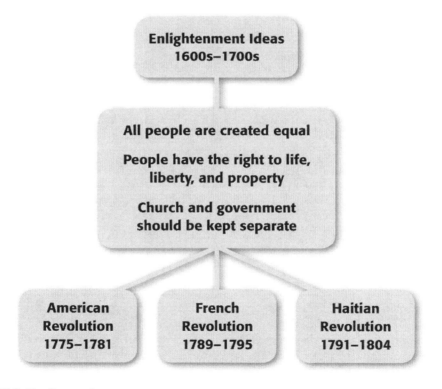

FIGURE 3.19. Concept map.

Explain that concept maps organize information to show related ideas. This concept map shows how Enlightenment ideas influenced political revolutions. Ask volunteers to read aloud each box of the concept map. Guide a class discussion by asking the following questions:

- When did the Enlightenment occur?
- What are three important ideas of the Enlightenment? Which of those ideas do you personally feel is most important—why?
- Which three revolutions were influenced by Enlightenment ideas?

Now ask students to re-read the text independently. Come together as a class to answer and discuss the following questions:

- From which country did the colonists in North America fight for independence?
- Who was the ruler of France at the start of the French Revolution?
- From which country did Haiti gain its independence?
- Review the ideas of the Enlightenment thinkers. Which of those ideas do you personally feel is most important—why?

Resources for Teaching about the Enlightenment

King, D. (2005). *People at the center of the Enlightenment.* Farmington Hills, MI: Blackbirch Press.
Murray, S. (2005). *American Revolution.* New York: DK Children.
Rockwell, A. (2009). *Open the door to liberty.* Orlando, FL: Houghton Mifflin Books for Children.
Stewart, G.B. (2005). *People at the center of the French Revolution.* Farmington Hills, MI: Blackbirch Press.

Visual Aids, Stratified Questioning, and Guided Discussion: The Industrial Revolution: The Cases of Great Britain and Japan (Levels 1–4)

The Industrial Revolution marked one of the most dramatic turning points in human history. Major changes in technology, economics, and society heralded a new age, the effects of which are still palpable today. For students, understanding the conditions that led to the Industrial Revolution as well as the far-reaching ramifications is key to understanding contemporary world history.

In the following learning activities, students will explore why Britain was uniquely positioned to become the first industrial nation, Japan's entry into the industrial age, child labor, and the birth of the Romantic Movement.

Teaching Tip

- MindSparks (http://mindsparks.com) publishes many primary source and visual materials that "challenge students to think historically." Given the visual nature of the resources, many of them are especially appropriate for ELL students.

The Industrial Revolution: Activity 1

Start by projecting the image of a scene from Great Britain during the Industrial Revolution (Figure 3.20).

Guide the students through their analysis of the image by asking the questions in Activity 3.17. Disclose that the scene depicts Great Britain (point to Great Britain on a wall map or globe) during the Industrial Revolution and that you will be exploring why Britain became the first industrial nation in the world.

Via teacher explanation (and by providing scaffolded note taking for ELLs), explain why the following were important advantages for Britain to become the first industrial nation, including:

- stable government;
- capital from colonial trade;
- reliable financial system;
- accessibility of much of the country to navigable rivers;
- abundant mineral deposits;
- temperate climate;
- larger workforce (as more children lived past infancy);
- rural to urban migration;
- enclosure;
- natural resources available from their colonies.

CHRIST CHURCH AND COAL STAITH, LEEDS.

London. Published by J.T. Hinton N°4. Warwick Square March 1829

FIGURE 3.20. Christ Church and Coal Staith, Leeds, 1829.

Source: Science & Society Picture Library, Science Museum, London.

Then compare the later industrialization of Japan: Which of the British advantages above did Japan share? What did Japan lack that had been important in British industrialization and how did the Japanese compensate? What did the Japanese learn from the British experience? Although it came later, industrialization occurred at a much faster pace in Japan—why, do you think?

ACTIVITY 3.17. The Industrial Revolution: Great Britain questioning strategies

Stage	Strategy
Preproduction	Is this taking place in the city or the country? Point to the train in the scene. Point to the smoke. Do you see factories? Where?
Early production	How do you know there are factories? What are the people doing? What is the train carrying?
Speech emergence	What does this scene show? From what time period do you think this scene is? Do you think the people waving (in the foreground) work in the factories (in the background) in this scene?
Intermediate fluency	Would you like to live in this city? Why or why not? Would you guess that this city is old or new? Why? Do you think a lot of people are moving to this city? Why?

Teaching Tip

- Ask students to research what was happening in countries other than Great Britain and Japan during the Industrial Revolution.

The Industrial Revolution (Child Labor): Activity 2

As the need for labor grew, industry turned to children to run the machines in factories. Children worked for less and their smaller frames made them more nimble and allowed them to fit where adults did not. Conditions were miserable and, despite reform movements, continued to be dismal until the twentieth century.

You will need to prepare for this lesson by locating Elizabeth Barrett Browning's 1843 poem, *The Cry of the Children* (it can be found on a number of websites). You will need to create a poetry analysis worksheet (Activity 3.18) by inserting two lines of the poem in each box under the "Poem" column (the first one is as shown in the activity worksheet).

Start this lesson by projecting the first stanza of the poem while simultaneously distributing the poetry analysis worksheet. Read the stanza aloud once while students follow along. Then ask for volunteers as you paraphrase each line and fill in the worksheet with the paraphrased "translations." Lead the class in a discussion by asking:

- Who is crying? Why?
- To whom is the poet speaking ? Who are her brothers?
- What scenes come to mind as the poet conjures images of meadows and animals?

- What does the "playtime of others" mean?
- To what country is the poet referring?

Afterwards, explain that this is the opening stanza of Browning's famous poem about children working in Britain's coal mines. Efforts by concerned citizens led to a series of reforms known as the Factory Acts. These laws, designed to protect children and women, were passed in Britain between 1802 and 1891 (see Activity 3.19).

ACTIVITY 3.18. Poetry analysis worksheet

Poem	Paraphrase
Do ye hear the children weeping, O my brothers, Ere the sorrow comes with years?	

Lead students in a guided discussion by collectively answering the "Questions to consider." Bring closure to the lesson by asking: Which of the Factory Acts do you feel was most significant? Why?

The Industrial Revolution (Literature and Philosophy): Activity 3

In this activity, cross-curricular connections between language arts and social studies are made by using literary excerpts. With scaffolding and linguistic support, ELLs can develop language

FIGURE 3.21. Textile industries, George Spill & Co., 1855.
Source: Science & Society Picture Library, Science Museum, London.

skills while gaining a greater appreciation of the time period. Start by projecting the image of a factory complex from Great Britain during the Industrial Revolution (Figure 3.21).

Guide the students through their analysis of the photo by asking:

- Describe the scene. What is taking place?
- When do you think this is taking place? Where?
- Describe the people in the scene. What are they doing?
- What do you think takes place inside the waterproofers' building?
- What do you think the skylights are for on the building roofs?

Disclose that this picture depicts the premises of the George Spill & Co. factory premises in Great Britain during the Industrial Revolution. The clothing and footwear industry was becoming more and more mechanized, which, in turn, had significant effects on the lives of workers. It was not unusual for factory workers to be recruited from the countryside, brought to urbanized areas to work, and housed in company dormitories nearby. Reactions from workers and society in general were inevitable. One such reaction was Romanticism and Naturalism in art and literature, generally understood to have evolved as a reaction to industrialism. Poets such as William Blake and William Wordsworth idealized pastoral, rural life while providing scathing commentary on contemporary society and industry (also recall Browning's poem from Activity 3.18).

ACTIVITY 3.19. Factory Acts

Law	Major provisions	Questions to consider
Factory Act of 1802	All factory rooms are to be well ventilated and lime-washed twice a year. Children must be supplied with two complete outfits of clothing. The work hours of children must begin after 6 a.m., end before 9 p.m., and not exceed 12 hours a day. Children must be instructed in reading, writing, and arithmetic for the first four years of work. Male and female children must be housed in different sleeping quarters and may not sleep more than two per bed. On Sundays children are to have an hour's instruction in Christian religion. Mill owners are also required to attend to any infectious diseases.	Why would it be important to wash the factory rooms with a strong chemical such as lime? Why would the factory owners need to supply clothing for the children? How old do you think the "children" are? Why do the children sleep in factory housing? Why don't they go home? Why do you think that instruction in Christianity is considered necessary? What kinds of infectious diseases do you think the children had?
Factory Act of 1833	Emphasis was on the textile industry. Employment of children under nine in the textile industry is outlawed. The work day would begin no earlier than 5:30 a.m. and end no later than 8:30 p.m. Children (ages 13–18) must not be employed for more than 12 hours a day. Children (ages 9–13) must not work more than nine hours. Children (ages 9–13) must have two hours of education per day. Provided for routine inspections of factories.	Why do you think the textile industry was targeted in this legislation? Do you think that a nine-hour or 11-hour work day is appropriate for these ages? Do you think that a two-hour school day is appropriate for these ages? What do you think was taught during the two hours of education? Why do you think inspections were necessary?
Factory Act of 1844	Children (ages 8–13) could work for no more than 6 1/2 hours per day Women and young people now worked the same number of hours. They could work for no more than 12 hours a day during the week and nine hours on Sundays.	Do you think the changes in the number of work hours permitted were significant? Why would it be necessary to have a doctor verify employees' ages?

	Factory owners must wash factories with lime every 14 months. Ages must be verified by surgeons. Accidental death or injuries must be reported to a surgeon and investigated. Record keeping regarding the provisions of the act was mandatory; certificates of school attendance must be kept.	Why would an investigation need to be called for an accidental death or injury? What were the makers of the law trying to ensure through record keeping?
Factory Act of 1850	Children and women could work only from 6 a.m. to 6 p.m. in the summer and 7 a.m. to 7 p.m. in the winter. All work would end on Saturday at 2 p.m. The work week was extended from 58 hours to 60 hours.	Why would there be different hours for summer and winter? Were the changes in work hours significant with this law?
Factory Act of 1878	Now the Factory Code applied to all trades. No child under the age of ten was to be employed. Compulsory education for children up to ten years old. 10–14-year-olds could be employed only for half-days. Women were to work no more than 56 hours per week.	What were the most meaningful changes made by this legislation?
Factory Act of 1891	Requirements for fencing machinery made more stringent.	What is fencing machinery? Why would this law be important for workers?

Source: Spartacus Educational (www.spartacus.schoolnet.co.uk/IRchild.main.htm) and Book Rags (www.bookrags.com/Factory_Acts#Factory_Act_of_1878), both retrieved on July 18, 2007.

Another movement that evolved during this time is known as Realism. Through this medium, authors and artists provided realistic depictions of the social world. The novels of Charles Dickens presented social criticism of what he saw happening in the world via his engaging stories and memorable characters, such as those in his classics *Bleak House* and *Oliver Twist*.

Teaching Tip

- Read excerpts from Dickens's novels (simplifying and paraphrasing text as necessary) to further connect the social studies to language arts.

But perhaps no work produced during the Industrial Revolution had greater effects than Karl Marx's and Friedrich Engels's *Communist Manifesto* (1848). In it, Marx and Engels argue that all of human history is based on class conflict. In industrial societies this conflict pitted the bourgeoisie (those who control the means of production) against the proletariat (working class). Further, they suggest that the only appropriate course of action is for the proletariat to overthrow the bourgeoisie, eventually bringing about an egalitarian, classless society. Published in London, *The Communist Manifesto* was in reaction to much of what Marx and Engels witnessed and experienced when they came to live in Great Britain.

The final words of *The Communist Manifesto* are:

> Let the ruling classes tremble at a Communistic revolution. The proletarians have nothing to lose but their chains.
>
> They have a world to win. Workers of the world unite!

Ask students to consider life as a factory worker in Great Britain during the Industrial Revolution. Then have them use one of the following formats to describe their plight:

- a letter to the editor of a local newspaper;
- a personal diary/journal entry;
- an impassioned speech to a local board;
- a poem;
- a short story;
- a drawing;
- a political cartoon.

Extension Activity (Historical Biography)

Have students select a biography or trade book of a historical figure who lived during the Industrial Revolution. In addition to conducting additional research on the person, have students keep a "character diary" wherein they chronicle a week or more in the life of the person studied (Short, 1991). This strategy can be used for any time period in history.

Teaching Tip

- Biography.com and History.com provide short, accessible biographies of a number of historical figures.

Selected Internet Resources for Teaching about the Industrial Revolution

Child Labor Online Resources (www.readwritethink.org/lesson_images/lesson289/web-childlabor.html)

The Industrial Revolution (www.historyteacher.net/APEuroCourse/WebLinks/WebLinksIndustrial Revolution.htm)

Internet Modern History Sourcebook: Industrial Revolution (www.fordham.edu/halsall/mod/modsbook14.html)

Kid Info: The Industrial revolution (www.kidinfo.com/American_history/Industrial_revolution.html)

Open Directory Project: The Industrial Revolution (http://dmoz.org/Society/history/By_Time_Period/Eighteenth_Century/Industrial_Revolution/)

The Photographs of Lewis Hine (www.kentlaw.edu/ilhs/hine.htm)

Spartacus Educational (www.spartacus.schoolnet.co.uk/Irchild.main.htm)

A Web of English History (www.historyhome.co.uk/peel/factmine/factleg.htm)

Visual Aids, Role Playing, Guided Reading, and Stratified Questioning: Japanese Americans During WWII (Levels 1–4)

Racial and ethnic cleansing was a hallmark of the WWII era. The Holocaust is the most infamous case of this process, which was carried to the extent of mass murder. But many other cases of racial and ethnic persecution also occurred prior to, during, and following the European war (Naimark, 2001).

In the Pacific, the racial friction that had long characterized relations between Japan and the West played an important part in the war. Soon after Pearl Harbor was attacked by the Japanese on December 7, 1941, three Presidential Proclamations were issued granting the government broad authority to investigate suspects. Then, on February 19, 1942, Executive Order 9066 was issued by President Franklin D. Roosevelt. In effect, it allowed for the relocation of all persons of Japanese ancestry, both U.S. citizens and non-citizens, to inland camps, away from the Pacific military zone. It was explained as an effort to prevent espionage and to protect persons of Japanese descent from anti-Japanese attacks. The forced migration would eventually affect 117,000 Japanese Americans, two-thirds of whom were native-born U.S. citizens. One of the most enduring images of this order is the notice that was posted in and around the environs of San Francisco (Figure 3.22). An image of the posting of this order, at the corner of First and Front Streets in San Francisco, can be found at www.archives.gov/education/lessons/japanese-relocation/images/order-posting.gif.

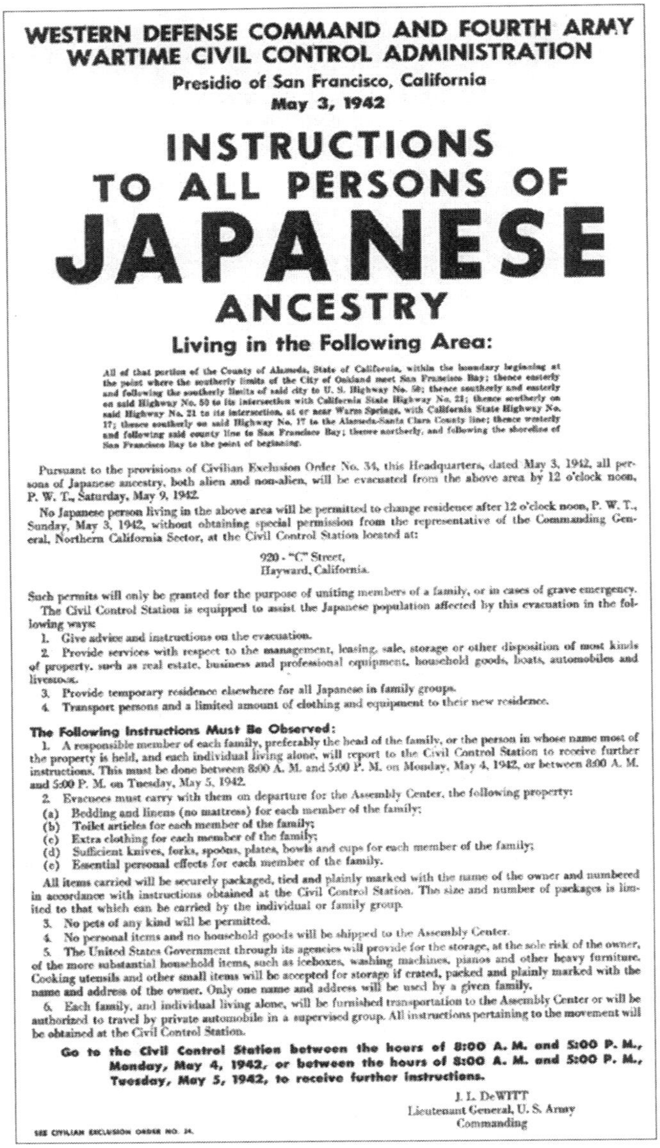

WESTERN DEFENSE COMMAND AND FOURTH ARMY
WARTIME CIVIL CONTROL ADMINISTRATION

Presidio of San Francisco, California
May 3, 1942

INSTRUCTIONS TO ALL PERSONS OF JAPANESE ANCESTRY

Living in the Following Area:

All of that portion of the County of Alameda, State of California, within the boundary beginning at the point where the southerly limits of the City of Oakland meet San Francisco Bay; thence easterly and following the southerly limits of said city to U. S. Highway No. 50; thence southerly and easterly on said Highway No. 50 to its intersection with California State Highway No. 21; thence southerly on said Highway No. 21 to its intersection, at or near Warm Springs, with California State Highway No. 17; thence southerly on said Highway No. 17 to the Alameda-Santa Clara County line; thence westerly and following said county line to San Francisco Bay; thence northerly, and following the shoreline of San Francisco Bay to the point of beginning.

Pursuant to the provisions of Civilian Exclusion Order No. 34, this Headquarters, dated May 3, 1942, all persons of Japanese ancestry, both alien and non-alien, will be evacuated from the above area by 12 o'clock noon, P. W. T., Saturday, May 9, 1942.

No Japanese person living in the above area will be permitted to change residence after 12 o'clock noon, P. W. T., Sunday, May 3, 1942, without obtaining special permission from the representative of the Commanding General, Northern California Sector, at the Civil Control Station located at:

920 - "C" Street,
Hayward, California.

Such permits will only be granted for the purpose of uniting members of a family, or in cases of grave emergency.

The Civil Control Station is equipped to assist the Japanese population affected by this evacuation in the following ways:

1. Give advice and instructions on the evacuation.
2. Provide services with respect to the management, leasing, sale, storage or other disposition of most kinds of property, such as real estate, business and professional equipment, household goods, boats, automobiles and livestock.
3. Provide temporary residence elsewhere for all Japanese in family groups.
4. Transport persons and a limited amount of clothing and equipment to their new residence.

The Following Instructions Must Be Observed:

1. A responsible member of each family, preferably the head of the family, or the person in whose name most of the property is held, and each individual living alone, will report to the Civil Control Station to receive further instructions. This must be done between 8:00 A. M. and 5:00 P. M. on Monday, May 4, 1942, or between 8:00 A. M. and 5:00 P. M. on Tuesday, May 5, 1942.
2. Evacuees must carry with them on departure for the Assembly Center, the following property:
   (a) Bedding and linens (no mattress) for each member of the family;
   (b) Toilet articles for each member of the family;
   (c) Extra clothing for each member of the family;
   (d) Sufficient knives, forks, spoons, plates, bowls and cups for each member of the family;
   (e) Essential personal effects for each member of the family.

   All items carried will be securely packaged, tied and plainly marked with the name of the owner and numbered in accordance with instructions obtained at the Civil Control Station. The size and number of packages is limited to that which can be carried by the individual or family group.
3. No pets of any kind will be permitted.
4. No personal items and no household goods will be shipped to the Assembly Center.
5. The United States Government through its agencies will provide for the storage, at the sole risk of the owner, of the more substantial household items, such as iceboxes, washing machines, pianos and other heavy furniture. Cooking utensils and other small items will be accepted for storage if crated, packed and plainly marked with the name and address of the owner. Only one name and address will be used by a given family.
6. Each family, and individual living alone, will be furnished transportation to the Assembly Center or will be authorized to travel by private automobile in a supervised group. All instructions pertaining to the movement will be obtained at the Civil Control Station.

Go to the Civil Control Station between the hours of 8:00 A. M. and 5:00 P. M., Monday, May 4, 1942, or between the hours of 8:00 A. M. and 5:00 P. M., Tuesday, May 5, 1942, to receive further instructions.

J. L. DeWITT
Lieutenant General, U. S. Army
Commanding

SEE CIVILIAN EXCLUSION ORDER NO. 34.

FIGURE 3.22. Japanese internment poster.

Source: National Park Service, www.nps.gov/history/nr/twhp/wwwlps/lessons/89manzanar/89facts2.htm.

In this exercise, students will consider what it might be like if they were to be forcibly evacuated and their likely response. Start by placing them in small groups of no more than four or five students and telling them that each group constitutes a "family." Distribute to each group an "Evacuation!" role sheet (Activity 3.20, based on wording from Executive Order 9066), reading aloud the "Background" section.

After sufficient time has been allotted for small group discussion and creation of packing lists, generate a whole-class discussion with the questions in Activity 3.21.

Conclude the lesson by revealing that the "Evacuation!" role sheet is based on Executive Order 9066 issued by President Franklin D. Roosevelt on February 19, 1942, just two months after the attack on Pearl Harbor. Ask students to alternately critique and defend the U.S. government's decision to relocate Japanese Americans during the war.

ACTIVITY 3.20. Evacuation!

Background
The United States has been attacked on U.S. soil by a hostile enemy. Unfortunately for you, your family's ancestry is the same nationality as that of the enemy. Although your family has lived and worked in the United States for the last 75 years, your loyalty is now being called into question since the government is rounding up "suspects." Prejudice against you is also building up in the community and the government says that you need to be protected against hate acts. As a result, a Presidential Order has been issued and within the next 48 hours you must report to the Civil Control Station to be evacuated to a "Reception Center" far away.

You must bring with you:

- bedding and linen (no mattress) for each member of the family;
- toilet articles for each member of the family;
- extra clothing for each member of the family;
- sufficient knives, forks, spoons, plates, bowls, and cups for each member of the family;
- essential personal effects for each member of the family.

All items must be securely packaged, tied, and marked with the name of the owner and numbered in accordance with instructions received at the Civil Control Station. The size and number of packages are limited to what can be carried by the individual or family group.

What will you bring? List the items below.

(Remember that you are limited to that which you can carry.)

Bedding

Personal hygiene

Clothing

Eating utensils

Personal effects

ACTIVITY 3.21. Evacuation! questioning strategy

Stage	Strategy
Early production	Name one item of personal hygiene that you will take with you. Of the five categories of items, which is the most important to bring? Which list is longest? If you were quickly evacuated by the government, how would you feel?
Speech emergence	How did you decide what to include and what to exclude from your lists? How difficult was it to decide what to bring? What items were omitted from your "personal effects" list? Do you think it was fair for the government to move you and your family, given the situation?
Intermediate fluency	What do you think the Reception Center will be like? Has there ever been a time in U.S. history where certain people were targeted as potential enemies? Can you think of other examples in world history? Do you think the government is justified in relocating your family? How should you be compensated for this forced migration?

Teaching Tip

- Locate the song "Kenji" by Fort Minor (album: *The Rising Tide*) on iTunes or a similar music service and the lyrics on the Internet. This powerful rap song tells the story of one relocated Japanese American from the perspective of his son.

Life in the Relocation Centers

With their meager collection of personal belongings, families began their lives in the relocation centers established by the U.S. government. Living conditions were rudimentary and the centers were surrounded by barbed wire fences. Armed military police, housed in a separate compound, patrolled the perimeter. Although familiar routines such as socializing and schooling were soon established, limited opportunities for work, eating in common facilities, and sharing communal bathrooms disrupted other social and cultural patterns. People who were considered disloyal or a high security threat were sent to a detention center at Tule Lake, California. In this exercise, students will consider what life might have been like for children living in one of the relocation centers by examining poetry written by them.

Start by distributing a copy of (or projecting) a map of the relocation centers; the National Park Service provides several useful ones, such as Figure 3.23. Direct students to note how many camps there were and where they were located. Population statistics can be obtained from www.nps. gov/history/history/online_books/anthropology74/ce3g.htm. Tell them that today they will examine poetry written by Japanese American children from the Gila River Relocation Center (Activity 3.22). All students should have access to a dictionary or thesaurus (ELL students should also have a bilingual dictionary) during the exercise; they should note any new or unfamiliar vocabulary in the appropriate area of the worksheet, taking the time to look up and write down the translation or definition in the space provided. The exercise can be completed individually, in small groups, or as a whole-class activity.

FIGURE 3.23. Relocation centers map.

Source: National Park Service, Relocation Centers (Figure 3.9), www.nps.gov/history/history/online_books/anthropology74/ce3g.htm.

Bring closure to the lesson by telling students of the aftermath of the camps. As the war came to an end, the relocation centers were gradually vacated; most were abandoned by the end of 1945. Only one relocation center, Manzanar, has been designated a National Historic Site to "provide for the protection and interpretation of historic, cultural, and natural resources associated with the relocation of Japanese Americans during World War II" (Public Law 102-248).

Whereas some Japanese Americans returned to their home towns, others never returned, instead taking up residency in new cities around the nation. It was not until years later, in 1988, that Congress passed Public Law 100-383, acknowledging and apologizing for the injustice of the Japanese American relocation. The law also provided for a $20,000 cash payment to each person who was interned. You may wish the class to consider and debate the appropriateness and fairness of this gesture.

Teaching Tip

- *Sadako and the Thousand Paper Cranes* is a true story about a girl who lived in Japan during WWII. The children's millennium peace project and teacher resources can be found at www.sadako.org.

Selected Resources for Teaching about Japanese Americans during WWII

Ansel Adams's Photographs of Japanese-American Internment at Manzanar (Library of Congress) (http://memory.loc.gov/ammem/collections/anseladams)

Burton, J., Farrell, M., Lord, F., and Lord, R. (2000). Confinement and ethnicity: An overview of World War II Japanese American relocation sites. Retrieved from www.nps.gov/history/history/online_books/anthropology74/ce16.htm.

Camp Harmony Exhibit (www.lib.washington.edu/exhibits/harmony/exhibit/index.html)

Daniels, R., Taylor, S. L., and Kitano, H. H. L. (Eds.) (1986). *Japanese Americans: From relocation to redress.* Seattle: University of Washington Press.

ACTIVITY 3.22. Poetry by Japanese American children, Gila Relocation Center

Be Like the Cactus by Kimmi Nagata

Let not harsh tongues, that wag in vain,
Discourage you. In spite of pain,
Be like the cactus, which through rain,
And storm, and thunder, can remain.

New vocabulary words:

Questions to consider:
- To whom is the poem directed? Who is "you"?
- Why is the poet encouraging you to be "like the cactus"?
- What are the virtues of a cactus, according to the poet?
- Why do you think the poet chose the cactus and not some other plant? (Hint: in addition to its tenacity, point out where the Gila River Center is on the map.)

My Plea by Mary Matsuzawa

Oh God, I pray that I may bear a cross
To set my people free,
That I may help to take good-will across
An understanding sea.
Oh, God, I pray that someday every race
May stand on equal plane
And prejudice will find no dwelling place
In a peace that all may gain.

New vocabulary words:

Questions to consider:
- Who are the poet's "people"?
- What is the poet asking of God?
- To what prejudice do you think the poet is referring?

The Desert is My Home by Tokiko Inouye

The desert is my home;
I love its sun and sands,
I love its vastness, century's sleep;
It challenges, commands!
At night the cold stars crystallize,
Opalescent, free;
I exult in their ageless eyes,
Their silence envelops me.
This desert is my home,
This, the open plains
And endless sage beneath hot suns,
The sky and sudden rains.
From golden dawn to red sunset,
The desert beckons, calls—
I love its freedom wilderness, Unlimited
by walls.
And this will be my home;
The desert sands I'll plod,
Far out beneath its skies and stars,
To be alone with God.

New vocabulary words:

Questions to consider:
- What virtues does the poet find in the desert?
- Do you think the poet ever plans on leaving the desert? Why?
- How does this poem compare to the first two?
- Why do you think the tone of this poem is so different from the others?

Source: Downing (1945).

Documents and Photographs Related to Japanese Relocation During World War II (The National Archives) (www.archives.gov/education/lessons/japanese-relocation)

Houston, J. W. and Houston, J. D. (1983). *Farewell to Manzanar*. New York: Bantam Books.

Human Rights and the Japanese Internment Experience (www.eduscapes.com/ladders/themes/japanese.htm)

Oppenheim, J. (2006). *Dear Miss Breed: True stories of the Japanese-American incarceration during World War II and a librarian who made a difference*. New York: Scholastic.

War Relocation Authority Photographs of Japanese-American Evacuation and resettlement, 1942–1945 (www.oac.cdlib.org/findaid/ark:/13030/tf596nb4h0)

Role Playing and Cooperative Learning: Factory Life in the Twentieth Century (Levels 2–4)

After having studied factory conditions during the Industrial Revolution of the nineteenth century, students are often surprised to learn that many of the same dismal conditions can still be found in various parts of the world. In this lesson, we will use the case study of the 1985 Mexico City earthquake to create a role-playing exercise; this template can then be used in a number of other scenarios during the study of world history.

Start by duplicating "Temblor!" (earthquake in Spanish) and distributing to students so that they may follow along while you read aloud.

Temblor![2]

At 7:19 on the morning of September 19, 1985, Mexico City experienced one of North America's worst earthquakes. Thousands of people were killed, countless numbers were left homeless, and many more were left jobless since many office buildings cracked or toppled over. An estimated 800 small garment factories in Mexico City were destroyed that morning, killing over 1,000 garment workers and leaving another 40,000 without jobs.

September 19 was a Thursday—payday—and many of these workers were single mothers whose families depended on their wages. Many of the women were already at work at 7 a.m. and they became trapped inside the flattened buildings. Managers usually kept windows closed and doors locked to stop women from taking work breaks or stealing materials, so few of the women had any chance of escaping.

Some of these buildings held up to 50 different garment companies, several per floor. The floors and cement pillars on which they rested could hardly have been expected to hold the weight of heavy industrial sewing machines and tons of fabric, although no government inspector had ever complained.

Women outside the collapsed building who had arrived later tried to climb over the debris to rescue their coworkers trapped inside. Hastily mobilized government soldiers told them to get back and roped off the building. Within a day the company owners arrived, accompanied by the army. Equipped with cranes, soldiers began to pull away piles of fallen cement so that the owners could retrieve their machinery. Employees still standing in the sun on the other side of the ropes watched with mounting horror and indignation as their bosses and the soldiers chose to rescue sewing machines before women.

Teaching Tip

■ Interact (www.teachinteract.com) makes available hundreds of hands-on, experiential learning exercises, many of them appropriate for ELLs.

After reading the case study, answer any questions students may have. Tell them that they will be assigned to a group that will depict the event from one of four perspectives: factory owners, soldiers, the Mexican government, women workers. Explain that they will have a limited amount of time to read through their role sheets and compose a response (allow about 30 minutes for this portion of the activity).

Garment Factory Owners

You are stunned by the negative press your group has received. Most of you are small sub-contractors, although backed by foreign money. The government used you as a major part of its policy to pay off its debt. And now it seems that even the government is turning its back on you.

The women workers are clamoring for their money, but you were not insured and it will take much money to reconstruct the factory. You desperately brainstorm about whom you can call upon to help you out of this crisis.

You are being called "beasts" and "unfeeling monsters" in the press. Can you be blamed for wanting to salvage the equipment that you worked so hard to acquire?

As a group, you decide that you must inform the public of your plight and let people around the world know that you are not "unfeeling monsters."

You have 30 minutes to draft a press release to the news media as a group. Be sure to explain the situation from your point of view and ask for assistance from the community at large.

Compose your press release now.

Soldiers

You are the government soldiers who were hastily mobilized to keep order at the garment factory site. You felt bad roping off the area and telling the surviving women workers to get back. However, you were just following orders.

The real problems started when your regiment started removing piles of fallen cement in order for the owners to retrieve their machinery. Since then, there have been newspaper reporters, camera people, and protesters there around the clock.

Last night, the women set up a human road block and refused to budge for your cranes. You feel torn about what to do.

While the government figures out what to do, the commander for your regiment has given you a break of about 30 minutes. During this time, you are to write a letter to your parents back home. You feel this might do you good and might help you understand where you stand on the issue.

As a group, compose your letter now.

Mexican Government

You are all advisors to the president of Mexico. You are greatly saddened by the loss of life and property that the earthquake has caused in your capital city; this will no doubt worsen the economic situation in your country. You must analyze the situation quickly and advise the president how he should act.

The president has been seriously embarrassed by the mobilized women workers; they have publicized the army's role in removing the sewing machines. But most people don't understand that the garment factories had become an integral part of your policy to pay off Mexico's debt.

However, the women have gotten international publicity; the government has been made to look like a "monster" by most newspaper accounts. The reputation and image of the Mexican government must be salvaged; after all, you are in dire need of foreign investments.

The president is expecting a memo from you in about 30 minutes advising him as to the course of action he should take.

Compose your memo to the president now.

Women Garment Workers

You are the surviving women garment workers of the neighborhood known as San Antonio Abad in Mexico City. You are disgusted by the way that the factory owners have acted in prioritizing their machinery over people. You are sickened by the government's apparent conspiracy with the owners and are enraged that you have not been compensated for last week's labor and future lost work.

For the last week, you have built a human road block against the soldiers, owners, and the cranes. You have kept a constant watch outside the factory since the earthquake.

Just one hour ago, you received a telegram from the World Court. It has heard of your plight (you've been very successful at embarrassing the president by publicizing the army's role in removing the sewing machines before rescuing trapped women workers) and has sent a telegram to let you know that they are willing to pay for two of you to travel to their chambers so that they can hear your grievance.

You decide that, although all of you can't go, you should all have a say. You compromise and decide to write an impassioned speech that one of you (who goes on the trip) will read before the Court. Unfortunately, you have only 30 minutes to write the speech before the selected two must leave for the airport.

Compose your speech as a group now.

Teaching Tip

- Make a connection to U.S. history by discussing the Triangle Shirtwaist Factory fire and the similarities to the Mexico City earthquake.

Bring closure to the lesson by allowing students to read their group's response to the entire class. Discuss the similarities between factory life for workers in Great Britain during the Industrial Revolution and those experienced by the Mexican factory workers in 1985. You could also extend the discussion to include the contemporary maquiladora industry at the U.S.–Mexico border.

Selected Internet Sites about the 1985 Mexico City Earthquake

Dr. George P.C. (www.drgeorgepc.com/Tsunami1985Mexico.html)
History.com (www.history.com/tdih.do?action=tdihArticleCategory&id=50842)
National Geophysical Data Center (www.ngdc.noaa.gov/seg/hazard/slideset/3/3_slides.shtml)
Spinet (www.scieds.com/spinet/historical/mexico.html)

Further Reading and Resources

Enloe, C. (1989). *Bananas, beaches, & bases: Making feminist sense of international politics.* Berkeley: University of California Press.

Poniatowska, E. (1988). *Nada, nadie: Las voces del temblor.* Mexico: Ediciones Era.

Poniatowska, E. (1995). *Nothing, nobody: The voices of the Mexico City earthquake.* Philadelphia, PA: Temple University Press.

Rowbotham, S., and Mitter, S. (Eds.) (1994). *Dignity and daily bread.* New York: Routledge.

Selected Resources for Teaching World History

Analyzing Visual Primary Sources: World History (2007). Available through Social Studies School Service (www.socialstudies.com)

Awesome Library: K–12 Social Studies Lesson Plans (www.awesomelibrary.org/social.html)

Crocco, M. S. (2011). Teaching about women in world history. *The Social Studies,* 102 (1): 18–24.

DiGiacomo, R. (2000). *Short role-playing simulations for world history.* San Jose, CA: Magnifico Publications.

Dunn, R. E., and Vigilante, D. (Eds.) (1996). *Bring history alive: A sourcebook for teaching world history.* Los Angeles: National Center for History in the Schools.

Hyperhistory Online (www.hyperhistory.com/online_n2/history_n2/a.html)

Maestas, A., and Dai Zovi, L. (2006). *Ancient civilizations: Resource book for differentiated instruction.* McHenry, IL: Delta Publishing Group.

National Center for History in the Schools (www.sscnet.ucla.edu/nchs)

National Council for History Education (www.history.org/nche)

Pahl, R. H. (2011). *Breaking away from the textbook: Creative ways to teach world history,* 2nd edn., vols 1 and 2. Lanham, MD: Rowman and Littlefield.

Risinger, C.F. (2011). Teaching world history and global issues with the Internet. *Social Education,* 75 (5): 263–264.

Roupp, H. (1997). *Teaching world history: A resource book.* Armonk, NY: M.E. Sharpe.

Society for History Education (www.csulb.edu/~histeach/#AboutSHE)

Student's Friend—World History and Geography (www.studentsfriend.com/sf/sf.html)

Teacher Explorer Center World History Lesson Plan Links (http://ss.uno.edu/ss/Links/WhLp.html)

Teaching History (www.emporia.edu/socsci/journal/main.htm)

Williams, M., Ratté, L., and Adrian, R. K. (2001). *Exploring world history: Ideas for teachers.* Portsmouth, NH: Heinemann.

Wineburg, S., Martin, D., and Monte-Sano, C. (2011). *Reading like a historian: Teaching literacy in middle and high school history classrooms.* New York: Teachers College Press.

Women in World History (www.womeninworldhistory.com/resources.html)

World History Association (Woodrow Wilson Leadership Program for Teachers) (www.woodrow.org/teachers/world-history)

The World History Association (www.thewha.org)

World History Resources from Big Eye (www.bigeye.com/histworl.htm)

3.5
Government and Civics

For many social studies educators, citizenship education is a central focus. The National Council for the Social Studies (NCSS, 2006) requires that "social studies educators teach students the content knowledge, intellectual skills, and civic values necessary for fulfilling the duties of citizenship in a participatory democracy." The study of government and civics helps students learn about the U.S. political system, foreign governments, the purpose, structure, and functions of government, and an appreciation of their rights and responsibilities as citizens. Usually discussed in social studies are topics such as the U.S. Constitution, how laws are made, suffrage, and human rights, which are important for all students to understand.

For ELLs, the government or civics class may be their first exposure to the U.S. political system and democracy. Full participation in a democratic society requires an informed citizenry that is able to participate in government by thinking critically about issues, voting conscientiously, monitoring government officials' activities, and having an awareness of local, national, and world events.

In the social studies curriculum, civic principles and the political process are studied in courses such as civics, government, and political science. Topics related to government and civics are also covered in courses such as U.S. and world history and electives such as law and sociology.

At the elementary school level, young children learn early on about their membership in their community and, later in the upper elementary grades, about their simultaneous "citizenships" of their nation and of the world. These lessons are mostly infused into the general, overall curriculum and often manifested through folktales, legends, and biographies. For example, children may hear the story of Johnny Appleseed and its meaning for the common good. They will probably also hear stories on national holidays about Thanksgiving, Washington, Lincoln, and King. Elementary students also study national symbols, monuments, and landmarks. Good instruction at this level also attempts to distinguish myths such as Betsy Ross and the first flag (Loewen, 1995: 31–32) from material based on sound historical foundation. As students progress to the secondary curriculum, topics such as governance, political parties, and constitutional rights receive explicit attention. At the high school level, abstract concepts and principles such as power and authority, diplomacy and international organizations, and the role of public opinion are examined in some depth.

As secondary school social studies educators, part of our goal is to have students understand and question the role of government in society. We would like our students to develop tolerance for political dissent, a sense of civic duty, and a commitment to justice and a way how to best achieve it for all. Hahn (2001b), in particular, has called for an increase in democratic discourse and decision making in the social studies classroom. To these ends, we must use pedagogical strategies that encourage students to question, debate, think critically, and apply knowledge and skills to real-world problems. Fortunately, there are many strategies available. Instructional methods that incorporate cooperative learning, diagrams and charts, and case studies can be used effectively with all students, including ELLs, in the social studies classroom. For example, strategies such as graphic organizers, political cartoons, historic documents, and picture dictionaries help simplify abstract concepts into understandable components for students with various learning needs.

For all students, the formal study of government and civics is crucial in developing the awareness needed to be participating citizens in a democratic society. For ELLs, this curriculum is especially important for developing civic competence in their new homeland. Some ELLs also come from countries where citizens do not have a significant voice in government; they may not have a history of participating in democratic life. And, because ELLs often serve as a sort of bridge between the home and the outside world, these students may be their families' primary source of information on the American political system.

In this chapter, we highlight the use of graphic organizers, visuals, political cartoons, primary documents, political memorabilia, and small group learning. As discussed in Parts 1 and 2, these strategies provide a high-context learning environment for ELLs so they can develop language skills while learning content matter. The topics include the duties, responsibilities, and rights of citizens, political campaigns, voting requirements, and women's suffrage. The section at the end of the chapter suggests websites to include in the lesson plans or for further information on teaching government and civics. Additional Internet sites are annotated and included throughout the chapter.

Graphic Organizers and Visuals: The Duties, Responsibilities, and Rights of United States Citizens (Levels 1 and 2)

Students—especially those who have grown up under other forms of government—often have difficulty differentiating among the various duties, responsibilities, and rights that citizens have in the United States. It is not enough to define the terms for them; meaningful discussion accompanied by examples and visuals can help students understand the differences. In this activity, students develop a firm understanding of these key vocabulary words and will be able to give examples of each.

Teacher Preparation

First, you will need to obtain images that represent some of the basic duties, responsibilities, and rights of citizenship in the United States. We suggest the following:

Duties: obeying the law, paying taxes, serving on a jury, serving in the armed forces if called.

- For "obeying the law," for example, you could find an image of a police officer directing traffic and pedestrians and/or drivers obeying the officers' directions. Alternately, an image such as Figure 3.24 clearly shows a citizen heeding the posted speed limit.

FIGURE 3.24. "Obeying the law."

Text and visuals reprinted with permission by National Geographic/Cengage Learning. Cruz, B.C. and Thornton, S.J. (2013). *Gateway to social studies.* Boston, MA: National Geographic/Cengage Learning, p. 230.

- For "paying taxes," an image of someone writing out a check juxtaposed with a tax return can convey meaning. An image of a courtroom, with the jury clearly marked or circled can show how citizens serve in that capacity. Using a few well-chosen descriptors on a simple Internet image search can yield enormously helpful visuals.

Responsibilities: voting in elections, volunteering in community, staying informed, speaking up if something is unfair.

- To show voting in elections, a simple image of someone at a voting booth or placing his or her ballot into a ballot box may suffice, such as Figure 3.25.
- If necessary, the word "ballot" can also be illustrated with an illustration such as Figure 3.26.
- Someone reading a newspaper, serving as a "candy striper" in a local hospital, or speaking at a government meeting can depict staying informed, volunteering, or speaking up if something is unfair, respectively.

Rights: speak freely, meet peacefully, follow any or no religion, have a public trial if accused of a crime.

- Showing citizens demonstrating peacefully at a political rally (Figure 3.27) can convey the idea of freedom of speech and the right to assemble.
- Assembling a variety of religious symbols or houses of worship can show freedom of religion. A photo of a public trial can also be useful to depict "rights."

All of these images should be reproduced and placed on index cards, one image per index card. On the back of each index card, the image should be identified or explained in simple terms. Create a complete set of index cards for each pair or group of students that you plan to have.

FIGURE 3.25. "Voting in elections."

Text and visuals reprinted with permission by National Geographic/Cengage Learning. Cruz, B.C. and Thornton, S.J. (2013). *Gateway to social studies*. Boston, MA: National Geographic/Cengage Learning, p. 230.

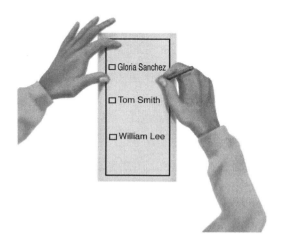

FIGURE 3.26. "Ballot."

Visual reprinted with permission by National Geographic/Cengage Learning. Cruz, B.C. and Thornton, S.J. (2013). *Gateway to social studies*. Boston, MA: National Geographic/Cengage Learning, p. 218.

FIGURE 3.27. "Freedom of speech and right to assemble."

Text and visuals reprinted with permission by National Geographic/Cengage Learning. Cruz, B.C. and Thornton, S.J. (2013). *Gateway to social studies*. Boston, MA: National Geographic/Cengage Learning, p. 231.

In-Class Activity

Have students fold a blank piece of paper into three columns. At the top of the columns ask students to write the words duty, responsibility, and right. Create a model three-column chart on the board. Explain each term in simple language, writing the definitions on the board as students write them on their papers:

Duty	Responsibility	Right
Things a citizen must do	Things a citizen should do	Basic freedoms citizens have

Divide students into pairs or small groups, distributing the sets of index cards to each group. Have students determine which activity belongs in which column. Allow time at the end of the class to come together as a whole group to discuss students' findings.

Extension/Assessment Activity

Have students take turns quizzing each other by considering the image on a given index card then reading the written text on the other side.

Peer Teaching and Visual Aids: Political Cartoons (Levels 2–4)

An accepted form of social commentary, political cartoons are often more accessible to ELL students than standard texts or prose because things are exaggerated and because most cartoons deal with one central idea. Primarily visual in nature, political cartoons lend themselves to being analyzed and interpreted, which encourages critical thinking by all learners. Easily recognized symbols quickly communicate an idea or feeling and cartoonists usually use humor or sarcasm to challenge opinion about issues.

Although useful with all students, the following activity can be especially helpful for ELL students still developing expressive skills in English. By pairing an ELL with an English speaker, ELL students can work collaboratively with a classmate on analyzing and creating their own political cartoon. This arrangement also provides ELLs with greater opportunities to practice speaking.

Adapting Bloom's taxonomy as an organizing tool, students can be guided through the analysis process. After presenting students with a cartoon, teachers can ask students to:

- identify standard symbols and central characters;
- describe activity taking place;
- analyze the cartoonist's point of view;
- determine the cartoonist's purpose;
- decide whether they agree or disagree with the cartoonist;
- draw their own cartoons.

Teaching Tip

- For ideas about peer teaching, access Page Kalkowski's helpful article, "Peer and Cross-Age Tutoring," at www.nwrel.org/scpd/sirs/9/c018.html.

This step-by-step process should be explained and demonstrated to students as a whole-class exercise first. Then, after the class analyzes two or three cartoons, cartoons can be distributed to pairs of students along with prompts to facilitate analysis. A dyad exercise may look something like Activity 3.23.

ACTIVITY 3.23. Political cartoon activity

Image of political cartoon here	Study the cartoon. Is there a caption or title? Do you see any symbols in this cartoon? What do they represent? Who or what are the central characters? Describe the activity taking place. What is the cartoonist's point of view? What is the cartoonist's purpose? Do you agree or disagree with the cartoonist's point of view? Why? Draw your own cartoon representing your viewpoint on the issue. If appropriate, include a caption.

So that the political cartoons are effective, make sure your students, including ELLs, are familiar with the issue the cartoon refers to. Keeping in mind lower-level ELLs, teachers should choose relatively simple, straightforward cartoons that have clearly identifiable symbols and characters. All ELLs regardless of language acquisition level will benefit from this activity by developing both receptive and expressive language skills.

In addition to the local or a national newspaper, political cartoons can be obtained from a number of reputable websites. Here are just a few:

- Cartoon Archives (www.pritchettcartoons.com/archives.htm)

    Editorial cartoons are organized on this site by topic and community level (international, national, municipal). The search engine is helpful in locating cartoons that address specific issues.

- The New York Times on the Web: Cartoons (www.nytimes.com/pages/cartoons/index.html)

    Organized by cartoonist, a great variety of recent cartoons are stored on this site, including Trudeau's Doonesbury and other nationally syndicated cartoonists.

- All newspapers (www.allnewspapers.com)

    Many of the newspapers and magazines in this collection from around the world include political cartoons appropriate for classroom use. Resources are organized by region, country, and type of resource.

- Political Cartoons and Cartoonists (www.boondocksnet.com/gallery/pc_intro.html)

    This site includes a brief essay on the history of political cartoons in the United States, along with a plethora of links to other political cartoon sites and a historical image gallery.

- Political Humor (http://politicalhumor.about.com)

    This site not only includes political cartoons, but also provides analysis of contemporary events, satire, and jokes about current scandals.

- Ucomics.com (www.ucomics.com/editorials)

    This comprehensive collection of outstanding editorial cartoonists—including the yearly Pulitzer Prize winners—is one of the best available on the Internet.

- Online newspapers (www.onlinenewspapers.com)

Teaching Tip

- Have students compare political cartoons from different countries, noting differences and similarities among cultures.

Teaching with Primary Sources (Levels 2–4)

Teaching with primary sources can bring a sense of immediacy and authenticity to the social studies classroom, stimulating critical thinking and analysis. Students often respond enthusiastically to these materials, excited by the idea of working with sources that constitute the historical record. Potter (2003) elegantly summarizes the unique benefits of using primary documents in teaching: "they are a part of the past; they are with us today; and touching them allows us, quite literally, to touch and connect with the past" (p. 372).

Primary sources include diaries, letters, memorabilia, clothing, coins, stamps, photographs, audio recordings, and motion pictures. For print materials, try to obtain an original. Having an original imparts a sense of authenticity that photocopies or word-processed transcriptions cannot convey as powerfully. For objects from the past, field trips to museums are highly recommended. It is important on these trips to consider beforehand how the objectives of the trip fit into your ongoing instructional program. Of course museum collections can often be accessed without leaving the classroom. Virtual field trips are widely available and many museums lend out museum artifact kits. Marcus *et al.* (2012) provide numerous suggestions for teaching with primary sources from museums.

For ELLs, the greatest challenge that historical documents can present is the inaccessibility of language. Often, documents are written in formal or archaic language, use complex terminology, or require a substantial amount of contextual knowledge in order to comprehend them. The historical context also gives rise to dated vocabulary and terms, colloquial expressions, and even unusual pronunciation of words. Nonetheless, there are a number of ways that these documents can be mediated and made more accessible to ELLs. For ideas on how to use primary sources with ELLs, see the U.S. history (3.3) and World History (3.4) chapters in this book. David Kobrin's (1996) *Beyond the Textbook* offers additional suggestions on using primary sources. For example, Kobrin uses the Renaissance as an extended example of collaborative group work (pp. 37–48), which complements the Renaissance exercises in this book's World History chapter (3.4).

Primary documents can be obtained from a number of places. Libraries, websites, and local archives can all provide materials appropriate for a social studies classroom. Students should also be encouraged to ask their families for journals, diaries, photographs, mementos, and other documents that can be used in instruction. ELLs might also be able to contribute to the classroom by bringing in documents from their homeland, explaining to students that they must be treated and used with the utmost care and respect.

NCSS features a regular section, "Teaching with Historical Documents," in its flagship journal, *Social Education*. Self-contained lesson plans use historic documents from the National Archives to teach history, civics, and other social studies disciplines. Examples include the First Act of Congress, a letter from U.S. president Millard Fillmore to the Emperor of Japan regarding that country's "closed country" policy, and the Order of Argument in *Brown* v. *Board of Education*.

The Internet has made it much easier for teachers to access historical documents. Local and national archives have begun to digitize their holdings and make them accessible to the public. Here are a few Internet sites that are especially helpful in this regard:

- The National Archives: America's Historical Documents (www.archives.gov/historical-docs)
  The National Archives provides digital images of famous documents such as the Declaration of Independence, the U.S. Constitution, and the Bill of Rights as well as lesser-known papers. Lesson plans and worksheets to guide analysis are also included.
- The Avalon Project (www.yale.edu/lawweb/avalon/avalon.htm)
  Maintained at Yale University, this site furnishes full-text documents that are critical for the study of law, government, and diplomacy. The documents are organized by time period, from before the eighteenth century to the twenty-first. Examples include the Athenian Constitution, the Monroe Doctrine, and the 9/11 Commission Report. Helpful chronologies of American history are also included for each time period.
- The Library of Congress: American Memory (http://memory.loc.gov/ammem/index.html)
  Users can browse this vast website by topics such as government, law, immigration, and presidents. The "Learning Page" (http://memory.loc.gov/learn/) on the site is a teacher's portal to lessons, activities, and features related to over 7 million documents.
- Hudson Library and Historical Society: Historical Archives (www.hudsonlibrary.org/ Hudson%20Website/Archives/Political-Artifacts/Political-artifacts.htm)
  Digital collection of political artifacts such as pins, posters, bumper stickers, and brochures and pamphlets. Their main site (www.hudsonlibrary.org/hudson%20Website/ Archives/archives.htm) also has facsimiles of letters, passenger lists, and photographs related to the Underground Railroad.
- EuroDocs (http://eudocs.lib.byu.edu/index.php/Main_Page)
  Transcriptions, facsimiles, and translations of documents related to European history.

Teaching Tip

▪ Aged-looking parchment paper can now be easily found in office supply stores. Print primary source documents from the Internet onto this special paper for authentic-looking facsimiles.

Using Bilingual Dictionaries and Graphic Organizers: Voting Rights (Levels 3 and 4)

The right to vote is a crucial component in exercising political rights and effecting political and social change. Suffrage is an important measure of full citizenship and often leads the way to obtaining other rights. Most secondary school students—given that they will shortly gain the right to vote—may be keenly interested in this topic. In these activities, students will determine the qualifications for voting eligibility and construct a timeline of voting rights in the United States.

Voting Rights: Voter Requirements (Activity 1)

Obtain a voting registration application from a local agency or by downloading from the Election Assistance Commission's website (www.eac.gov/docs/NVRA%20Update%2009–12–06.pdf). Distribute a copy of the application to students and instruct them to review the General Instructions, Application Instructions, and State Instructions (for your state). Make sure each ELL student is equipped with a bilingual dictionary to aid in translation. Then, have them fill out the form as if they were planning to submit it. As noted in Part 1, writing and engaging in interviews and applications are suggested instructional strategies for ELLs at the higher levels of language ability.

 After allowing sufficient time to complete this task, lead a discussion of voting requirements by asking, "To be eligible to vote. . .":

▪ Must you be a citizen of the United States?
▪ Must you be born in the United States?
▪ Must you be 18 years or older?
▪ Must you have a permanent address?
▪ Can you be a convicted felon?
▪ Do you have to pay a fee?
▪ Must you be able to read and write?
▪ Must you be a property owner?
▪ What proofs of identification can you use to register?
▪ Must you select a political party affiliation?
▪ What special instructions does our state have?

 You can also distribute these questions to ELL students the night before so they can complete them at home ahead of time. Bring closure to the lesson by comparing present voter requirements with those in the past.

> **Teaching Tip**
>
> ■ Cross-cultural comparisons of voting regulations make for an interesting lesson on global citizenship.

Voting Rights: Timeline of Voting Rights in the United States (Activity 2)

Understanding the chronology of voting rights legislation helps students comprehend the many challenges that have faced Americans since the inception of the nation. ELL students will particularly benefit from the graphic nature of the timeline, showing clearly the chronological development of voting rights laws. Some ELLs may not be familiar with chronological timelines (as noted in Part 2); this simplified activity is an excellent way to introduce them to the concept. In this activity, students should be provided with a blank template of "Voting Rights in the United States: A Timeline" or it should be projected on a screen in the classroom for students to follow along and fill in on their own paper.

Voting Rights in the United States: A Timeline

1776
1820
1848
1868
1869
1870
1876
1882
1887
1890
1920
1943
1947
1964
1965
1971
1975
1990
1993

Voting Rights in the U.S.: A Timeline (Teacher's Notes)

1776:   Nearly everywhere, only white, male, land owners can vote (although women and free African-American men could vote for a time in a few places).

1820:   Although owning property is no longer required for whites to vote, poll taxes and literacy tests are used for eligibility.

1848:   Seneca Falls Convention is held, to appeal for women's suffrage.

1868:   The 14th Amendment states that any eligible 21-year-old male has the right to vote.

1869:   Wyoming Territory is first to revive the issue of women's suffrage.

1870: The 15th Amendment is passed, granting African-American men suffrage: the right to vote cannot be denied "on account of race, color, or previous condition of servitude."

1876: When Wyoming achieves statehood, it also becomes the first state to grant women suffrage.

1882: Congress passes the Chinese Exclusion Act denying citizenship and voting rights to Chinese immigrants and their descendants.

1887: The Dawes Act grants suffrage to Native Americans who give up their tribal affiliations.

1890: Laws are passed in some southern states to limit the voting rights of African Americans (e.g., poll tax, literacy tests).

1920: The 19th Amendment grants women the right to vote.

1943: The Chinese Exclusion Act is repealed, giving Chinese immigrants the right to citizenship and suffrage.

1947: Native Americans are granted the right to vote in every state (an earlier ruling barred Native Americans living on reservations from voting because they pay no state taxes).

1964: The 24th Amendment is passed, outlawing the poll tax.

1965: The Voting Rights Act is passed, banning literacy tests and racist voting practices.

1971: The 26th Amendment lowers the minimum voting age from 21 to 18.

1975: Amendment to the Voting Rights Act allows for voting materials to be printed in the languages of non-English speakers.

1990: The Americans with Disabilities Act mandates access to the polls and to the ballot for all voters.

1993: The Voter Registration Act—also called the "Motor Voter Law"—simplifies registering by permitting citizens to register by mail, when they obtain their driver's license, or at government agencies.

In addition to asking clarifying and probing questions throughout the explanation, the activity can be debriefed by asking:

- Why did some people get the right to vote before others?
- Who still cannot vote in the United States? Should any of these groups be allowed to vote?

Selected Internet Sites for Teaching about Voting

The Democracy Project (PBS) (http://pbskids.org/democracy/vote)

Elections The American Way (Library of Congress) (http://lcweb2.loc.gov/learn/features/election/home.html)

Fair Vote (www.fairvote.org/righttovote/timeline.htm)

Kids Voting Classroom (www.kidsvoting.org/classroom/curriculum.htm)

Kids Voting USA (www.kidsvotingusa.org/index.cfm)

Vote Kids (www.votekids.org)

Voting Rights (eNotes) (http://law.enotes.com/everyday-law-encyclopedia/voting-rights)

Voting Rights Act (ACLU) (www.votingrights.org/timeline/)

Language Development through Simplifying Complex Text and Using Visual Aids: Women's Suffrage (Levels 3 and 4)

In the activities that follow, modifications are made to make social studies content more accessible to ELL students while supporting language development. In the first activity, students will simplify complex text into more manageable passages, translating into comprehensible English. In the second activity, historical images and photographs will be used as visual aids in analysis. The teacher will need a short lecture on women's suffrage history before the students can complete the exercise outlined below.

Most scholars agree that in the United States the 1848 Seneca Falls Convention was a turning point in the women's suffrage movement. Women then had few legal and political rights in the United States. Women could neither vote nor participate in governmental affairs. Moreover, many professions and educational careers were effectively barred to women. In the domestic sphere, married women's property and wages legally belonged to their spouses and, in the relatively rare case of a divorce, custody of children was usually automatically awarded to the father (Osborn, 2006).

The two-day gathering in Seneca Falls, New York, resulted in the *Declaration of Sentiments*. Written in the style and form of the *U.S. Declaration of Independence*, this document spurred discussion and debate throughout the nation regarding women's appropriate roles in society.

Women's Suffrage: Declaration of Sentiments (Activity 1)

In this learning activity, students will be asked to reflect on both *Declarations* and analyze the writers' intentions. They will also consider the strong anti-suffrage movement that existed at the time. For the first activity, students will be required to translate the opening of each document into contemporary English (Activity 3.24) and compare and contrast the main points of both. English speakers and ELLs alike should use a dictionary (and perhaps a thesaurus) to assist in the translations. ELLs in early stages of language emergence could have two translation columns (one for English and one for their home language).

After the students have translated the *Declarations*, stimulate class discussion by asking the following questions, simplifying as needed:

- What intolerable conditions spurred the American revolutionaries to write the *Declaration of Independence*?
- What conditions were considered intolerable by the writers of the *Declaration of Sentiments*?
- Why do you think the Seneca Falls activists used the style and form of the U.S. *Declaration of Independence*?
- What "truths" are considered by each *Declaration* to be "self-evident"?
- How do the "truths" differ in each *Declaration*?

Women's Suffrage: Anti-suffrage Movement

Today's students often find it difficult to believe that there was an anti-suffrage movement that was popular and influential at the time. In addition to many men, not all women supported female suffrage. The arguments against suffrage ranged from women being incapable of making important political decisions to views about women's physical constitution to protecting marriage

ACTIVITY 3.24. Women's suffrage: *Declaration of Sentiments* (Activity 1)

The *U.S. Declaration of Independence*	Translation
When, in the Course of human Events, it becomes necessary for one People to dissolve the Political bands which have connected them with another, and to assume, among the Powers of the Earth, the separate and equal Station to which the Laws of Nature and of Nature's God entitle them, a decent Respect to the Opinions of Mankind requires that they should declare the Causes which impel them to the Separation. We hold these Truths to be self-evident, that all Men are created equal, that they are endowed, by their Creator, with certain unalienable Rights, that among these are Life, Liberty, and the Pursuit of Happiness. When, in the course of human events, it becomes necessary for one portion of the family of man to assume among the people of the earth a position different from that which they have hitherto occupied, but one to which the laws of nature and of nature's God entitle them, a decent respect to the opinions of mankind requires that they should declare the causes that impel them to such a course. We hold these truths to be self-evident: that all men and women are created equal; that they are endowed by their Creator with certain inalienable rights; that among these are life, liberty, and the pursuit of happiness . . .	

and family. In the following activity, students will examine a historical political cartoon and photographs and consider the challenge that women's suffrage posed to the status quo and analyze the reasons for the resistance.

Allow students to view "The apotheosis of suffrage" cartoon (the image can be captured at the online site of the Library of Congress Prints and Photographs Division, www.loc.gov/rr/print, by entering "apotheosis" in the search field, or you can scan the image or make a handout by using Figure 3.28). Make similar arrangements for the photographs in Figures 3.29 and 3.30.

FIGURE 3.28. The apotheosis of suffrage. 1896.

Credit: George Yost Coffin, artist. Cartoon Drawings, Prints and Photographs Division, Library of Congress (http://hdl.loc.gov/loc.pnp/cph.3a13267).

Viewing/Discussion Questions: Political Cartoon

1.   Ask students to read the title at the top of the illustration.
2.   Can you identify any of the characters? (The three prominent figures are Elizabeth Cady Stanton, George Washington, and Susan B. Anthony).
3.   Why is Anthony sounding a trumpet?
4.   (Juxtapose Brumidi's fresco in the U.S. Capitol Rotunda with the political cartoon.) Why do you think the cartoonist chose to draw the image in the style of the Capitol Rotunda? (Brumidi's original artwork, on which this cartoon is based, can be accessed at www.access. gpo.gov/congress/senate/brumidi.)
5.   What is the cartoonist's position on women's suffrage?
6.   Do you think this cartoon helped or hurt the women's cause?

Viewing/Discussion Questions: Historical Photographs

1.   What do the signs say in each photo (Figures 3.29 and 3.30)?
2.   Who is standing in front?
3.   In what year(s) do you think these photos were taken?
4.   In what country do you think these photographs were taken?
5.   What is the main purpose of each office?

Writing Activity

After telling students a bit about the arguments, in this instance, made for/against women's suffrage at the time, have students write a persuasive piece either in support of or against the issue. You could also have them write it from the perspective of someone living in the United States before WWI. Since some ELL students may be unfamiliar with the genre of persuasive writing, distributing and discussing examples beforehand would be useful.

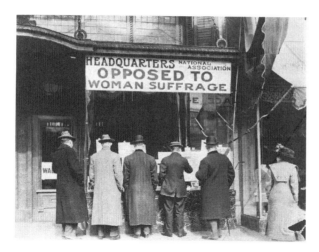

FIGURE 3.29. Men looking in the window of the National Anti-Suffrage Association headquarters. 1911.

Credit: Harris & Ewing. Women—Politics and Suffrage, Prints and Photographs Division, Library of Congress (http://hdl.loc.gov/loc.pnp/cph.3a26270).

FIGURE 3.30. Women's Suffrage Headquarters, Cleveland, Ohio. 1912.

Prints and Photographs Division, Library of Congress (http://hdl.loc.gov/loc.pnp/cph.3a52979).

Selected Resources for Teaching about the Anti-Suffrage Movement

Anti-Suffrage Movement and Sentiments (Western New York Suffragists) (http://winningthevote. org/res_anti.html)

Anti-Suffrage Arguments and Activists (About.com) (http://womenshistory.about.com/od/ suffrageanti/AntiSuffrage_Arguments_and_Activists.htm)

By Popular Demand: Votes for Women's Suffrage Pictures, 1850–1920 (LoC) (http://memory.loc. gov/ammem/vfwhtml/vfwhome.html)

Crawford, E. (1999). *Women's suffrage movement: A reference guide 1866–1928*. New York: Routledge.

Fawcett, M. (2002). *Women's suffrage: A short history of a great movement.* Boston, MA: Adamant Media Corporation.

International Woman Suffrage Timeline (About.com) (http://womenshistory.about.com/od/suffrage/a/intl_timeline.htm)

Law, C. (1997). *Suffrage and power: The women's movement 1918–1928.* London: IB Tauris.

Leaders of the Women's Suffrage Movement (Teacher Vision) (www.teachervision.fen.com/womens-history/resource/5100.html)

Seager, J. (1997). *State of the women of the world atlas.* New York: Penguin.

Women's Suffrage Resources (San Francisco State University) (http://userwww.sfsu.edu/~crdodson/online_class_2%20wmns%20sfrg.htm)

Cooperative Learning, Computer Technology, and Alternative Assessments: Political Bumper Stickers (Levels 1–4)

In the social studies classroom, bumper stickers can be very useful in summarizing the issues of the day even when studying a past presidential election or analyzing contemporary concerns. For ELLs in particular, the simplified text and visual nature of this type of propaganda provide contextual cues that aid comprehension.

In this activity, ask students to locate political bumper stickers for any presidential campaign. Instruct them to analyze their purpose and effectiveness. After some class discussion, have the students design their own for an upcoming election. Divide the class into pairs, with each pair assigned a specific presidential election. ELLs should be paired with supportive English speakers who can assist them in negotiating meaning from the resource materials. The first few times this strategy is used in the classroom, the teacher needs to tell/show/instruct the native English speaker what being a good partner is and what things they should be doing to help the ELL. Preproduction students can pick up quite a bit of content knowledge given the visual nature of the materials in this exercise.

For this learning exercise, secure a computer lab at your school and deliver a brief lecture on locating images on the Internet. (Note: Some of your ELLs may not be familiar with computer technology; clearly, they may need additional instruction and support in Internet research or in capturing images from the Internet.) Instruct students to go to a large search engine such as altavista.com or yahoo.com, select the "images" tab, and enter the appropriate search terms with Booleans or quotation marks as the search engine requires (e.g. "Nixon AND bumper sticker"). As part of your briefing orientation, you should demonstrate the search process, locate a bumper sticker, and guide them through the image-capturing process as well as through the analysis of the material (see Activity 3.25). Two helpful websites that have images of historical bumper stickers are:

- Hudson Library and Historical Society: Historical Archives (www.hudson.lib.oh.us/hudson%20website/Archives/Political-Items/political-bumper-stickers.htm)
- The National Archives: Presidential Libraries (www.archives.gov/presidential-libraries/index.html)

After students have completed the exercise, you can have them design their own bumper sticker. They could either create one for an upcoming election in their community or at the national level, or design an alternative bumper sticker for the election they investigated. In either case, they should be asked to explain their choice of colors, symbols, and slogans.

Political Campaign Bumper Stickers

Instructions to Students

In this activity, you and a partner will search the Internet for bumper stickers that were used in a particular presidential election. Try to locate at least five. Using Activity 3.25, analyze each bumper sticker by filling in the information. Print out each image and submit with your completed chart.

Extension Activity

With your partner, design your own alternative political bumper sticker for an upcoming election in our community or nation. Be prepared to defend your choice of colors, symbols, and slogans.

ACTIVITY 3.25. Political campaign bumper stickers activity

Presidential Election of (Year) _____
Major Candidates: _____

Bumper sticker	Which candidate and political party are featured in this bumper sticker?	What colors, symbols, and slogans are used?	Why do you think these colors, symbols, and slogans were used?	How effective is this bumper sticker?

Visual Aids and Graphic Organizers: Executive Powers (Levels 1–4)[1]

The president of the United States is often described as the most powerful person on Earth. But what powers—as enumerated and described by the Constitution—does the president really have?

In this exercise, students will examine Article II of the U.S. Constitution and become familiar with the powers and roles of the president. For ELLs, include a visual presentation of information filled with contextual clues as well as a graphic organizer that will aid in comprehension.

Start by having students consider the various roles each of them hold in their daily lives—both in and out of school. Have them individually create a list of those roles.

Show them a PowerPoint presentation of (or otherwise project) images of various types of roles that students are likely to hold (e.g., son/daughter, sibling, student, athlete, part-time employee, member of band or choir, school club member). As you show each labeled image, read the role, being sure to enunciate clearly, and ask students to raise their hands when they see a role that they identified on their lists. After you show all the images, ask for volunteers to share roles that are on their lists but were not shown by the teacher. Ask students to consider how one individual can have so many different roles. Tell them that today they will be examining the many roles and duties of the president of the United States.

Start by distributing a Describing Wheel graphic organizer (one can be downloaded from http://eduplace.com/graphicorganizer/pdf/wheel_eng.pdf, or you can just have students create their own). Instruct students to write "U.S. President" in the center Topic oval (Figure 3.31). Ask them to think about what documents they should consult in order to fill out the Describing Wheel (probe and prompt until they say the Constitution). For recently arrived ELLs, you may need to provide more direct instruction and support materials since they likely would not have the schema necessary to brainstorm on the U.S. presidency.

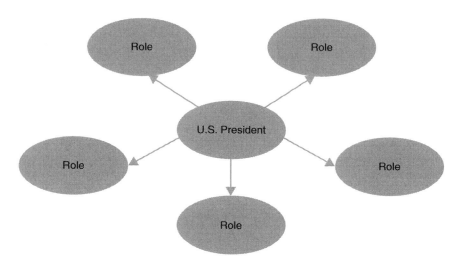

FIGURE 3.31. U.S. presidency brainstorm.

U.S. Presidency Brainstorm

Distribute Article II of the U.S. Constitution (it can be downloaded from www.founding fathers.info/documents/constitution.html), directing students' attention especially to Section 2. Working in pairs and/or with bilingual dictionaries, have students write down the roles of the president on each of the spokes, noting too some words that describe each role.

After students have completed the assignment, have these six headings noted on the board (an illustrative image accompanying each should be identified for ELLs at lower levels of language proficiency, as noted below):

- Chief Executive (example image: president in Oval Office);
- Chief Diplomat (example image: president meeting with foreign dignitaries);
- Head of State (example image: president at press conference);
- Legislative Powers (example image: president before Congress or signing bill);
- Commander-in-Chief of the Armed Forces (example image: president with military).

Ask for volunteers to come up to the board and write descriptors for each role under the terms. Augment students' contributions as needed so that they have complete descriptions for each role.

- Chief Executive: acts as administrative head of the government; meets with the Cabinet; signs bills; issues executive orders; appoints government officials.
- Chief Diplomat: negotiates with foreign governments on behalf of the United States; appoints ambassadors; makes treaties; supports or opposes actions of other nations.
- Head of State: ceremonial head of United States; speaks to nation on topics of interest; meets with officials and heads of state from other countries.
- Legislative Powers: can recommend legislation to Congress; has veto power.
- Commander-in-Chief of the Armed Forces: civilian head of the military; can order troops into battle or send overseas.

Bring closure to the activity by having students consider and discuss the many ways the president can influence life in the United States, being sure to involve ELLs by asking questions using simplified language and noting important terms on board or word wall.

Extension Activity

Have students role play in this instance each of the roles, creating simple skits and dialogues that illustrate each role. For ELLs in the early levels of language acquisition, you could provide dialogue scaffolding. That is, have already written out a potential dialogue but, instead of giving out the whole dialogue, you give one student what person "A" says, and another what "B" says. This then allows them to reconstruct the dialogue. Alternately, you give both only the part of "A" and they have to reconstruct part "B."

Selected Resources for Teaching about the U.S. Presidency

American President: An Online Reference Resource (www.millercenter.virginia.edu/academic/americanpresident)

Drake, S. E. and Vontz, T. S. (2000). Teaching about the U.S. Presidency. ERIC Digest, ED447064 (www.ericdigests.org/2001–3/presidency.htm)

teAchnology: U.S. Presidents Teaching Theme (http://teachers.teach-nology.com/themes/social/presidents)

U.S. Presidency Resources (www.teachervision.fen.com/us-presidency/executive-branch/1765.html?detoured=1)

Teaching Tip

- Have students maintain a current events board by having volunteers (or assigning students to) bring in newspaper articles and post them accordingly.

Local News	State News
National News	World News

Selected Resources for Teaching Government and Civics

The American Promise (www.farmers.com/FarmComm/AmericanPromise)

The Avalon Project (www.yale.edu/lawweb/avalon/avalon.htm)

Ben's Guide to the U.S. Government for Kids (http://bensguide.gpo.gov)

Center for Civic Education (www.civiced.org)

CIA for Kids (www.cia.gov/cia/ciakids)

Civics Online (http://civics-online.org/teachers)

Core Documents of U.S. Democracy (www.gpoaccess.gov/coredocs.html)

Federal Bureau of Investigation (www.fbi.gov/fbikids.htm)

FirstGov (www.firstgov.gov)

Justice for Kids (www.usdoj.gov/kidspage)

National Standards for Civics and Government (www.civiced.org/stds.html)

Office of the Clerk: Kids in the House (http://clerkkids.house.gov)

Project Vote Smart (www.vote-smart.org)

Public Agenda (www.publicagenda.org)

Short, D. J., Seufert-Bosco, M., and Grognet, A. G. (1995). *By the people, for the people: U.S. government and citizenship*. McHenry, IL: Delta Systems.
   This text on American government and citizenship education is designed with the special needs of ELL students in mind. It prepares students for mainstream government and civics classes while promoting their English language development.

Thomas (http://thomas.loc.gov)

U.S. Census Bureau (www.census.gov/dmd/www/teachers.html)

U.S. Department of Justice (www.usdoj.gov/kidspage/kids.htm)

U.S. Department of State for Youth (http://future.state.gov)

White House Kids (www.whitehouse.gov/kids)

3.6
Economics

According to the National Council on Economic Education (NCEE), less than half of American high school students have adequate understanding of basic economic principles. Further, an NCEE survey of states reveals that a commitment to offer or require economic and finance education is severely lacking. As a result, the majority of students do not acquire the essential, real-life economic skills that are required to be informed consumers, wise savers and investors, and productive workers (NCEE, 2007).

Specialized economics courses are most commonly offered at the high school level; however, economic concepts appear, explicitly or implicitly, in just about any social studies course. Analysis of economic concepts and relationships should receive direct attention in geography, history, and civics courses. By the same token, one of the ten themes that form the framework of the social studies standards, "Production, Distribution, and Consumption," is most obviously economic in character. But economics is relevant, in varying degrees, to the other nine themes as well (National Council for the Social Studies, 2010).

Economic literacy is a significant part of general education. For example, some acquaintance with economics is necessary to read the newspaper intelligently, appraise government decisions, appreciate the bases of U.S. foreign policy, and secure a mortgage. Economics is, in other words, relevant to the demands of contemporary living and being an engaged citizen.

Although opportunities to study economics in depth should be available for deeply interested students, this should not be confused with the aforementioned purposes of economics in general education. Thus economics for general education should inform, for example, the teaching of U.S. history courses, if these courses are to be complete. From this perspective, economics educator Mark Schug (2007) warns: "Not economics as a long list of concepts embalmed in huge textbooks written for use in Econ 101 and 102." Rather, Schug continues, an "economic way of thinking" should be infused in U.S. history courses (p. 61).

As educators, we may have a special responsibility to ELL students to promote their economic literacy. Since many of them are newly arrived immigrants, they may be entirely unfamiliar with the U.S. economic system. Nevertheless, these students and their families become participating members of the economy before they are fluent in English. Often, as noted in the previous chapter, it is the ELL student who serves as a cultural bridge between the home and society at large.

In the following learning activities, we have tried using instructional strategies that support ELLs while affording all students the opportunity to explore concepts and issues likely to be found in an economics curriculum. Topics such as international trade, goods and services, personal budgeting, and consumer credit are crucial in developing a basic economic literacy.

Visuals and Simplified Text to Develop Key Vocabulary (Levels 1 and 2)

Building vocabulary is an essential first step in developing economic literacy for all students, regardless of linguistic ability. Economics has specific terminology that students must understand before they can go on to master complex concepts and processes. In this activity, simplified text coupled with visuals help students acquire key vocabulary in order to understand economic systems.

Distribute photocopies of the following text:

> People create economic systems in which they produce, sell, and use goods and services. Payment with money is just one way that people pay for goods and services. In some societies, people also barter, or exchange things as forms of payment.[1]

Read aloud the text while students follow along on their handouts; ask them to underline or highlight the key vocabulary in bold script.

Tell students that they will now go back and review each of the key vocabulary words in the passage so that they can better understand what the text says. Start by focusing on one word, exchange. Project the vocabulary chart below or create your own on the board.

Word	Explanation	Sample Sentence	Visual Cue
exchange (verb)	to trade one thing for another	People exchange money for the things they want or need.	

FIGURE 3.32. Vocabulary chart: Exchange.
Visual reprinted with permission by National Geographic/Cengage Learning. Cruz, B.C. and Thornton, S.J. (2013). *Gateway to social studies*. Boston, MA: National Geographic/Cengage Learning, p. 17.

Point out the sound that the consonant blend *ch* makes in the word exchange and that in this passage it is a verb. Read aloud the explanation. Read aloud the sample sentence. Direct students' attention to the visual cue. Ask: What are the two people exchanging? (One person is giving money to another person who is giving a bag of fruit or vegetables.)

In pairs, have students create vocabulary charts for the other key vocabulary in the passage. Images can be found in magazines or on the Internet.

Graphic Organizers and Role Playing: "Half a Loaf is Better than None":[2] International Trade and Development (Levels 3 and 4)

Economic development is a hotly debated topic throughout the developing world. Historically, foreign investment has provided many of these countries with capital, technological skills, and training. In recent years, "outsourcing" has become a common term, often used by transnational corporations faced with an increasingly competitive world market and rising labor costs in their own nations. Many have sought to cut their labor costs by relocating their labor-intensive operations abroad. In this lesson, students will analyze some of the consequences that these transnational flows of labor and capital have had for workers in the Caribbean and recognize how production decisions in one country may be affected by economic conditions in other countries.

Start by directing students to think about the region known as the Caribbean. You might want to point out the region on a wall map or ask them to find it in a textbook map. Then, as a class, construct a brainstorming web on the board (Figure 3.33). Write "Caribbean" in the center, asking for terms or phrases that come to mind ("level 1" descriptors). As you write those words on the board around "Caribbean," connect the level 1 words with lines to "Caribbean." You can also have students generate additional terms ("level 2" words) that are elicited by the level 1 descriptors.

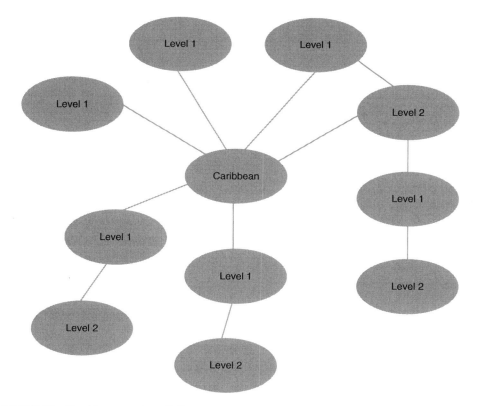

FIGURE 3.33. Caribbean web activity.

Teaching Tip

- Obtain Caribbean tourism posters from a travel agency and have students analyze how the region is portrayed.

Caribbean Web Activity

Another possible strategy for the webbing activity is to simply provide students with markers and have them come to the board and add their words to the web themselves. This approach encourages a more hands-on, collaborative exercise. After about five to ten minutes of the webbing activity, review the class's collective web on the Caribbean. Ask students if they think that the region might be a good one for a U.S. company to invest in and set up operations. What are some compelling reasons to do so? What would be some challenges?

Tell students that they are going to participate in an activity designed to simulate how some companies may do business in foreign countries. Stating both the social and academic goals of the activity at the outset is important before embarking on group work. Students need to clearly understand what is expected of them and non-ELLs need to be told explicitly how they are to work collaboratively with ELL students.

Teaching Tip

- Stating both the social and academic goals before embarking on group work is an important step in achieving educational objectives.

Before you begin the modified role playing exercise, you should review some or all of the following terms (they can also be posted on the classroom's word wall):

- development;
- developing nations;
- transnationalism;
- transnational and multinational corporations;
- capital investments;
- internationalization of labor/capital;
- Export Processing zone;
- Free Trade zone;
- outsourcing;
- offshoring;
- high-wage economy;
- low-wage economy.

Orient students to the role-playing activity by reading or paraphrasing the following (ELLs may need to have a print copy to follow along).

General Progress Corporation (GPC): Briefing

You are executive chiefs of a large transnational corporation heavily involved in the manufacturing and marketing of personal computers. Recent developments in the computer field have put tremendous pressure on your company to cut production costs to a bare minimum. Given this, you will be aggressively seeking to offshore, or relocate, much of your assembly process outside the United States, resulting in a major reduction of your labor costs. Your goal today is to set up an assembly plant in a developing country that has a large, low-wage labor pool. After extensive research, your company has decided that the Caribbean basin offers the best possible environment for your operation. Because of unemployment rates and large foreign debts, certain Caribbean countries are eager to increase foreign investment to help in their development plans. Your company views this situation as a win–win scenario: a great investment opportunity for you and a development opportunity for them. You have narrowed your country choices to three: Liberté, Barbudos, and Costa Fuerte.

General Progress Corporation

Project Activities 3.26 and 3.27 on the board or screen, reviewing the characteristics of each country and then the conditions that each offers GPC. You will need to paraphrase or explain certain terms as you present the information, pausing to answer any clarifying questions students might ask.

Teaching Tip

- Teachers not familiar with role playing as a teaching strategy should prepare by carefully reading through all materials first and even conducting a "dry run" of the exercise with colleagues or a select group of students.

After reviewing the two charts, generate a class debate and discussion by asking (and paraphrasing as needed):

- In which country should GPC set up its offshore assembly plant? Why? (Allow for one or two students to defend each country as a choice, explaining their rationale.)
- How might business leaders justify their interests in relation to the needs of developing countries?
- Why might some developing nations enter into a less-than-fair (to their citizens) business arrangement with a transnational company?
- Do for-profit businesses have an ethical or moral imperative to conduct business in an equitable (to their employees) manner?
- What are the challenges and opportunities involved in business transactions between transnational firms and developing countries?

ACTIVITY 3.26. Country characteristics

Liberté	Barbudos	Costa Fuerte
Poorest country in the region, with 80% living under the poverty line	Economically stable country with one of the highest standards of living in region	Economically stable, but dependent on other socialist countries
Mostly rural; two-thirds of the people are peasants who farm small plots of land	95% of the people are literate; mixture of urban and rural dwellers	99.7% literacy rate; mixture of urban and rural dwellers
60% of the children are malnourished and there is a high infant mortality rate	Infant mortality rate is comparable to that of the United States	Infant mortality rate is lowest in region and life expectancy is high
Widespread unemployment and underemployment	Unemployment is just under 10%	Unemployment rate is just 2%
History of harsh authoritarian governments	One of the oldest democracies in the Western Hemisphere	One of the few Marxist states in the region

ACTIVITY 3.27. Conditions offered

Liberté	Barbudos	Costa Fuerte
Export Processing Zone	Export Processing Zone	Export Processing Zone
Tax holiday: 20 years	Tax holiday: 8 years	Tax holiday: 8 years
Geographic proximity: 450 miles from Miami, the nearest shipping port	Geographic proximity: 350 miles from Miami, the nearest shipping port	Geographic proximity: 125 miles from Miami, the nearest shipping port
Large pool of unskilled labor	Pool of semiskilled workers	Small pool of workers
Acceptable monthly wage: $105	Acceptable monthly wage: $185	Acceptable monthly wage: $125
Political stability: dictatorship with good track record of maintaining order; threats to authority squelched	Political stability: parliamentary democracy with strong pro-labor and human rights record	Political stability: benevolent dictatorship; no viable threats to authority
No organized labor movement intervention	Long traditions of labor unions	No organized labor movement, but heavy government

Closure: Have students visit the website of the International Labour Organization (ILO) (www.ilo.org/global/lang--en/index.htm), a United Nations agency that brings together governments, employers, and workers to promote decent work conditions throughout the world. The ILO provides an online library, labor standards for workers and employers, and descriptive statistics of labor markets.

Extension Activity

Explore the role of ethics in a free market economy. Wight and Morton's (2007, National Council on Economic Education) *The Ethical Foundations of Economics* is an excellent resource to use as a springboard in this exploration.

Visual Aids, Realia, Total Physical Response, and Stratified Questioning Strategy: Goods and Services (Levels 1–4)

A basic understanding of what constitutes goods and services is important in a free market economy. In this lesson, students will be able to distinguish between needs and wants and between goods and services.

Start by orienting students to the terms goods, services, needs, and wants. For ELLs in the early stages of language development, be sure to have some realia or images to illustrate examples of each vocabulary word; alternatively, using total physical response to physically illustrate each vocabulary word can also be effective in aiding comprehension.

- consumption: spending by consumers on goods and services;
- goods: tangible objects—made, grown, hunted, mined, raised by people—that satisfy people's needs or wants;
- services: intangible activities or jobs that people perform that satisfy people's needs or wants;
- needs: things considered necessary by people;
- wants: things desired by people; people have unlimited wants.

Distribute a copy of the personal consumption log sheet (Activity 3.28) to each student in class. Tell them that they will need to keep a log of all the goods and services that they use from the time they get home today to the time they get to school tomorrow morning. Remind them to consider all items and services they come into contact with, even if they are not self-evident (e.g., electricity, water, appliances). They are to catalog each good or service under the appropriate column and check off whether they consider it to be a need or a want.

ACTIVITY 3.28. Personal consumption log sheet

GOODS Objects made, grown, or gathered by people	SERVICES Activities or jobs performed by people	NEEDS Things considered necessary by people	WANTS Things desired by people

ACTIVITY 3.29. Goods and services questioning strategy

Stage	Strategy
Preproduction	Point to some goods on your list. Find some services on your list. Which goods are "needs" on your list? Which services are "wants" on your list? Do you have more goods or more services on your list?
Early production	Do you think more people had needs or wants on their lists? Give some examples of goods you had on your list. Give some examples of services your partner had on his/her list. What are the top five most important goods and services on your list?
Speech emergence	Describe some of the services on your list. How might your list differ from someone living in the developing world? If you had to eliminate one good and one service from your list, which would they be?
Intermediate fluency	Why do people have unlimited wants? What are some items considered as needs by people that are probably wants? How typical do you think your personal consumption log is to that of the "average" American? Consider how your personal consumption log would have been different if you had lived 100 years ago.

The next day, have students share and compare their log sheets with a partner, adding items to their own list that they may have forgotten or overlooked. Then generate a discussion by following the questioning strategy in Activity 3.29.

Extension Activity

Contrast students' wants and needs in the "goods" category with images from *Material World: A Global Family Portrait* (www.pbs.org/wgbh/nova/worldbalance/material.html). See extension activity in this chapter's Personal Budgeting lesson, below.

Teaching Tip

- Add a realia component to this lesson by having students bring in one good (or representation of a service) logged on their personal consumption sheet.

Visual Aids and Cooperative Learning: The Economic Concept of Scarcity (Levels 2–4)

Students can easily grasp the economic concept of scarcity. The idea that resources are limited, but that humans' needs and wants are unlimited, can be illustrated with a number of examples and case studies to which students can relate, particularly in the case of economic goods. However, they sometimes have a more difficult time understanding why a particular resource or good is scarce.

In this lesson featuring webquests,[3] students will consider why gold is a precious, scarce commodity and the factors that contribute to its high price.

Create a PowerPoint presentation of (or otherwise project) images of gold in different forms—in antiquity, art, coinage, gold bars, contemporary jewelry, dentistry, computer technology, even edible gold in food. The World Gold Council (www.gold.org) provides several useable graphics. Engage the class in a discussion, using this question: "Why do people—throughout history—value gold so much?" Jot down students' responses on the board. Through probing and prompting, ask them to consider the qualities/characteristics underlying these reasons (e.g., it is scarce, easily exchanged, malleable, ductile, resistant to corrosion, a symbol of wealth/prestige, retains polish).

Tell students that they will be participating in a webquest in which they will explore the major issues surrounding the precious metal. Assign students to dyads, pairing ELL students with a partner who can assist them with language. Using the Gold Webquest Worksheet, have students visit websites, gather data, and answer the questions.

Gold Webquest Worksheet

1. www.bullion.org.za/welcome.htm (select "Mining Education")
    What percentage of the world's known gold reserves is in Russia?
    What percentage of the world's known gold reserves is in South Africa? What country is ranked second in production?
    What percentage of the world's gold does Peru produce?
    Why do some countries rank higher in gold reserves but lower in gold production?

2. www.responsiblegold.org/role_of_gold.asp
    Developing countries account for how much of the world's gold output? What benefits does gold mining bring to these countries?
    How much of jewelry manufacturing takes place in the developing world? How does gold play a role in the purchase of a home in Vietnam?
    How does gold play a role in the financial security of Muslim or Hindu women? How is gold used in industry and medicine?

3. www.u-s-history.com/pages/h753.html
    What does it mean when a nation is "on the gold standard"? When and why was the gold standard adopted?
    Which metal predated gold as the standard for the world's currency? Which country was the first to adopt the gold standard?
    Until when did the gold standard prevail in most industrialized countries?

4. http://geopubs.wr.usgs.gov/open-file/of00–144/of00–144.pdf
    What are five items in the house that contain gold?
    What are other metals that are commonplace in the house?

After allowing students to complete the webquest in pairs, regroup as a class and discuss their findings. Bring closure to the lesson by analyzing the pros and cons of gold mining and gold's role in society. Ask students to summarize the factors that contribute to gold's high price.

Selected Resources for Teaching about Gold

American Museum of Natural History: Gold (www.amnh.org/exhibitions/gold/incomparable/mining.php)

Ciddor, A. (1995). *The goldfields: Through children's eyes.* South Melbourne, VIC: Macmillan Education Australia.

Fetherling, G. (1997). *The gold crusades: A social history of gold rushes, 1849–1929.* Toronto, ON: University of Toronto Press.

Henderson, J. W. (2001). *Global production networks and the analysis of economic development.* Manchester, UK: Manchester Business School.

Cooperative Learning: Setting Priorities and Making Choices: A Lesson in Personal Budgeting (Levels 3 and 4)

Being a responsible consumer entails making choices and decisions based on limited resources. When making both short-term and long-term economic decisions, students must learn the importance of living within their means. In this lesson, students will have an opportunity to reflect on their priorities and how spending choices must be made within the context of a finite income.

Start by telling students that they will be creating a personal budget based on average income and expense figures in the United States. In preparation for the lesson, you will need to find the average U.S. income for someone without a high school diploma, a high school graduate, and a (four-year) college graduate. For example, Activity 3.30 gives the average figures for the year 2006.

ACTIVITY 3.30. Average income table

No high school diploma	$18,734
High school graduate	$27,915
College graduate (bachelor's)	$51,206

Source: www.firstbook.org/site/c.lwKYJ8NVJvF/b.2637397/k.C72F/Literacy_in_the_US.htm

Assign students to small groups to complete the assignment (groups of two or three would be ideal), each group randomly assigned to one of the three levels of educational attainment. Inform each group of their income; they are to write this figure in the "income" column of their personal budget worksheet (Activity 3.31). They are then to allocate a dollar amount for each of the budget items under "Fixed expenses." They should use a calculator to ensure that the amounts in both columns are reconciled.

After allowing sufficient time to complete the activity, ask for volunteers from each of the three levels of educational attainment to share their budgets with the rest of the class. (You should project their budgets with a document projector or create outline overhead transparencies of the personal budget worksheet so that students can fill them out and project them for all to see.) Generate a class discussion by encouraging students to consider:

- Which expenses did they feel were the most important?
- Which expenses received the smallest allocation?
- Which expenses could be eliminated altogether?
- What is the impact of one's educational attainment on quality of life?

ACTIVITY 3.31. Personal budget worksheet

Income (wages, after taxes)	Fixed expenses
	Shelter (rent or mortgage)
	Utilities (gas, electricity, etc.)
	Telephone
	Food (groceries, eating out)
	Health
	Insurance
	Medicine
	Transportation
	Car/public transportation
	Car insurance
	Car repair
	Gas
	Entertainment
	Cable TV, film rentals
	Computer
	Hobbies
	Vacations
	Clothing
	Work-related
	Non-work
	Miscellaneous
	Personal hygiene
	Gifts
	Charity

Teaching Tip

■ Have students research the average salaries in the United States for a variety of jobs, noting how much and what kind of education or training is needed for each.

Extension Activity

Menzel, P., Mann, C. C., and Kennedy, P. (1995). *Material world: A global family portrait.* San Francisco, CA: Sierra Club Books.

    Share with students this fascinating look at the material possessions of families throughout the world. Vivid photographs chronicle the contents of "average" families' homes moved outside in order to create visible representations of standards of living. Contrast the relative standards of living by having students compare families within countries as well as country-to-country. A PBS website also includes many of the images: www.pbs.org/wgbh/nova/worldbalance/material.html. The Social Studies School Service (www.socialstudies.com) also sells a teaching kit that includes a CD, curriculum guide, charts and posters, and reproducibles.

Graphic Organizers and Cooperative Learning: Consumer Credit and Debt (Levels 2–4)

Credit cards have become a fixture in daily U.S. life. They are so widespread that many students are surprised to learn that the system has been in place only since the 1950s, with Diner's Club, American Express, and Carte Blanche being the first general purpose credit cards. Since then, consumer debt has usually risen every year.

Credit cards are used as a substitute for money. Consumers are given a line of credit, against which they can borrow, to make purchases. In return for this concession, credit card companies charge businesses a small fee (which gets passed on to the consumer) and charge consumers interest based on the balance they carry on the card. In this lesson, students will explore the benefits and disadvantages of having credit cards and learn about the spiraling credit card debt that is forcing many individuals into bankruptcy. (Note that PBS has an excellent collection of lesson plans on this topic: www.pbs.org/opb/electricmoney/teaching_guide/eMoney_Lesson_two.pdf).

Start by asking students to consider the many uses and benefits of having credit cards, as well as the disadvantages that such a convenience potentially holds. Have them write those down in a two-column format that may look something like Activity 3.32.

ACTIVITY 3.32. Credit cards

Benefits	Disadvantages
Source of credit	Higher interest rate than other types of
Convenient	consumer loans
Can use for purchases by phone or Internet	Debt
Safer than cash	Late fees
Emergencies	Credit limits
Protection for certain types of transactions	Targeting young people (often in college, while
Points/rewards systems	they are accruing education loans)
Advantages for merchants	Hidden costs
	Identity theft/credit card fraud

Given that students might have limited directed experience with credit cards, they may need to be probed and prompted with specific cases and examples in order to generate a comprehensive list. You might consider conducting this activity as a think–pair–share so that students first have the opportunity to think independently, then share their lists with another student, and then finally discuss as a whole class.

Bring closure to the lesson by asking: According to the Federal Reserve, consumer debt hit a record $11.44 trillion in March 2012. Why do you think there has been such an increase in consumer debt?

Extension Activity

Bring in several credit card applications and have students examine the terms, conditions, and "fine print." Have them locate interest rates, late penalties, transaction fees, grace periods, etc.

Visual Aids and Stratified Questioning Strategy: Advertising (Levels 1–4)

Advertising is a multibillion dollar industry in the United States. In addition to advertisements on television, radio, and in magazines, people are bombarded by marketing through billboards, websites, email, on the sides of buses, and in schools. Additionally, covert forms of advertising (such as product placement in television shows and in movies) further pitch products to potential consumers. Many of these potential consumers are people under the age of 18 who constitute an important and growing sector of the purchasing public. In this activity, students will have an opportunity to analyze print advertisements and consider how advertisers attempt to influence consumers' purchases.

Prepare for this lesson by collecting popular magazines and tearing out advertisements, collecting enough for everyone in the class (this activity can be done individually or in pairs). Guide students' analyses by having them complete the advertisement analysis worksheet in Activity 3.33.

ACTIVITY 3.33. Advertisement analysis worksheet

What product is being sold?

What is the advertiser promising or claiming? What does the advertiser say the product will do?

To whom are they trying to sell?

Are there any testimonials in the commercials? Do you think the information in the commercial is true?

How could you find out if the advertiser's claims are true?

Why might advertisers not always tell the truth?

In which magazine do you think this advertisement appeared?

Would you buy the product based on this advertisement?

Alternative Strategy

Project an advertisement on a screen and analyze as a class, using Activity 3.34 as a guide.

Extension Activity

Have students design their own advertisement for this (or another) product. This activity can be particularly effective as an application-level exercise if you first discuss the main types of advertising used in the industry.

Selected Internet Sites for Teaching Economics

Cool Bank (www.coolbank.com)
Consumer Education for Teens (www.wa.gov/ago/youth)
Economic Education Web (http://ecedweb.unomaha.edu)

ACTIVITY 3.34. Advertising questioning strategy

Stage	Strategy
Preproduction	Point to the product being sold. Find the name of the product. Are there any people in the advertisement?
Early production	What product is being sold? To whom are they trying to sell? Are there any testimonials in the commercials? (Explain that a "testimonial" is a person speaking about a product s/he has used; often testimonials in ads are by famous people.) In which magazine do you think this advertisement appeared?
Speech emergence	What is the advertiser promising or claiming? What does the advertiser say the product will do? (If the ad includes a testimonial:) Why do you think that particular person was used in this advertisement? How could you find out if the advertiser's claims are true? (Determine whether anyone in the class has used the product.) If you have used this product, is everything in the advertisement true? In addition to magazines, where else do you see products advertised?
Intermediate fluency	Why might advertisers not always tell the truth? Can you think of any instances in history when advertisers have made claims that later were exposed as false or even detrimental to human health? What might be a more effective way to advertise this product? In addition to for-profit corporations, what other groups or organizations advertise?

Economic Literacy Project (http://woodrow.mpls.frb.fed.us/sylloge/econlit/more-resources.html)

Electric Money (PBS) (www.pbs.org/opb/electricmoney/teaching_guide/eMoney_Lesson_two.pdf)

Federal Reserve (www.federalreserveeducation.org)

Foundation for Teaching Economics (www.fte.org)

It All Adds Up (www.italladdsup.org)

Kids' Almanac: Business and Technology (www.yahooligans.com/content/ka/index.html)

Kids' Money (www.kidsmoney.org)

Mid-Continent Research for Education and Learning (www.mcrel.org/compendium/Subject Topics.asp?SubjectID=15)

The Mint (www.themint.org)

Money Instructor (www.moneyinstructor.com)

National Association of Economic Educators (http://ecedweb.unomaha.edu/naee/naeepamp.htm)

National Center for Research in Economic Education (www.cba.unl.edu/additional/econed/ncree.html)

National Council on Economic Education (www.ncee.net)

A Pedestrian's Guide to the Economy (www.amosweb.com)

Teenpreneurs Club (www.blackenterprise.com/S0/Pageopen.asp?Source=Articles/DEFAULT.htm)

Understanding USA (www.understandingusa.com)

U.S. Treasury Department (www.treas.gov)

Young Biz (www.youngbiz.com)

Youth Link (www.ssa.gov/kids/index.htm)

3.7
Anthropology, Sociology, and Psychology

Anthropology, sociology, and psychology are sometimes collectively referred to as the behavioral sciences. They often focus on the understanding of how social institutions influence humankind's lives and thinking, which is widely considered to be an important goal of the social studies. All three subjects generally play a subsidiary role to the social studies mainstays of geography, history, civics, and economics.

Nonetheless, the behavioral sciences are embedded in virtually all social studies courses. For example, authorities deem the sociological construct of material culture and the anthropological construct of culture essential to the teaching of world history (Levstik & Barton, 2001; Merryfield & Wilson, 2005). In addition to being embedded in history courses and the like, anthropology, sociology, or psychology is sometimes offered as a stand-alone course. Usually these are elective courses in high schools.

Sociology and anthropology have similar underpinnings in that they both encompass the study of human interactions, group processes, and cultural change and diffusion. Having knowledge and appreciation of other cultures and their values and priorities is a social studies imperative. As Egbert and Simich-Dudgeon (2001) have noted, "Social studies students need to have a high level of cultural knowledge" (p. 22). Psychology is centered more on the individual, focusing on humans' behavior as they interact with their environments. This content area is often particularly interesting to adolescents given their heightened sense of personal identity and individual development.

Although the time afforded the behavioral sciences is limited, they can still make distinctive and valuable contributions to social studies learning. For example, topics in anthropology and sociology can challenge adolescents' simplistic or conformist conceptions of cultural and social norms. Immersed in their sociocultural milieu, they seldom reflect upon these norms. In a related vein, adolescent preoccupation with identity formation and peer groups often draws them to psychological subject matter. Years ago, some curricula were even designed to bring together the developmental level of the students and the requirements of the subject (e.g., Hertzberg, 1966).

More broadly, there may be greater freedom to pursue student interests in courses built around behavioral sciences than in staples such as U.S. history, in which teachers often feel pressured to "fight the Civil War by Christmas."

The following learning activities showcase a number of topics and issues that are appropriate for study in sociology, anthropology, and psychology. To orient students and set the tone, you may want to start with the perspective consciousness exercise, Mental Cartography.

Cooperative Learning and Visual Aids: Mental Cartography[1] (Levels 1–4)

That everyone has a unique view of the world is an important concept to grasp in the study of culture and society. In Robert Hanvey's (1982) influential global education treatise, "An Attainable Global Perspective," he outlines five dimensions that help students develop such understanding. The first dimension, perspective consciousness, is defined as an awareness on the part of an individual that his or her view of the world is not universally shared and, further, that this viewpoint is shaped by influences that escape conscious detection. This recognition is significant in the examination of "deep and hidden layers of perspective that may be . . . important in orienting behavior" (Hanvey, 1982, p. 162).

In this exercise, students will have an opportunity to draw from memory a map of the Western Hemisphere, labeling as many natural and human-made features as possible. They will compare their "mental maps" with others' mental maps, noting similarities and differences in their renditions. After comparing their maps with "real" ones, they will then be able to make some observations about perspectives, viewpoints, and how personal experience can shape one's view of the world. This activity can certainly also be done in a geography class. The cooperative learning approach used will afford ELL students the opportunity to develop their expressive language skills with peers. The visual supports of maps will aid in comprehension of the content matter.

Start by removing or covering up any wall maps that you may have in your classroom. Provide each student with a blank piece of paper. Ask them to close their eyes and envision the Western Hemisphere (you may need to explain this term and briefly describe what the region encompasses; in the case of preproduction ELLs, it would be appropriate to briefly show them a map of the Western Hemisphere first and motion that they are to draw the region from memory). Direct them to see in their mind's eyes any natural physical features such as mountains, rivers, and oceans. Also have them consider any human-made structures they could identify such as specific countries, states, and cities, major highways, and certain destinations they may be familiar with such as the White House and Disneyworld.

Ask them to open their eyes, take out a pencil, and draw their mental map, taking care to label as many features as possible. Assure them that technical drawing skill is not important; what is important is that they have a rough outline of the region, including as many features as they are able to identify. Allow about 15 minutes for this part of the exercise.

Then ask students to share their maps with someone else in class, noting as many similarities and differences as possible. Allow five minutes for sharing. Have them repeat the sharing with another person and ask them to return to their seats.

Distribute a "real" map of the Western Hemisphere (or have them look in a textbook or project on a screen) and have them compare their mental map of the region with the "official" one. Stimulate class discussion by asking:

- How accurate do you think your maps are?
- How accurate do you think they should be?
- In your map and in your classmates' maps, which places seemed to be included most? Why?
- Which places and features seemed to be omitted from your mental maps? Why do you think?
- What observations and generalizations can you make?

Close the lesson by defining "perspective" and discussing how one's personal experiences can influence one's view of the world.

> **Teaching Tip**
>
> - Ask students to consider how their personal experiences—having lived in or visited a place, having friends from a particular locale—can influence their perception or knowledge of a location.

Visuals, Graphic Organizer, and Modified Assessment: Religions of the World (Levels 1 and 2)

Religion is an important aspect of culture that should be explored in the social studies. In sociology and anthropology, the function and purposes of religion, as well as its myriad practices, are an established part of the curriculum. In this activity, students will consider the world's most followed religions and learn how to read a pie chart.

Start by obtaining images that represent various religions (e.g., the star of David, a cross, a crucifix, Islam's star and crescent, and the yin/yang symbol). Display these to students and ask students what all these symbols, as a group, represent (religion). Have them examine each symbol individually and ask them to write down the name of the religion that corresponds to each image.

Explain that a pie chart shows a circle divided into parts; the size of the parts can then be compared. Pie charts are particularly useful for showing information in percentages. Point out that the larger the percentage, the larger the pie slice. Project (or distribute via photocopies) a pie chart of the world's religions (Figure 3.34).

Help students analyze the data by asking the following questions:

- Which religion has the most followers? (Christianity)
- Which religion has the second largest number of followers in the world? (Islam)
- What percentage of people in the world are followers of Hinduism? (13)
- What percentage of the world's population follows no religion? (15)
- Tell students that, although these are the world's largest religions, there are over 4,000 religions in the world.

Extension Activity

Have students select a religion they would like to know more about and allow them to conduct independent research. They could then create posters or collages using images to represent the religion (e.g., symbols, house of worship, special holidays).

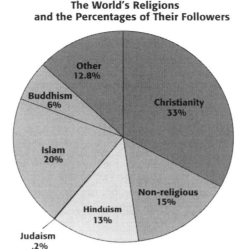

FIGURE 3.34. The world's religions and the percentages of their followers.

Text and visuals reprinted with permission by National Geographic/Cengage Learning. Cruz, B.C. and Thornton, S.J. (2013). *Gateway to social studies*. Boston, MA: National Geographic/Cengage Learning, p. 16.

Modified Assessment

ELLs do best on assessments that provide language scaffolding. A paper-and-pencil assessment on this topic can be made more accessible to ELLs by reproducing the pie chart and asking students to interpret it using similar questions to those posed in class. If multiple-choice questions are constructed, offering just three options (as opposed to the traditional four or five) can also make the assessment more manageable for students. Last, if a fill-in-the-blank section is included on the test, providing a word bank with possible answers can also reduce stress for students, allowing them to better show their understanding on the test.

Visual Aids, Realia, Object-Based Learning: Archaeological Artifacts (Levels 1 and 2)

Text adapted with permission from National Geographic/Cengage Learning.
Cruz, B.C. and Thornton, S.J. (2013). *Gateway to social studies*.
Boston, MA: National Geographic/Cengage Learning, pp. 50, 57.

Archaeologists and historians surmise much of early human history from artifacts that people left behind. The interpretation of art, tools, household objects, and cave drawings give glimpses into the way people lived in the past. This activity, while aimed at students at the early levels of linguistic proficiency, can easily be adapted for students able to express themselves more fluently in English.

Start by obtaining some visuals of early human artifacts from each of the following categories: tools, pottery, jewelry, and toys/games. Print these images and affix double-sided sticky tape on the back of each. Be sure to make an "answer key" of what each item is, what culture/society it came from, and approximately when it was created.

Instruct students to create a four-column chart in their notebooks, labeling each column with the four categories (model by creating a chart on the board for them to emulate). Make sure students understand what each category represents by having a modern-day item of each category in the form of realia, holding up an example of each category as you write the term at the top of each column.

Next, hold up one image at a time, allowing students to examine each picture. Then give the picture to a student and motion for him or her to place it in the appropriate column on the board. Ask students to indicate with a show of hands if they think the image was placed in the correct column. Reveal the correct answer, providing any pertinent information you deem important. Repeat with each image.

Explain that each of these items is an artifact. Have students write the definition of the term in their notebooks (a tool, ornament, or other object that was made by a human being). Tell students that much of what we know about ancient peoples is based on the artifacts they left behind.

Homework

Ask students to select five artifacts to help people in the future understand our society today. Have students write or draw their lists, picking one item to bring to school the next day. Have students share their lists and items, discussing how each item could give clues to a future archaeologist about life in today's society.

Extension Activity for Levels 3 and 4

Ask students to consider the possibility of erroneous interpretation of artifacts. How can archaeologists be sure that their interpretation of an item is correct if no accompanying written record was left? What are the possible problems that historians may encounter when they find an ancient object? Could future archaeologists make incorrect interpretations of one of the items they selected from their home? What are some alternate explanations for each of the items they selected?

Simplifying Complex Language: Cultural Anthropology: Seeing Through Others' Eyes (Levels 3 and 4)

Comparing how the ideas of one's culture might be viewed from other vantage points—or transpection—is a key skill for developing cross-cultural awareness (Hanvey, 1982). Far from being an easy skill to develop, students need multiple opportunities to look at the world through the eyes of others.

This lesson is primarily intended for students at levels 3 and 4 who, with additional time allowed, can read the essay "The Sacred Rac" (Ponzi, 1974) about a group of people with a fixation for something known as a "rac." Depending on the reading level of your students, you may also wish to read it together as a group, pausing to paraphrase or explain certain terms or vocabulary. You could also consider utilizing total physical response to act out the main concepts in the essay. As discussed in Part 2, total physical response integrates both verbal and physical communication so that students can "code break" language. In addition to being useful in vocabulary building, it is effective for students who are primarily kinesthetic learners.

In the essay, despite a multitude of problems generated by the rac, the people continue to venerate and protect the beast, even going into debt for its upkeep and maintenance. Conclude the reading with thought-provoking and discussion-generating questions:

- What is happening to the rac population?
- What implications do the rac have for people's health?
- In what ways are rac a detriment to Asu society?
- Why do the Asu want to possess so many rac?
- What do you think the Asu should do about the rac?

After discussing the students' perceptions and recommendations about the rac, ask students if U.S. society has any problem similar to the rac. After some discussion, point out that "Asu" and "rac" spelled backward are "USA" and "car."

Compare and contrast the two approaches—emic and etic—that can be used to study and describe a society's culture.

Emic

First introduced by linguistic anthropologist Kenneth Pike (1954), the emic perspective can be loosely understood as the insider's point of view. Emic knowledge is crucial for developing an empathetic understanding of a culture and cultural anthropologists employ it in their fieldwork.

Etic

The etic perspective, on the other hand, is often described as an outsider's account. Etic knowledge is needed for cross-cultural comparisons because such studies of contrast require standard categories and reference points.

Most cultural anthropologists agree that both emic and etic knowledge are valuable and necessary for understanding a culture.

Tell students that they will now have the opportunity to serve as anthropologists. In a style similar to "The Sacred Rac," they are to observe and write about a common American pastime, event, or location. Some ideas include a shopping mall, a football game, a school pep rally, a commencement ceremony, and a tanning salon. Instruct them to observe this location or event from the perspective of someone outside the culture. They should take notes during their observation (much the way anthropologists keep field notes) to aid them in their analysis and writing later.

Their concluding project will be an essay, written in the manner of "The Sacred Rac." You might consider having students exchange essays and try to guess what American pastime, event, or location is being described.

Teaching Tip

- If your students are at a more advanced reading level, Horace Miner's "Body Ritual of the Nacirema" (*American Anthropologist*, 58, June 1956) is another excellent, classic reading that embodies the concept of transpection.

Alternative Assessments: Sociology: Surveys and Opinion Polls (Levels 2–4)

Surveys and the accompanying statistical data are mainstays in sociology. Using interviews and questionnaires, sociologists gather information from randomly or specially selected people that are representative of a particular population. These data are then considered generalizable to a given populace. In this activity, students will analyze survey methodology and create their own surveys. If you wish, you can also afford students the opportunity to administer their surveys, gather and analyze the data, and report their findings.

Start by orienting students to surveys, what they measure, and how they are conducted. Two good sources of information are the Gallup organization (www.gallup.com) and the University of Michigan Library's Statistical Resources on the Web: Sociology (www.lib.umich.edu/govdocs/stsoc.html). You should also provide students with the findings of a few surveys, including charts and diagrams that graphically represent the survey findings. Since some students may not be familiar with surveys at all, you could conduct an informal survey of the class on a topical issue as a way to orient them to the purpose and construction of surveys. For example, you could conduct a simple survey about which radio station is listened to most by students in class; by just a show of hands or by collecting their responses on a slip of paper, you could tally them up and provide simple statistics.

Discuss the findings of a few surveys and have students analyze the structure and construction of the questionnaires (wording, number of questions, demographic data, etc.). Compare and contrast open-ended versus closed-ended questions and Likert scale responses. Ask students to consider the advantages of surveys and questionnaires and their limitations.

Teaching Tip

- Consider conducting an informal survey of the class on a topical issue to orient them to the purpose and construction of surveys.

Tell students that they will now have the opportunity to construct a survey of their own. For this activity, they can work individually or in pairs or small groups. Have students use the Steps in Survey Design (see below) to guide their project.

If students are afforded the opportunity to administer their surveys, you will need to further direct them as they analyze and categorize the data. In addition to reporting their findings in a traditional paper, you should also encourage them to create visual representations (charts, graphs, etc.) of their data collection. These graphic organizers could form the centerpieces of student-created posters that could then be shared with others in the class. Note: For ELLs in the early levels of language acquisition, you can allow them to administer the survey in their home language to other ELLs to ensure that they get the point of the lesson.

Steps in Survey Design

1. Select your topic
   Pick a topic that is of interest to you and about which you have formulated some hypotheses. Also consider selecting a topic about which most people have a strong opinion. Some possible topics: capital punishment, compulsory education, foreign policy, immigration, and politics.
2. Research your topic
   Conduct some background investigation on your topic by conducting Internet and library research.
3. Write the survey questions
   Decide whether you want open-ended or closed-ended questions. If you choose open-ended, avoid writing questions that are vague, wordy, or difficult to understand. Also avoid questions that are so broad that they will elicit too many types of answers that will later be difficult to categorize. If using closed-ended questions, consider using a Likert-type scale (e.g., strongly agree, agree, disagree, strongly disagree). Some ELLs may be unfamiliar with this strategy; they would, of course, need additional explanation of the terms and how a continuum works.
4. Directions to respondents
   If it is a written questionnaire, write a concise, clear explanation of how to complete and return it. If it will be an oral survey, write a brief introduction that the researcher will read at the beginning.
5. Background information
   Decide what background information is important to know about the people being surveyed. To consider: age, gender, political orientation, educational background.
6. Sampling
   Decide on the appropriate sample size for your study and what sampling technique would be best.
7. Piloting
   After you construct your survey, "pilot" (that is, test) it on one or two peers for trouble-shooting.

Teaching Tip

- Statistics in Schools is an educational program created by the U.S. Census Bureau that explores the value and use of statistics in everyday life. The website (http://www.census.gov/schools) has portals for both students and teachers.

Selected Resources for Teaching about Surveys

Basics of Developing Questionnaires (www.managementhelp.org/evaluatn/questnrs.htm)

Cool Surveys (www.coolsurveys.com)

Creating Good Interview and Survey Questions (Purdue University) (http://owl.english.purdue.edu/owl/resource/559/06)

Fink, A. and Kosecoff, J. (1998). *How to conduct surveys: A step-by-step guide.* Thousand Oaks, CA: Sage.

Phi Delta Kappa/Gallup Poll of the Public's Attitudes Toward the Public Schools (www.pdkintl. org/kappan/kpollpdf.htm)

Problems to be Aware of When Constructing Questions (www.sociology.ohio-state.edu/jbb/ IntroWi00/SocWi00surveyprobs.htm)

Survey Research (www.socialresearchmethods.net/kb/survey.php)

What is a Survey? (www.whatisasurvey.info)

Visual Aids, Graphic Organizer, and Effective Closure: Psychology: Identity Formation (Levels 1–4)

The formation of identity is a process that is especially interesting to most adolescents given their stage in life. This developmental process is understood as a person's understanding of him- or herself as a unique individual, separate from, yet connected to, others. Many psychologists have written about the various processes, issues, and events that can shape an individual's development and self-concept. In addition to the well-known works of Sigmund Freud, Erik Erikson, Lawrence Kohlberg, and Carol Gilligan, the topic of identity formation can be effectively discussed and illustrated using historical biographies.

In this lesson integrating art, students will study the life and work of the Mexican artist Frida Kahlo, paying special attention to notable life events and how those events shaped her self-identity and work. Students might have heard of Kahlo, given that there have been several plays and films produced about her life and work. The remarkable and bittersweet story of this great Mexican artist provides an excellent opportunity to examine how life events can have a dramatic impact on identity formation.

After constructing a biographical timeline of Kahlo's life, students will have an opportunity to reflect on their own lives and create an autobiographical timeline. The lesson capitalizes on two powerful strategies for ELLs in social studies classrooms: biographies, which bring historical figures to life, and art, which can graphically illustrate concepts to students learning a language. The timeline also provides a graphic representation of chronology.

In preparation for this lesson, you should consider reading one of the several excellent biographies that exist on the artist. You will need to create overhead transparencies or develop a PowerPoint presentation of Kahlo's artwork. Most of the images can be easily found on the Internet. We suggest the following pieces:

- *Self-Portrait in Velvet Dress* (1926);
- *My Dress Hangs There* (1932);
- *On the Border* (1932);
- *Self-Portrait with Cropped Hair* (1934);
- *Self-Portrait Dedicated to Leon Trotsky* (1937);
- *Las Dos Fridas* (1939);
- *Diego on My Mind* (1940);
- *Self-Portrait with Thorn Necklace* (1946);
- *The Wounded Deer* (1946);
- *Tree of Hope* (1946);
- *Death in My Thoughts* (1953).

You can also locate other images of Kahlo in childhood, in body casts, and at art shows that will illustrate the key points in the timeline.

You will then need to construct a timeline for the years covered and have students fill in events as they attend to your lecture/PowerPoint presentation. As a suggestion, we have included teachers' notes on the key points in Kahlo's life, which you may want to expand.

After students have completed the timeline activity, generate discussion by asking:

- What kinds of hardships did Frida Kahlo endure as a child and as an adult?
- How did she deal with these hardships?
- What role did art play in how she responded to adversity?
- As you review her biographical timeline, what are the key events that shaped her self-identity?

Closure: An exit ticket is a five-minute, end-of-class exercise that can be an efficient way to check for comprehension and gather feedback from students. It can provide an opportunity to determine students':

- understanding of key concepts;
- remaining questions;
- attitude towards the content or instructional methodology.

For this lesson, the exit ticket question is: What do you think of Frida Kahlo's work? Which piece did you like best—why?

Students' responses can be written on a scrap sheet of paper, an index card, or you can reproduce an exit ticket, as in Figure 3.35.

Give students time at the end of the lesson to complete their exit ticket and turn it in on the way out of class. Review students' tickets before the next class so that any concepts can be clarified, questions answered, or suggestions can be incorporated in the following day's lesson.

Extension Activity

Ask students to consider how their biographical timelines might look if they were to construct one. What key events would they identify on their timelines? Have students then create an autobiographical timeline of their own, starting with their birth year and identifying key events in subsequent years. As an alternative strategy, you can have students draw a self-portrait in the style and manner of Kahlo, noting and including people and things important to them.

We would be remiss if we didn't mention that both the self-portrait activity and the personal timelines are, necessarily, highly self-reflective. Students may disclose aspects of their personal histories that can be upsetting or emotional. Although this is a possibility, the exercises can also elicit awareness about the importance of finding healthy outlets for difficult or painful emotions and situations. Kahlo's life, in particular, can point out how art can be a therapeutic vehicle for individuals.

EXIT TICKET

What do you think of Frida Kahlo's work so far?

_____

_____

Which piece did you like best – why?

_____

_____

FIGURE 3.35. Exit ticket.

Teaching Tip

■ Select an artist from a culture or country represented by one of the ELLs in your class. Prepare a presentation based on the Frida Kahlo example in this lesson.

Frida Kahlo: Teachers' Notes

1907: Born in Mexico to Guillermo Kahlo, a German immigrant, and his Mexican wife, Matilda Calderón Kahlo.

1913: Frida contracts polio, which affects her right leg.

1922: Frida starts attending "La Prepa," a school for the best and smartest students; she plans on being a medical doctor.

1925: Frida is in a horrible bus accident that changes her life forever. Is bed-ridden for a year, during which time she begins to paint.

1926: Paints first self-portrait, _Self-Portrait in Velvet Dress_; today, she is known mostly for her self-portraits.

1928: As she starts painting more, she visits the famous Mexican painter, Diego Rivera, for his advice. He confirms that she has talent and encourages her to keep painting. They become friends and soon fall in love.

1929: Diego and Frida marry.

1932: Frida and Diego travel to Detroit, where Diego has a commission to paint a mural. But Frida does not enjoy her time in the United States, in large part because she suffers a horrible miscarriage while in Detroit.

1934: When they return from the United States, they move into the twin houses in San Angel with studios for each. When Frida discovers that Diego has been having a secret love affair with her sister, Cristina, she sinks into a depression and paints several disturbing paintings.

1937: Leon Trotsky arrives in Mexico and stays with Diego and Frida for a while. Frida has an affair with Trotsky and paints a self-portrait for him.

1939: When Diego finds out about the love affair, he is furious and asks for a divorce. Frida and Diego officially divorce in November. She completes her major work, *Las Dos Fridas.*

1940: Trotsky is assassinated. Diego travels to San Francisco, partly because he has been commissioned to do a mural, partly because he is avoiding the law. He calls for Frida and she joins him. While in San Francisco, they remarry.

Frida's 1925 accident continues to hurt her body and almost every year of her life she has to have an operation.

1950: Frida spends most of the year in the hospital because of spinal surgery and infections.

1953: A bittersweet year: Although she is honored in a premier art show in Mexico, Frida's leg has to be amputated.

1954: Frida dies in her sleep at the age of 47.

Selected Resources for Teaching about Frida Kahlo

The Artchive (www.artchive.com/artchive/ftptoc/kahlo_ext.html)

Cruz, B. C. (2001). Frida Kahlo: A personal view of Mexican culture. *Social Studies and the Young Learner*, 14 (2): 20–24.

Cruz, B. C. (1996). *Frida Kahlo: Portrait of a Mexican painter.* Springfield, NJ: Enslow.

Herrera, H. (1983). *Frida: A biography of Frida Kahlo.* New York: Harper & Row.

Herrera, H. (2002). *Frida Kahlo: The paintings.* New York: Harper Perennial.

Kahlo, F. (2005). *The diary of Frida Kahlo: An intimate self-portrait.* New York: Harry N. Abrams.

Las Mujeres: Frida Kahlo (www.lasmujeres.com/fridakahlo/life.shtml)

Lowe, S. M. (1991). *Frida Kahlo.* New York: Universe Publishing.

National Museum of Women in the Arts (www.nmwa.org/legacy/bios/bkahlo.htm)

Rivera, G. and Colle, M.-P. (1994). *Frida's fiestas.* New York: Clarkson Potter.

Resources for Teaching Sociology, Anthropology, and Psychology

American Anthropological Association (www.aaanet.org)

American Psychological Association (www.apa.org)

American Sociological Association (www.asanet.org/index.ww)

ArchNet (www.lib.uconn.edu/ArchNet)

ASA Teaching and Learning Resources (http://www.asanet.org/teaching/resources.cfm)

Association for Psychological Science (Teaching Resources) (http://psych.hanover.edu/aps/teaching.html)

The Gallup Organization (www.gallup.com)

Kinship and Social Organization (www.umanitoba.ca/faculties/arts/anthropology/kintitle.html)

Library of Congress American Folklife Center (http://lcweb.loc.gov/folklife)

Online Psychology Laboratory (www.opl.apa.org)

Smithsonian Institution Libraries, Anthropology on the Internet for K–12 (www.sil.si.edu/SIL Publications/Anthropology-K12)

Teachers of Psychology in Secondary Schools (TOPSS) (www.apa.org/ed/topsshomepage.html)

World Wise Schools (Peace Corps Global Education) (www.peacecorps.gov/wws/guides/looking/index.html)

3.8
Controversial Issues in the Social Studies Classroom

For many educators, the heart of a social studies classroom is the discussion of controversial issues, both historical and contemporary. Topics such as immigration, foreign policy, and ethnicity stimulate thought and dialogue and can bring relevance to the curriculum for students. ELL students will learn about vital issues in their new home and the world at large. They will also benefit from the hands-on, engaged strategies that are used to explore controversial issues such as cooperative learning, kinesthetic activities, and role playing. It is uncommon to find a course called "Controversial Issues" or its equivalent. But there is potential to address controversial issues in any social studies course. Take the topic of ethnicity. This could readily be addressed from a present-day perspective in a Sociology course. It could just as well be addressed in a U.S. History course. In a unit on WWII, for instance, students could examine the concept of gangs and attacks on Mexican Americans in Los Angeles (Ramirez, 2012). This historical treatment offers the added benefit of providing context for understanding related issues in today's society. All issues involve disputes between two or more parties. Issues of a controversial nature are loosely defined as "unresolved questions of public policy that spark significant disagreement" (Hess & Posselt, 2002). They are often complicated matters on which people usually hold strong beliefs based on differing backgrounds, experiences, and values (Oxfam, 2006). Issues such as population, the environment, immigration, and race and ethnicity are in the news on a daily basis, generating debate and often discord. As noted, current issues nearly always have parallels in the past. Levstik and Barton (2001) point out, "historical perspective helps students develop a broader view of current controversies" (p. 126). Whether the issue is in the past or the present, discussion of such issues of public concern is at the very core of a democracy.

Harwood and Hahn (1990) point out the importance of treating controversial issues in the social studies classroom, including:

- preparing students for their roles as citizens in a participatory democracy by having the classroom serve as a sort of experiential laboratory for democratic purposes;

- improving critical thinking skills by constructing hypotheses, evaluating evidence, and gaining insights by engaging in dialogue with others;
- developing interpersonal skills by listening, responding, and cooperating.

Perhaps the most compelling reason why social studies educators should encourage open dialogue is the likely effect it has on civic engagement (Hahn, 2001a). For example, Hahn (1996) has reported that positive correlations have been found between an open classroom climate and levels of political efficacy, interest, and participation. Students in such classrooms, it is argued (Rossi, 2006), are more likely to have confidence in public officials and less likely to be distrustful of government, although some question whether this is always a good thing.

However, many teachers shy away from the debates that frequently ensue when controversial issues are introduced to the social studies classroom. Curricular resources are sometimes poorly adapted to assist educators in facilitating the exploration and discussion of contentious issues. Feeling ill equipped to manage such a discussion, teachers may be afraid that arguments will disrupt the classroom. Other teachers do not believe they (or their students) are knowledgeable enough about the topics for debate to lead anywhere worthwhile. Still others fear that some students will dominate the discussion while others will "opt out."

Fortunately, there are a number of things teachers can do to have successful discussions in their classrooms (Parker, 2001; Hess, 2004). For instance, creating a "safe" learning environment where students feel free to discuss, disagree, and debate is critical for classroom treatment of controversy. An open classroom climate is a significant predictor of support for democratic values, participation in political discussion, and political engagement (Torney-Purta *et al.*, 2001).

As Rossi (1996) points out, the challenge for the teacher is to generate interest in a topic within a climate where civil discourse is prized. Having a classroom management plan in place and understood by students is an important first step. Students must understand the rules of debate and civil discourse. Additionally, a number of other guidelines have been offered (Harwood & Hahn, 1990):

- Teachers should prepare themselves and their students by studying an issue and identifying multiple resources and perspectives.
- Teachers need to maintain the focus and direction of discussions.
- Teachers should model respect when listening and responding to students.
- Students should be asked to present evidence to support their positions.
- Teachers should strive to ensure intellectual balance and encourage participation from all students.
- Teachers may or may not express personal opinions when appropriate, but they should not promote their position in the classroom.

Oxfam (2006) lists six roles a teacher can play when discussing controversial issues:

- Committed: teacher is free to express own views but care must be taken that this does not lead to a biased discussion.
- Objective or academic: teacher informs students of all possible perspectives without stating own viewpoint.
- Devil's advocate: teacher assumes an oppositional standpoint to challenge existing beliefs.
- Advocate: after presenting all possible perspectives, teacher states own position, encouraging students to formulate own opinions.

- Impartial chairperson: using either students' statements or published sources, teacher makes certain that all positions are presented but does not state own viewpoint.
- Declared interest: teacher starts by declaring own viewpoint, then presents all possible opinions as objectively as possible, allowing students to judge teacher's bias.

Rossi (2006) suggests three models for discussing controversial public issues in the classroom, varying in purpose, size of the group, preparation, role of the teacher, and role of the student. In all three models, the teacher functions as an observer, but retains a certain amount of control by having selected the controversy, providing background information, conducting the debriefing session after the debate, and assessing student performance. The three models are:

- Scored discussion: a peer-led conversation among a small group of students based on an open-ended question, without the intervention of the teacher during the discussion; the discussion is assessed by the teacher using a prescribed point system for academic skills as well as interpersonal behavior.
- Structured academic controversy: a peer-led discussion in a small group setting requiring students to reach consensus decisions on conflicts after examining different perspectives on the issue.
- Advocate decision making: a peer-led, decision-making, small group activity that maximizes individual participation, with all students having a role enabling each of them to take and defend a thoughtful position on a contemporary or historical public question.

Active learning approaches are also often used when investigating controversial issues. Role playing, mock trials, town hall formats, and the like can be very effective in helping students think through the issues, formulate a position, and explore alternative perspectives.

Finally, another strategy that can be used for the discussion of controversial issues is technology-based discussion. Instant messaging, text messaging, blogs, chat rooms, and the like can provide technology-savvy students a more comfortable and familiar forum for discussion. Merryfield (2000) found in a study of her university students that they were more apt to broach sensitive issues such as "racism, white privilege, and homophobia" in online discussions. For ELLs, the extra time afforded by an asynchronous format method can be beneficial: it can help them structure their thoughts, find appropriate vocabulary, and check their grammar.

Having students with different cultural backgrounds can prove to be both a challenge and a benefit in the social studies classroom. On the one hand, different cultural perspectives may lead ELLs to develop interpretations and arrive at results that are surprising to other students. On the other hand, these same results can serve as "teachable moments" rich with learning opportunities (Egbert & Simich-Dudgeon, 2001, p. 22).

The following teaching ideas will afford you with some opportunities for exploring controversial issues in standard social studies courses and will also demonstrate how ELLs can effectively participate in these explorations.

Cooperative Learning, Kinesthetic Activities, and Stratified Questioning Strategy: The Paper Chase (Levels 1–4)

One of the most important skills students can learn is how to navigate a newspaper. In this classic social studies activity, students engage in a scavenger hunt through a newspaper, learning about standard formats and locating customary features while simultaneously learning about news in their community, nation, and world.

Place students in cooperative learning groups of four or five. Give each group one marker, one complete newspaper, and a paper chase checklist sheet (see below). Explain to students that they are to work cooperatively to locate, in their newspapers, all the items listed on the sheet. As they find an item, they are to check it off their sheet.

After the activity, point out the features of the newspaper by using Activity 3.35 as a guide, modified for each level of language development in your classroom.

Teaching Tip

- Have ELLs in the early stages of language acquisition select an article that piques their interest. Then ask them to mark all the words they know in red and the ones they don't know in yellow. Have them look up unknown words in their dictionary.

The Paper Chase

This activity is a race designed to get you around and about the newspaper. The more quickly you get to know the newspaper and its contents, the better your chances of winning. Group organization and teamwork are key factors. Work in groups of four or five persons. Using a magic marker or other colored pen, find and circle each of the following items in the newspaper:

- the names of three government leaders from other countries;
- the name of the U.S. president;
- two crimes mentioned, pictured, or described;
- an article critical of some aspect of government;
- a consumer help column;
- an editorial;
- an article of world importance;
- a down stock;
- mention of a local problem or issue;
- an advertisement for tires;
- an ad for a secretary;
- an ad for a mechanic (any type);
- a comic strip;
- the horoscope;
- a political cartoon.

If your group is the first one finished, double-check your news items to be certain that you have found examples of all of the above; if so—*victory*!

ACTIVITY 3.35. Paper chase questioning strategy

Stage	Strategy
Preproduction	Point to section A. Point to the section of the newspaper that has mostly world news. Where is the sports section? Which section has mostly local news?
Early production	What type of news is usually found in section A? In section B? What is your favorite part of the newspaper? Which parts of the newspaper shows the opinions of the editors?
Speech emergence	Why do we use newspapers? For what purposes? On which page did you find the political cartoons? Why aren't they in the same section as the comic strips? Where are the horoscopes? Why are they located in that section of the newspaper?
Intermediate fluency	What do all newspapers have in common? Are there any special sections of the newspaper that appear only on certain days? Why is there typically no market report in Monday's newspaper?

Teaching Tip

- On www.english-trailers.com/index.php, you can find film trailers that can be viewed purely for enjoyment while students develop language skills. For example, you could ask students to watch three trailers and compare them, or watch a trailer and tell someone else about it. If you don't have time to work out your own lessons, some clever teachers in Japan have designed a site (English Trailers, www.english-trailers.com) where you can watch a trailer and complete a range of cloze and quiz activities they have designed to go with the movie clip.

Teaching Tip

- Adaptable for ELLs, FRONTLINE activities (www.pbs.org/frontlineworld/educators/index.html) are designed to take up no more than one or two class periods. Activities are tied to national standards and can be customized or adapted to your particular needs. Activities are offered in the following categories: culture, geography, economics, history, and politics.

Using Technology, Audio-Visual Materials, and Cooperative Learning: Controversial Issues at Home and Abroad (Levels 2–4)

Utilizing newspapers from around the world can be an effective way to expose students to alternative perspectives on a variety of issues. The World Wide Web has made this strategy feasible for most classrooms. In this exercise, students will investigate an issue by consulting newspapers from different countries. Using an inquiry chart research strategy, students are provided with a structured framework for examining critical issues. Students will also sharpen their research skills by consulting at least three news sources, noting the newspapers they used to cull their information. After consulting at least three sources, they will summarize their findings for each country. Then, after considering the U.S. government's position on the issue and contrasting it with the positions of at least two other countries, they will formulate their own stance on the issue.

Start by having students select an issue of interest (you may also consider assigning students the issues to ensure broad-based coverage of a variety of timely topics). Then, using the list of newspapers found on the following page, have students investigate the issue by completing the inquiry chart (Activity 3.36). You might consider ensuring that newspapers from the countries represented by the ELLs in your class are included in the activity.

ACTIVITY 3.36. Inquiry chart for controversial issues

Issue: _____
_____
_____

Country: United States   Country: _____

Source #1:

Source #2:

Source #3:

Summary:

What I think/believe: _____

Another downloadable example of an inquiry chart can be found at www.readingquest.org/pdf/ichart.pdf.

After completing their research, you can have students share their findings in dyads, small groups, or the whole group, or by posting their inquiry charts on a bulletin board.

Extension Activity

Guide students in listening and/or viewing news broadcasts on given issues. Students can transcribe the broadcasts, be provided with transcripts, or complete cloze passages to assure comprehension (Brinton & Gaskill, 1978).

> **Teaching Tip**
>
> ▪ Comparing political cartoons from various countries' newspapers can be a fascinating and enlightening way to develop higher-order analytical skills and cross-cultural awareness.

> **Teaching Tip**
>
> ▪ Have students compare different news media by investigating a story via the Internet, a newspaper, television, and the radio.

World and U.S. Newspapers on the Internet

Access World News (http://infoweb.newsbank.com)
　　U.S. newspapers as well as full-text content of key international sources; easy-to-search database with a world map.
Awesome Library (www.awesomelibrary.org/news.html)
　　Selection of U.S. and world news, organized by subject and country.
Christian Science Monitor (www.csmonitor.com)
　　Daily online newspaper that strives for a global perspective.
Nettizen (www.nettizen.com/newspaper)
　　Online newspaper directory, organized by region and featuring headlines from around the world.
News Directory.Com (www.ecola.com)
　　Links to English-language newspapers and magazines throughout the world—organized by region, continent, and country.
Newspaper-News (www.newspaper-news.com)
　　Current events information organized by country and region.
Online Newspapers.Com (www.onlinenewspapers.com/)
　　Links to thousands of newspapers throughout the world—in English as well as other languages.
U.S. Newspaper Links (www.usnpl.com)
　　Links to newspapers and TV stations throughout the United States.
USF Virtual Library (www.lib.usf.edu/virtual/newspapers)
　　Electronic newspapers and databases.

Political Cartoons, Values Clarification, and Role Playing: Immigration: Whom Should We Allow In? (Levels 1–4)

Controversy over immigration has been around since the time of the 13 English colonies. Immigration policy has been a topic of public debate from time to time throughout the history of the United States, including during the last decade.

This exercise allows students to consider whether some people are considered more valuable as citizens than others. Acting as a facilitator, the teacher must be prepared for spirited student discussion and some potentially prejudiced viewpoints. Despite these caveats, this exercise underscores legitimate difficulties of choice that confront us, especially when those choices concern our fellow human beings. Although this lesson can be modified for other levels, it is most appropriate for students at the intermediate fluency stage.

Start by distributing a copy of the historical cartoon "Looking Backward" by Joseph Keppler (it can be found on several Internet sites) or projecting it in another manner so that all students can view. This cartoon originally appeared in the political humor magazine *Puck* on January 11, 1893. In the cartoon, Keppler criticized the hypocrisy of wealthy businessmen who opposed immigration by depicting the shadows of their own immigrant origins. Guide the students through the analysis of the cartoon by using the following questioning strategy:

- How many figures do you see in the cartoon?
- How are the people dressed?
- Where is the scene taking place?
- Where has the man in the foreground come from?
- What are the men on the dock saying with their outstretched arms?
- Who are the shadowy figures behind the rich men?
- What is the cartoonist trying to say?
- When do you think this cartoon was drawn?
- What similarities can you draw between this cartoon and today?

Teaching Tip

- Before embarking on a class discussion of a controversial issue, be sure to have ground rules and classroom management procedures well established.

Strategy

1. Place students in groups of three or four. Explain that they are a panel of U.S. immigration officials who will be reviewing the backgrounds and credentials of 10 people trying to gain entry into the United States. Because immigration is restricted to certain quotas per year, only four of the applicants can be allowed in.
2. Distribute "Whom Should We Allow In?" (below) to each student, allowing ELL students to have access to their bilingual dictionaries. Direct students to read silently through the cases first and, individually, rank order them from most desirable (1) to least desirable (9). After everyone has ranked the applicants as individuals, each group is to discuss its rankings and which immigrant characteristics should be prioritized, and to decide which four applicants will be allowed entry into the United States. (Alternate strategy for preproduction ELLs: You may also want to first present the scenarios with visuals and gestures and then group students to make rankings.)
3. Ask each group to write their list of four (in rank order) on the board.
4. As a class, discuss the rankings and the discussions that led to their final decisions. Ask: "Whom did you pick first? Why?"

5. Bring closure to the lesson by leading a discussion using the following questions:
    - What is the most important thing to help you decide who can come to the United States?
    - Should everyone who comes to the United States to live know English first?
    - Should political immigrants be given priority over those who immigrate for economic reasons? (If necessary, explain that a political immigrant is someone who comes to live in the United States because his or her political beliefs are not the same as the government's political beliefs in his/her country. An economic immigrant comes to live in the United States to find better job prospects. You might also want to discuss refugees and asylum seekers.)
    - Would your rankings be different if you could place certain conditions on the applicants (e.g., ineligibility for public assistance, learning English, etc.)?
    - In what ways are the profiles of the immigrants stereotypical?
    - What might happen if the United States decided to stop all immigration into the country?
    - Do you think the United States will ever need to stop immigration entirely? Why or why not?

Whom Should We Allow In?[1]

Ricardo Flores
1. 34-year-old farmer from small town in Mexico where there is guerrilla violence.
2. Has a family (wife, mother, and four children) who will come with him.
3. Skilled agricultural worker who is willing to accept any work available; wife and mother also willing and able to work.
4. Can speak only Spanish.

Chandra Patel
1. 42-year-old physician from India.
2. He and his family (wife and three children) want a new start in the United States.
3. Dr. Patel is internationally well known as a cardiologist.
4. Will move to Atlanta where his uncle and two cousins live.

Michael Collins
1. 29-year-old computer programmer from Ireland.
2. Has a high level of education and experience in computer science.
3. Has no family or friends in the United States.
4. Is HIV-positive.

Francine Bouvier
1. 21-year-old fashion model from France.
2. Well known in the United States; has been on the cover of several magazines.
3. Wants to become an American citizen eventually.
4. Speaks little English but is starting a language course soon.

Lydia Martínez
1. 65-year-old retired school teacher from Cuba.
2. Is sick and cannot get necessary medicines and treatment in her native country.
3. Has two children in Miami who are willing to give her a home.
4. Speaks only Spanish.

Li Chang

1. 25-year-old factory worker from China.
2. He and his wife have one child but would like to have more (the "one-child policy" in China makes it difficult for them to have another child).
3. Would like to settle in San Francisco, where there is a large Asian community.

Sonya Petrov

1. 14-year-old gymnast from Russia.
2. She and her parents would like to move to the United States to increase Sonya's career prospects; they have hopes of her joining the American Olympic team.
3. All three are fluent in English.

François Pamphile

1. 50-year-old taxi driver from Haiti.
2. Single, no family.
3. Cannot make a living in Port-au-Prince because of his country's political and economic problems.
4. Speaks French, Creole, and some English.

Hans Koch

1. 34-year-old German with a criminal record.
2. Has been studying English for the past year.
3. Is willing to work at any job available, although he has training as a diesel mechanic.

Closure: Create a "Tweets of the Day" wall in your classroom by dedicating a bulletin board to this activity or covering a wall with butcher paper and providing students with markers (Figure 3.36). At the end of the lesson, allow five to ten minutes for students to come up to the wall and write a tweet (140 characters or less) expressing what they learned that day.

FIGURE 3.36. Tweets of the day.

Alex Sarsfield, Alonso High School, Tampa, Florida.

Teaching Tip

- A "Tweets of the Day" wall will work in just about every social studies course. It is a useful way to gauge student learning and can serve as a visual summary of the course content. And because tweets are by definition very short, ELLs may feel more comfortable writing them than a longer, more traditional written response.
(The idea for this activity was provided by Mr. Alex Sarsfield, Alonso High School, Tampa, Florida.)

Useful Internet Sites on Immigration

The American Immigration Home Page (www.bergen.org/AAST/Projects/Immigration/index.html)
    Various topics in immigration are examined, including why people immigrate, how immigrants have been treated during different time periods, illegal immigrants, and questions of assimilation.
The Ellis Island Immigration Museum (www.ellisisland.com)
    Information about visiting the site, special events, and related links. Online audio tours and movie clips are available.
The Ellis Island Foundation (www.ellisisland.org)
    Free passenger and genealogy searches. A history of the island as well as a timeline and photo albums are also included.
Immigration Past and Present: A Simulation Activity (www.rims.k12.ca.us/SCorE/activity/immigration)
    In this high school-level simulation developed by a school teacher, students play a number of roles (immigrants, lobbyists, members of a commission) while having to select from among four policy options. Included on the website are teaching notes, suggested discussion questions, and links to other websites and materials.
Immigration in American Memory (http://lcweb2.loc.gov/ammem/ndlpedu/features/immig/immig.html)
    Part of the Library of Congress's American Memory project, this website helps students understand immigration from various historical perspectives. It includes interviews, posters, sound recordings, and many historical photographs. Teacher-tested lessons, interactive vocabulary games, and recipes are additional classroom-ready resources offered.
Project Vote Smart Issues: Immigration (www.vote-smart.org/issues/IMMIGrATIon)
    Vote Smart is a citizenship education website dedicated to providing multiple viewpoints on a wide range of issues. The web page on immigration includes links to dozens of organizations, representing a broad political spectrum.

Simplified Text, Guided Note Taking, Visual Aids, and Cooperative Learning: Human Rights (Levels 2–4)

The study and discussion of human rights (the basic rights and freedoms all people have simply by virtue of being human) provide an opportunity for students to develop their thinking on this important global issue. Some students may be surprised to learn that not all people on the globe believe in these basic rights and that certainly many people don't enjoy them. This activity makes use of the work of the United Nations and allows students to clarify their own values pertaining to human rights. Because the concept of human rights is fairly abstract, this activity conveys meaning through illustrations and simplified text and students practice note taking and summarizing.

First, collect illustrations of basic human rights, such as:

- a person with his or her head bowed and hands clasped in prayer (right to worship);
- a person dropping a ballot into a ballot box (right to vote);
- students in a classroom (right to an education);
- children eating a meal (right to nourishment);
- a person being examined in a doctor's office (right to medical care).

An example of such a collage is Figure 3.37.

Project the images and ask students to identify the basic right in each illustration. Ask the class if they believe each of these rights should be guaranteed to all people everywhere and briefly discuss.

In dyads, lead students in a think–pair–share exercise.

Think: What rights should all people have? Make a list on your paper.

Pair: Share your list with a partner. Which rights did you both list? Did your partner list a right that you did not have on your list?

Share: Create an inclusive class list on the board, asking for volunteers to share ideas from their lists.

FIGURE 3.37. Collage of human rights.

Visuals reprinted with permission by National Geographic/Cengage Learning. Cruz, B.C. and Thornton, S.J. (2013). *Gateway to social studies*. Boston, MA: National Geographic/Cengage Learning, p. 123.

Transition to the United Nations Declaration of Human Rights

Obtain a copy of the "plain language version" (http://www.un.org/cyberschoolbus/human rights/resources/plain.asp), further simplifying and editing before photocopying, according to your students' linguistic needs. Create a two-column handout with the text on one side and space for students' notes on the other. As you read through the text together as a class, encourage students to make notes and write definitions and explanations of terms on the right-hand side. Ask students to decide whether all of these rights are worthy to pursue for all people in all countries. Are there any that are missing?

Extension Activity

Students at levels 3 and 4 can be asked to write a letter to an elected official about a right they feel is especially important. The United Nations site has a "Right to Write" page (http://www.un.org/cyberschoolbus/humanrights/resources/letter.asp) with helpful hints.

Teaching Tip

- The United Nations Cyber Schoolbus website (http://www.un.org/cyberschool bus/humanrights/resources.asp) offers definitions of commonly used terms, a fact sheet, and links to additional human rights resources.

Kinesthetic Learning and Critical Thinking: Taking a Stand[2] (Levels 2–4)

After students research and thoughtfully analyze an issue, they will invariably come to their own conclusions and develop their own positions. In this activity, students will consider a statement and "take a stand"—both literally and philosophically—on an issue.

For this exercise, you will need to create five large signs that have the following words written on them:

1. I completely agree.
2. I somewhat agree.
3. I am unsure.
4. I somewhat disagree.
5. I completely disagree.

Post these signs around the classroom in five distinct, separate areas. Once posted, paraphrase and explain to the students what each of the positions mean, using facial expressions and hand gestures to clarify meaning.

Tell the students that you will read a statement about a particular issue (to aid ELLs' comprehension, you should also write the statements on the board or have them projected for all to view; you could also allow ELLs to take them home the night before so they have additional time to translate, read, and comprehend the statements). Upon reflection, students should move to stand by the sign that best represents how they feel about the issue. After students move to their places, you may select two or more students to explain their positions; let students know that they may move to another sign if, after hearing a convincing argument, they change their mind on an issue.

Taking a Stand: Issue Statements

(Note: Feel free to pick and choose issues that are appropriate for your class. Also, you may need to restate or paraphrase certain statements so they are understood by all students in your class. Finally, you should consider creating some issue statements that reflect issues in your local community.)

Immigration
- Only people who speak English should be allowed entry into the United States.
- There are too many people in the United States already; immigration to the United States should be stopped immediately.

Environmental Resources
- If people can afford it, they should be allowed to use as many resources (water, petroleum, electricity, etc.) as they want.
- People should be given tax incentives if they conserve non-renewable resources.

Population
- The United States should put a limit on the number of children Americans have.
- People should be allowed to have as many children as they want.

Religion
- Religions that advocate hate against any particular group should be outlawed.
- All religions have a right to exist and be practiced.

Trade
- The United States should trade only with countries that purchase goods from the United States.
- Americans should buy only items that are manufactured in the United States.

Euthanasia
- People should be allowed to kill themselves if they are terminally ill.
- Doctors who help terminally ill patients to die should be imprisoned.

Cloning and Stem Cell Research
- All cloning research should be stopped immediately.
- The U.S. government should fund stem cell research.

Genetically Modified Crops
- We should take advantage of better crops obtained through genetic modification.
- Genetically modified crops should be banned until long-term studies on the effects on human health can be completed.

Gay Rights
- Sexual orientation should not be a consideration for a marriage license.
- Gay couples should be allowed to adopt children.

Animal Rights
- Animals should have the same rights as humans.
- Cosmetics tested on animals should be banned.

Race/Culture/Ethnicity
- Racial and ethnic groups should forget their differences and put being American first.
- People should stop "hyphenating" their identities (e.g., Mexican American, African American, etc.).

Cooperative Learning, Critical Thinking, and Research Skills: The Dead–Red Sea Canal (Levels 3 and 4)

Increasingly, the Middle East has become a region of interest and controversy in social studies classrooms. It also figures prominently in that more and more of our ELLs hail from Middle Eastern countries.

Located near the West Bank with Israel to the west and Jordan to the east, the Dead Sea is a hypersaline (almost nine times saltier than the ocean) lake, considered to be the lowest point on Earth. It has figured prominently in Middle Eastern history since at least biblical times. In recent years, the water level in the Dead Sea has been declining at alarming rates. Over the last 100 years, the water level has plunged 80 feet and in the last 20 years alone the sea has been reduced by a third (Watzman, 2007). This shrinkage is due chiefly to the siphoning of the Jordan River, the Dead Sea's principal tributary. Using dams, canals, and pumping stations, Israel, Jordan, and Syria divert 90–95 percent of the water for drinking and crop irrigation.

To address this problem, a 110-mile-long canal that would direct water from the Red Sea to the Dead Sea has been proposed. In addition to making fresh water available to drought-prone countries through desalinization, the Dead–Red Sea Canal would also create needed hydro-electricity because of the great differences in water levels, which would cause cascading water that would generate hydropower.

But not everyone supports the proposed canal. Some worry about unintended, negative ecological impacts such as increased seismic activity as well as creating an imbalance in the natural environment because of the chemical incompatibility of Red Sea and Dead Sea water. Some countries, such as Egypt, have expressed concern about providing Israel with water for its nuclear program.

In this jigsaw activity, students will have the opportunity to consider various viewpoints and analyses of the canal proposal and will brainstorm on possible solutions. The case study also is useful to prompt a discussion about global citizenship and interdependence and the various constituencies that must be taken into consideration in public and environmental policy.

Start by obtaining five or six articles on the subject. Some suggestions are:

Allbritton, C. (2007). Dead Sea on life support. *The Washington Times*, August 12, p. A01.
Friends of the Earth Middle East. Red–Dead conduit. www.foeme.org/projects.php?ind=51.
Israel Ministry of Foreign Affairs (2002). The Red Sea and the Mediterranean Dead Sea canals project. August 10. www.mfa.gov.il/MFA/MFAArchive/2000_2009/2002/8/The%20red%20Sea%20and%20the%20Mediterranean%20Dead%20Sea%20canals.

Kress, R. (2007). World Bank promotes Dead–Red Sea canal. *The Jer*

Mattar, S. (2006). Red Sea might save Dead Sea. *Live Science*, Decem̃
strangenews/061212_ap_shrinking_sea.html.

Milistein, M. (2006). Diverting Red Sea to save Dead Sea coɪ
National Geographic News, December 14. http://news.natior.
061214-dead-sea.html?source=rss.

Tal, D. (2007). Dead Sea falling. *Globes* (Tel Aviv, Israel), July 18. http://new.ₒ
globes/DocView.asp?did=1000233520&fid=980.

Ser, S. (2006). The Med–Dead/Red–Dead headache. *The Jerusalem Post*, July 13. www.jpos.
servlet/Satellite?c=JPArticle&cid=1150885986651&pagename=JPost%2FJPArticle%2FShow
Full.

Watzman, H. (2007). Israel's incredible shrinking sea. *New York Times*, July 29, p. WK 11 (or
International Herald Tribune, July 31, p. 6).

After reviewing the articles yourself, place students in heterogeneous groups, assigning one article to each group, taking ELL students' language ability levels into consideration (you can also provide ELL students with a copy of the article the day before so that they can review it at home prior to the in-class activity). All students should have dictionaries or thesauruses available to assist in comprehension. Each group is to read the article, summarize it, discuss the major tenets, and prepare a five-minute presentation for the rest of the class. You can guide this analysis by using the following questions (and having them written on the board for reference):

- Who wrote the article? What organization does s/he represent?
- What are the main points of the article?
- According to the article, what are the main benefits of the proposed canal?
- According to the article, what are the major disadvantages of the proposed canal?
- What is the author's position on the proposed canal?

After the group analyses have been completed, allow each group to present its findings to the rest of the class. Using all the information provided, have students debate the various issues in a whole-class discussion.

Extension or Alternate Activity (Brainstorming)

Lead the class in a guided brainstorming activity, by following these guidelines:

1. After they have been briefed on the issue and considered the different perspectives, ask students to (individually) generate a list of as many solutions as they can possibly think of. Encourage them to think creatively, without thought of cost, feasibility, or politics.
2. After about ten minutes of "the sky is the limit" brainstorming, ask students to look over their lists and select their top three ideas. They are then to share their ideas with a peer, soliciting feedback on the viability of each idea.
3. Have them review their top three ideas again and, based on their peer feedback, select their best idea.
4. Have students share their ideas with the rest of the class and compose a class list of possible solutions.

closure to the lesson by having students consider how the costs and benefits of any
al that affects the environment must be weighed by governments when exploring solutions
orld or regional problems.

Resources for Teaching about the Dead Sea Canal

Allbritton, C. (2007). Dead Sea, dying river: How politics and conflict are killing one of the world's cultural treasures. *The Star-Ledger* (Newark, NJ), July 29, p. 2.

Dead Sea Canal (www.american.edu/ted/deadsea.htm)

Dead Sea–Red Sea canal could cause quakes. Reuters News Service (July 25, 2005) www.planetark.com/dailynewsstory.cfm/newsid/31801/newsDate/27-Jul-2005/story.htm.

Memorandum of Understanding (Terms of Reference) for Red–Dead Project (www.ezekielproject.org/terms_of_reference.shtml)

Saving the Dead Sea by using the Red Sea (www.msnbc.msn.com/id/16152686)

Selected Resources for Teaching Controversial Issues

Choices Program (Brown University) (www.choices.edu)

Citized (www.citized.info/pdf/briefing/Student_Briefing_Controversial_Issues.html)

Controversial Public Policy Issues (www.learner.org/channel/workshops/civics/workshop7)

Headliners (www.headliners.org/homepage.htm)

Hess, D. (2001). Teaching students to discuss controversial public issues. Bloomington, IN: ERIC Clearinghouse for Social Studies/Social Science Education. Available online at www.vtaide.com/png/ErIC/Controversial-Public-Issues.htm.

Opposing Viewpoints (Gale) (www.gale.com/opposingViewpoints)

Oxfam's Cool Planet for Teachers (www.oxfam.org.uk/coolplanet/teachers/controversial_issues/index.htm)

Population Education (www.populationeducation.org)

Population Reference Bureau (www.prb.org)

Social Education, Volume 60, number 1, January 1996

StreetLaw.org: Tips for Teaching about Controversial Issues (www.streetlaw.org/controversy2.html)

Taking Sides (Dushkin) (www.dushkin.com/takingsides)

Teachable Moment: Teaching on Controversial Issues: Guidelines for Teachers (www.teachablemoment.org/high/teachingcontroversy.html)

Teachernet: Teaching about Controversial Issues (www.teachernet.gov.uk/wholeschool/behaviour/tacklingbullying/racistbullying/preventing/controversialissues)

Tolerance.org: Controversial Subjects in the Classroom (www.tolerance.org/teach/activities/activity.jsp?ar=761)

U.S. Census 2000 (www.census.gov/dmd/www/schmat1.html)

Resources

Internet Resources for Teachers

The following are general ELL teaching resources that can be found on the Internet. Annotations have been provided to assist you in your selections. The sites have been selected for accuracy, credibility, and durability. We have tried to give priority to sites whose sponsors have longstanding reputations for service to the public good (e.g., professional organizations, museums, government organizations, colleges, and universities). Nonetheless, keep in mind that, because the Internet is fluid, you will need to review content carefully. If a URL does not work, enter the resource's name or title into a search engine to find a current Web address. Remember, too, to check individual chapters (geography, government and civics, etc.) for content-specific websites.

Professional Organizations

American Association for Applied Linguistics (http://www.aaal.org)
American Council on the Teaching of Foreign Languages (www.actfl.org) Computer-Assisted
    Language Instruction Consortium (https://calico.org)
ESL etc. (http://www.esletc.com)
International Association of Teachers of English as a Foreign Language (http://www.iatefl.org)
Modern Language Association (www.mla.org)
National Association for Bilingual Education (NABE) (www.nabe.org)
National Council for the Social Studies (www.nss.org)
National Network on Early Language Learning (http://nnell.org)
Teachers of English to Speakers of Other Languages (TESOL) (www.tesol.org)

Professional Journals and Magazines

Heritage Language Journal (www.heritagelanguages.org)
Internet TESL Journal (http://iteslj.org)
International Journal of Bilingual Education and Bilingualism (http://www.tandfonline.com/toc/rbeb20/current)
Journal of Teaching English with Technology (http://www.tewtjournal.org)
Language Learning and Technology (http://llt.msu.edu)
Learning Languages Journal (http://www.nnell.org/publications/journal.html)
Multicultural Perspectives (http://nameorg.org/resources/publications)
Social Education (http://www.socialstudies.org/socialeducation)
TESL-EJ (http://www.tesl-ej.org/wordpress)

Research Centers and Institutes

Center for Applied Linguistics (www.cal.org)
  CAL's self-described mission is "improving communication through better understanding of language and culture." Links to research reports, resources, and training services are all provided.
Center for Research on Education, Diversity & Excellence (CREDE)
  Government-funded center designed to conduct research and disseminate knowledge to improve the education of marginalized students. Individual research projects are housed at various universities, for example Center for Applied Linguistics (www.cal.org/crede), Center for Multilingual Multicultural Research (www-rcf.usc.edu/~cmmr/crede.html), and UC Berkeley (http://crede.berkeley.edu).
Center for Research on the Educational Achievement and Teaching of English Language Learners (CREATE) (http://www.cal.org/create)
  This national center conducts research and publishes briefs on a number of topics related to ELLs, most of them downloadable from their website.
Dr. Cummins' ESL and Second Language Learning Web (http://iteachilearn.org/cummins/index.htm)
  Based on the work of Jim Cummins, makes available research and publications on second language learning and literacy development.
Education Alliance at Brown University (http://www.alliance.brown.edu/ae_ells.php)
  This center, dedicated to equity and excellence for all students, has English language learners and diverse students as two of its six areas of expertise.
Educational Policy Information Clearinghouse (www.eplc.org/clearinghouse_ell.html)
  Links to information resources, research, and reports are provided on this site. Users can also sign up for a free news service.
An ELT Notebook (http://eltnotebook.blogspot.com)
  This blog for English language teachers of all levels of experience serves as a forum to exchange ideas, opinions, and teaching strategies.
Joint National Committee for Languages & the National Council for Languages and International Studies (http://www.languagepolicy.org)
  This joint commission is based on the belief that all Americans must be given the opportunity to be proficient in English as well as at least one other language. This organization tracks hearings, appropriations, and legislation in Congress and other government bodies.

Let Everyone Participate (www.lep.gov)
> LEP.gov promotes fair language access to federal programs and serves as a clearinghouse, providing and linking to information, tools, and technical assistance regarding Limited English Proficiency and language services.

National Clearinghouse for English Language Acquisition and Language Instruction Education Programs (www.ncela.gwu.edu)
> Funded by the U.S. Department of Education, this clearinghouse collects, analyzes, and disseminates information about language instruction educational programs for English language learners.

National Institute on the Education of At-Risk Students (http://www2.ed.gov/offices/OERI/At-Risk/index.html)
> The At-Risk Institute supports a range of research and development activities designed to improve the education of students at risk of educational failure because of limited English proficiency, poverty, race, geographic location, or economic disadvantage.

Office of English Language Acquisition (OELA) (www.ed.gov/oela)
> The twofold mission of OELA is to ensure academic success for English language learners and immigrant students by attaining English proficiency and assist in building the nation's capacity in critical foreign languages.

Tapestry at the University of South Florida (http://tapestry.usf.edu)
> Series of free video lectures by experts in the field of teaching English to Speakers of Other Languages (ESOL). Topics include legal issues and ESOL, special education and ESOL, content instruction, and dialect diversity.

WISE: Working to Improve Schools and Education (http://www.ithaca.edu/wise/bilingual)
> This site features current reports, articles, and immigration information as they relate to language learning and bilingual education.

Classroom Teaching Resources

Culture Grams (www.culturegrams.com)
> Although this site requires a registration fee, many school libraries and districts opt to subscribe so that the entire faculty has access to these highly informative profiles purporting to provide "an insider's perspective on daily life and culture, including the history, customs, and lifestyles of the world's people."

Dave's ESL Café (www.eslcafe.com)
> This "Internet meeting place" can be accessed by teachers and students alike. The easily navigated site offers resources such as idioms, pronunciation help, a photo gallery, and an "idea cookbook" for teachers.

Differentiated Instruction (http://www.xmarks.com/site/www.frsd.k12.nj.us/rfmslibrarylab/di/differentiated_instruction.htm)
> Links, strategies, and tools for effectively reaching all students in a heterogeneous educational environment.

English Club: ESL Videos (http://www.englishclub.com/esl-videos)
> A collection of short (less than 15 minutes) films and video clips on a variety of topics, some with subtitles. Some of the shorts are accompanied by quizzes and classroom materials.

English Forum (www.englishforum.com/00/teachers)
> Links for ESL teachers, dictionaries and reference books, and online exercises and quizzes that can be used with students.

English Language Learning (www.isbe.state.il.us/bilingual/htmls/ellparents.htm)
  Created by the Illinois State Board of Education, this site provides resources (print and video) in several languages.
ESL Connect (www.eslconnect.com/links.html)
  This gateway site offers links to scores of other useful ESL sites. The sites are helpfully organized by topics such as ESL lessons, homework help, crosswords and puzzles, and English teaching ideas.
ESL Infusion (http://www.eslinfusion.oise.utoronto.ca/Home/index.html)
  Offering a practical guide for content teachers on how to infuse the curriculum to meet the needs of ELLs; visitors can also access resources, post questions, share teaching ideas, test their knowledge, and more.
ESL-Kids (www.esl-kids.com)
  Free printable flashcards, worksheets, and games that can be used with ELL students.
ESL Kidstuff (www.eslkidstuff.com)
  Although geared for elementary students, this site nonetheless provides some useful materials such as flashcard images, games, and printables.
ESL Lesson Plans and Resources (www.csun.edu/~hcedu013/eslplans.html)
  Links to dozens of lesson plans, resources, and other learning activities.
ESL Lounge (www.esl-lounge.com)
  Teachers can download free lesson plans, learning activities, and worksheets for ESL classroom teaching. Other resources include board games, flashcards, and song lyrics ready for use.
ESL Printables (www.eslprintables.com)
  This website offers teachers an opportunity to exchange resources such as worksheets, lesson plans, and learning activities. For each contribution you send, you can download ten printables free of charge.
ESL Teacher Resources (Purdue University) (www.owl.english.purdue.edu/owl/resource/586/01)
  Links to professional resources, both theoretical and practical. The list includes links to organizations and journals of interest to language teachers and language policy developers, as well as online teaching and reference materials.
Gateway to 21st Century Skills (www.thegateway.org)
  Free and easy access to thousands of lesson plans and other teaching resources.
its-teachers (www.its-teachers.com)
  Quarterly online magazine for English language teachers. In addition to articles and research, you will also find practical classroom applications.
Kathy Schrock's Guide to Everything (www.schrockguide.net)
  Links to a wealth of resources for foreign language instruction and ESL education.
Lanternfish (http://bogglesworldesl.com)
  Printable teaching resources such as worksheets and flashcards are provided, along with real-world language applications.
Learn English through Song (www.letslets.com/teach_english.htm)
  Designed as a supportive resource for ELLs, this website teaches English grammar, vocabulary, and pronunciation using specially written English language songs.
Letters from Home: An Exhibit-Building Project for the Advanced ESL Classroom (www.postal museum.si.edu/educators/4b_curriculum.html)
  Intended for grades 8 and above, these enrichment materials help build language and communication skills. The dynamic power of personal letters is highlighted in this collection while students develop English proficiency.

Linguistic Funland: Resources for Teachers and Students of English (www.tesol.net/tesl.html)
    Materials, activities, and links are provided in addition to "fun sites" that can be utilized by
    teachers in the classroom.
Mark's ESL World (www.marksesl.com/?source=sft)
    A "gateway" site featuring links for teachers, students, and the international ESL community.
Pearson ELT (English Language Teaching) (http://www.pearsonelt.com)
    This site provides teachers' resources, sample exams, and helpful teaching tips as well as a
    community forum.
Purdue Owl: ESL Teacher Resources (https://owl.english.purdue.edu/owl/resource/586/1)
    Collection of links that lead to both theoretical and practical professional resources.
Reading Quest: Making Sense in Social Studies (www.readingquest.org/strat)
    Useful collection of strategies and resources for helping students develop reading compre-
    hension skills in the social studies. In addition to detailed instructions for each strategy,
    handouts, charts, and blackline masters are also included for many of the strategies.
Resources for English as a Second Language (www.usingenglish.com)
    The ESL Teacher Resources section provides handouts and printable materials, professional
    articles, lesson plans, and links to other sites. Tests and quizzes are also available on the site, as
    is a discussion forum for other ESOL educators.
Selected Links for ESL Teachers (http://iteslj.org/ESL3a.html)
    In addition to lesson plan and assessment ideas, this site includes language-appropriate readings
    for students, articles and research papers, and games and activities for language learning.
Tapping into Multiple Intelligences (www.thirteen.org/edonline/concept2class/mi/index.html)
    This online workshop allows visitors to explore how multiple intelligences can be used to
    accommodate ELLs.
Teaching Diverse Learners (TDL) (www.lab.brown.edu/tdl/index.shtml)
    TDL is dedicated to enhancing the capacity of teachers to work effectively and equitably with
    all students. It includes information about teaching and learning strategies; assessment; policy;
    strategies for working with families; and organizations.
Teachnology (http://teachers.teach-nology.com/web_tools)
    Games, glossaries, and printable page-making tools are some of the resources available to
    teachers on this site.

Culturally Responsive Teaching/Pedagogy

Almanza de Schonewise, E. and Klingner, J.K. (2012). Linguistic and cultural issues in developing
    disciplinary literacy for adolescent English language learners. *Topics in Language Disorders*, 32
    (1): 51–68.
    The authors argue for a culturally sensitive, research-based practice when working with ELLs
    that includes: understanding of the second language process, issues related to culture, attention
    to assessment, pedagogy that takes into consideration both language development and content
    area learning.
Banks, J. and Banks, C. (2010). *Multicultural education: Perspectives and issues.* Hoboken, NJ: John
    Wiley.
    Written by two leading scholars in the field, this book explores theories, research, and best
    practice.
Chartock, R.K. (2010). *Strategies and lessons for culturally responsive teaching: A primer for K-12
    teachers.* New York: Pearson.

Includes general suggestions for becoming a culturally responsive teacher, for building classroom community, and for reducing prejudice. Of particular note is the chapter on addressing the needs of ELLs.

Critical Multicultural Pavilion. (http://www.edchange.org/multicultural)

Teacher resources, curriculum, printables, and links to professional articles on critical multicultural education.

Culturally Responsive Instruction in the ELL Classroom. (http://www.colorincolorado.org/educators/reachingout/culture)

Tips, resources, and links for culturally sensitive teaching and ELLs.

Education Alliance at Brown University. (2005). *Leading with diversity: Cultural competencies for teacher preparation and professional development.* Available from: http://www.alliance.brown.edu/pubs/leading_diversity/index.php.

This resource outlines cultural competencies that all teachers should master in the areas of culture, language, and race and ethnicity.

Gay, G. (2000). *Culturally responsive teaching: Theory, research, and practice.* New York: Teachers College Press.

Using real-world classroom vignettes and examples from successful programs, this book examines how to better address the needs of today's diverse student population.

Haynes, J. (2011). *Culturally responsive teaching and English language learners.* Retrieved from http://www.everythingesl.net/inservices/culturally_responsive_teaching_06718.php.

Haynes applies Geneva Gay's work on culturally responsive teaching to effective practices for English language learners.

Irvine, J. and Armento, B. (2001). *Culturally responsive teaching: Lesson planning for elementary and middle grades.* New York: McGraw Hill.

In addition to general principles of effective lesson planning, this book includes examples of content-specific lessons for use in diverse classrooms.

Irvine, J. J., Armento, B. J., Causey, V. E., and Cohen, J. (2000). *Culturally responsive teaching: Lesson planning for elementary and middle grades.* New York: McGraw-Hill.

Although primarily intended for elementary and middle school, this book can be very useful in helping teachers plan content-specific lessons for today's diverse classrooms and learn to create and use such lessons in their classrooms.

Lindsey, R. B., Roberts, L. M., and Campbell Jones, F. (2005). *The culturally proficient school: An implementation guide for school leaders.* Thousand Oaks, CA: Corwin Press.

The reflective exercises included in this book are particularly helpful for teachers and administrators wanting to effect positive change in their schools.

Morgan, H. (2012). *Improving schooling for cultural minorities: The right teaching styles can make a big difference.* Retrieved from http://www.eric.ed.gov.

Exploration of how cultural communication patterns cans lead to home–school conflicts and result in low academic achievement. Guidelines that ameliorate the problems are offered.

Nieto, S. (2009). *The light in their eyes: Creating multicultural learning communities.* New York: Teachers College Press.

This important book in the field examines theories, policies, and practices dealing with culturally responsive pedagogy, placing the classroom teacher at the center of the movement.

Pang, V. O. (2010). *Multicultural education: A caring-centered, reflective approach.* San Diego, CA: Montezuma Publishing.

A practical approach for what a teacher needs to know to create a positive classroom environment that meets the academic needs of all learners.

Pang, V.O., Stein, R., Gomez, M., Matas, A., and Shimogori, Y. (2011). Cultural competencies: Essential elements of caring-centered multicultural education. *Action in Teacher Education*, 33 (5–6): 560–574.

This article explores caring-centered multicultural education and enumerates those competencies essential for K–12 educators, including reflecting on cultural biases and misconceptions, implementation of ELL strategies, teaching content-area knowledge and skills, and developing critical thinking.

Principles for Culturally Responsive Teaching (http://www.alliance.brown.edu/tdl/tl-strategies/crt-principles.shtml)

A definition and discussion of what is entailed in culturally responsive pedagogy.

Robins, K. N., Lindsey, R. B., Lindsey, D. B., and Terrell, R. D. (2006). *Culturally proficient instruction: A guide for people who teach* (2nd edn). Thousand Oaks, CA: Corwin.

This book includes case studies, reflective exercises, and classroom activities for a number of different teaching environments and student populations.

Shade, B. J., Kelly, C.A., and Oberg, M. (1997). *Creating culturally responsive classrooms.* Washington, DC: American Psychological Association.

Published by the APA, the authors draw on cognitive and educational research to explore culture and styles of learning.

Teaching Diverse Learners (http://www.alliance.brown.edu/tdl/tl-strategies/crt-research.shtml)

Links to current research related to culture, learning style, and effective instruction.

Teaching Tolerance: An Introduction to Culturally Relevant Pedagogy (http://www.tolerance.org/blog/introduction-culturally-relevant-pedagogy?newsletter=TT062210)

This short video features experts in the field discussing how to enact culturally relevant pedagogy in the classroom.

Clip Art and Images

In addition to all the large search engines (AltaVista, Google, Yahoo, etc.), the following are useful sites to access royalty-free clip art and line drawings for educational use.

#1 Clip Art (http://www.1clipart.com)

ABC Teach Clip Art (http://www.abcteach.com/directory/clip_art)

Classroom Clip Art (http://classroomclipart.com)

Clip Art History (http://www.clipart-history.com)

Clip Art Links for Teachers (http://sciencespot.net/Pages/refdeskclips.html)

Cool Clips (http://www.coolclips.com)

Discovery Education: Free Teacher Resources (http://www.discoveryeducation.com/teachers/index.cfm?campaign=flyout_teachers)

DK Clip Art (http://www.clipart.dk.co.uk)

Flickr Photo (http://www.flickr.com/explore)

Free Educational Clip Art (http://www.teacherfiles.com/clip_art.htm)

Kid's Image Search Tools (www.kidsclick.org)

Microsoft Office Online Clipart (http://office.microsoft.com/en-gb/images)

My Florida Digital Warehouse (http://myfdw.com)

NCRTEC: Using Pictures in Lessons (www.ncrtec.org/tl/camp/lessons.htm)

Open Clip Art Library (http://openclipart.org)

Pics4Learning (http://www.pics4learning.com)

A Picture Paints: Clip Art for Language Teachers (http://www.miscositas.com/APicturePaints.pdf)

Royalty-Free Clip Art Collection for Foreign/Second Language Instruction (http://tell.fll.purdue.edu/JapanProj/FLClipart)

UVic's Language Teaching Clipart Library (http://hcmc.uvic.ca/clipart)

Virtual Picture Album (http://www.carla.umn.edu/LCTL/VPA)

Print and Associated Resources for Teachers

There is a wealth of resources available to teachers offering practical research findings and advice on teaching ELL students. This section provides an annotated list of reader-friendly research articles and texts for teachers who would like to read more on specific subjects/topics. Also provided is a list of instructional materials that teachers can use in classrooms to help accommodate ELLs.

Best Practice in ELL Instruction

Association for Supervision and Curriculum Development (no date). *Differentiated instruction resources*. Retrieved from www.ascd.org/portal/site/ascd/menuitem.3adeebc6736780dddeb3ff db62108a0c.

Barr, S., Eslami, Z.R., and Joshi, R.M. (2012). Core strategies to support English language learners. *The Educational Forum*, 76 (1): 105–117.

Best Evidence Encyclopedia. http://www.bestevidence.org/teachers.htm.

Calderón, M., Slavin, R., and Sánchez, M. (2011). Effective instruction for English learners. *The Future of Children*, 21 (1): 103–127.

Chamot, A. U. and O'Malley, J. M. (1987). The Cognitive Academic Learning Approach: A bridge to the mainstream. *TESOL Quarterly*, 21 (2): 227–249.

Echevarria, J. and Goldenberg, C. (1999). *Teaching secondary language minority students*. Center for Research on Education, Diversity & Excellence. Retrieved from www.cal.org/crede/pubs/ResBrief4.htm.

Faltis, C. J. and Wolfe, P. M. (Eds.) (1999). *So much to say: Adolescents, bilingualism, and ESL in the secondary school*. New York: Teachers College, Columbia University.

Fern, V., Anstrom, K., and Silcox, B. (no date). Active learning and the limited English proficient student. *Directions in Language and Education*, 1 (2). Retrieved from www.ncela.gwu.edu/pubs/directions/02.htm.

Genesee, F., Lindholm-Leary, K., Saunders, W., and Christian, D. (Eds.) (2006). *Educating English language learners: A synthesis of research evidence*. New York: Cambridge University Press.

Hansen-Thomas, H. (2008) Sheltered instruction: Best practices for ELLs in the mainstream. *Kappa Delta Pi Record*, 165–169. Available from: http://www.dentonisd.org/51238713151612/lib/51238713151612/Kappad_Delta_Pi_Record_Article_on_SIOP.pdf.

Lewis-Moreno, B. (2007). Shared responsibility: Achieving success with English language learners. *Phi Delta Kappan*, 88 (10): 772–775.

Linquanti, R. (1999). *Fostering academic success for English language learners: What do we know?* Retrieved from www.wested.org/policy/pubs/fostering/index.htm#sect5.

Lucas, T. (1993). What have we learned from research on successful secondary programs for LEP students? A synthesis of findings from three studies. *Focus on middle and high school issues:*

Proceedings of the Third National Research Symposium on Limited English Proficient Student Issues. Washington, DC: U.S. Department of Education.

Mihai, F. M. (2010). *Assessing English language learners in the content areas.* Ann Arbor, MI: University of Michigan Press.

Olmedo, I. M. (1993). Junior historians: Doing oral history with ESL and bilingual students. *TESOL Journal,* 2 (4): 7–10. Available at www.ncela.gwu.edu/pubs/tesol/tesoljournal/juniorhi.htm.

Olmedo, I. M. (1996). Creating contexts for studying history with students learning English. *The Social Studies,* 87 (1): 39–43.

Patchen, T. (2005). Prioritizing participation: Five things that every teacher needs to know to prepare recent immigrant adolescents for classroom participation. *Multicultural Education,* 12 (4): 43–47.

Rance-Roney, J. (2009). Best practices for adolescent ELLs. *Educational Leadership,* 66 (7): 32–37.

Short, D. (1993). *Integrating language and culture in middle school American history classes.* Santa Cruz, CA: National Center for Research on Cultural Diversity and Second Language Learning.

Short, D., Echevarria, J., and Richards-Tutor, C. (2011). Research on academic literacy development in sheltered instruction classrooms. *Language Teaching Research,* 15 (3): 363–380.

Tambini, R. F. (1999). Aligning learning activities and assessment strategies in the ESL classroom. *Internet TESL Journal,* 5 (9). Retrieved from http://iteslj.org/Articles/Tambini-Aligning.html.

Tedick, D.J. and Cammarata, L. (2012). Content and language integration in K–12 contexts: Student outcomes, teacher practices, and stakeholder perspectives. *Foreign Language Annals* 45 (1). Retrieved from http://onlinelibrary.wiley.com/doi/10.1111/j.1944-9720.2012.01178.x/abstract.

TESOL (1997). *ESL standards for preK–12 students.* Alexandria, VA: TESOL.

Thomas, W. P. and Collier, V. P. (2002). *A national study of school effectiveness for language minority students' long-term academic achievement.* Berkeley, CA: Center for Research on Education, Diversity & Excellence.

Truscott, D. M. and Watts-Taffe, S. (1998). Literacy instruction for second-language learners: A study of best practices. *National Reading Conference Yearbook,* 47: 242–252.

Walqui, A. (2000). *Strategies for success: Engaging immigrant students in secondary schools.* Retrieved from www.cal.org/resources/digest/0003strategies.html.

Cultural and Newcomer Information

Axtell, R. E. (1997). *Gestures: The do's and taboos of body language around the world.* New York: John Wiley.

Informational guide about gestures and signals, organized by country.

Boyson, B. A. and Short, D. J. (2003). *Secondary school newcomer programs in the United States* (Research Report 12). Santa Cruz, CA/Washington, DC: Center for Research on Education Diversity & Excellence.

Presents the findings of a four-year research study that sought to identify and document programs that helped immigrant students make the transition into U.S. schools.

Center for Applied Linguistics (2006). *Refugee families & refugee youth.* Washington, DC: CAL.

Two videos—*A New Day* and *Be Who You Are*—help refugee families and refugee youth adjust to their new lives in the United States. Family adjustment, school life, and learning English are some of the topics covered. http://www.cal.org/resources/pubs/refugee-families-and-refugee-youth-videos-and-companion-facilitator%27s-guide.html.

CultureGrams (2006). New York: Ferguson Publishing Company. http://www.culturegrams.com/.
Concise cultural reports covering 25 categories, including history, religion, family, and economy.

Dresser, N. (1996). *Multicultural manners: New rules of etiquette for a changing society.* New York:
John Wiley.
An overview of the correct behavior to use in a wide range of cross-cultural situations.

Flaitz, J. (2006). *Understanding your refugee and immigrant students: An educational, cultural, and
linguistic guide.* Ann Arbor, MI: University of Michigan Press.
The focus of this book is focused on the 18 countries that contribute a majority of refugees and
immigrants to the United States and includes interviews with students, information about
specific schooling traditions, and country profiles. Also provided is information about
teacher–student relationships, discipline and class management, and appropriate non-verbal
communication, taking into account refugee and immigrant students' cultural and educational
backgrounds.

Franquiz, M.E. and Salinas, C.S. (2011). Newcomers developing English literacy through historical
thinking and digitized primary sources. *Journal of Second Language Writing,* 20 (3): 196–210.
Using three historical lessons as exemplars, the authors argue that the integration of historical
thinking and primary sources enhances both the acquisition of English and social studies
content learning.

Henze, R. and Hauser, M. (2000). *Personalizing culture through anthropological and educational
perspectives.* Washington, DC: Center for Research on Education, Diversity & Excellence.
The premise of this book is that teachers can use students' prior knowledge and skills as rich
resources for teaching and learning, helping to create culturally responsive schools.

Ioga, C. (1995). *The inner world of the immigrant child.* Mahwah, NJ: Lawrence Erlbaum.
Incorporating the voices and artwork of immigrant children, this book is a teacher's description
of the cultural, academic, and psychological adjustments that these students must make.

Leaks, R. and Stonehill, R.M. (2008). *Serving recent immigrant students through school-community
partnerships.* Retrieved from http://www.education.com/reference/article/Ref_Serving_Recent.
Explores the growth in immigrant student populations and explains how community-based
organizations can help ease the transition for newcomer students.

Levitan, S. (Ed.) (1998). *I'm not in my homeland anymore: Voices of students in a new land.* Toronto,
ON: Pippin Publishing.
Collection of short stories written by immigrant students, reflecting on their experiences.

Lucas, T. (1996). Promoting secondary school transition for immigrant adolescents. *ERIC Digest.*
Washington, DC: ERIC. Retrieved from http://www.eric.ed.gov/PDFS/ED402786.pdf.
Focuses on three ways that educators can help immigrant adolescents learn a new language and
culture while simultaneously providing academic support. Positive home–school relations and
programs for parents are also discussed.

Matluck, B. J., Alexander-Kasparik, R., and Queen, R. M. (1998). *Through the golden door:
Educational approaches for immigrant adolescents with limited schooling.* McHenry, IL: Delta
Systems Publishing Group.
This book examines the needs of recent immigrant students who enter middle school and high
school with little or no prior formal schooling and with low literacy skills. The critical features
of successful secondary school programs for these students are described and guidelines for
school administrators and teachers are provided.

Padrón, Y. N., Waxman, H. C., and Rivera, H. H. (2002). *Educating Hispanic students: Obstacles and
avenues to improved academic achievement.* Berkeley, CA: Center for Research on Education,
Diversity & Excellence.

This report examines factors that must be considered when planning for effective instruction of Hispanic students.

Short, D. J. (2002). Newcomer programs: An educational alternative for secondary immigrant students. *Education and Urban Society,* 34 (2): 173–198.

Based on the findings of a national study, this article explores the growth of newcomer programs in urban middle and high school settings, discussing implications for successful practice.

Short, D. (2004). *Creating access: Language and academic programs for secondary school newcomers.* Washington, DC: Center for Applied Linguistics.

Describes the most salient features of effective newcomer program, while providing illustrative case studies and offering practical advice for implementation.

ELLs with Special Needs

Barka, J. H. and Bernal, E. M. (1991). Gifted education for bilingual and limited English proficient students. *Gifted Child Quarterly,* 35 (3): 144–147.

Bermudez, A.B. and Marquez, J.A. (1998). *Insights into gifted and talented English language learners.* San Antonio, TX: Intercultural Development Research Association. Retrieved from http://www.idra.org.

Bulgren, J., Deshler, D.D., and Lez, B.K. (2007). Engaging adolescents with LD in higher order thinking about history concepts using integrated content enhancement routines. *Journal of Learning Disabilities,* 40 (2): 121–133.

Castellano, J. A. (Ed.) (2003). *Special populations in gifted education: Working with diverse gifted learners.* Boston, MA: Pearson Education.

Castellano, J. A. and Díaz, E. I. (Eds.) (2002). *Reaching new horizons: Gifted and talented education for culturally and linguistically diverse students.* Boston, MA: Allyn and Bacon.

Esquivel, G. B. and Houtz, J. C. (Eds.). (2000). *Creativity and giftedness in culturally diverse students.* Cresskill, NJ: Hampton Press.

Ford, D.Y. and Grantham, T.C. (2003). Providing access for culturally diverse gifted students: From deficit to dynamic thinking. *Theory Into Practice,* 42 (3): 217–225. Retrieved from http://muse.jhu.edu/journals/theory_into_practice/v042/42.3ford.html.

Harris, B., Plucker, J.A., Rapp, K.E., and Martinez, R.S. (2009). Identifying gifted and talented English language learners: A case study. *Journal for the Education of the Gifted,* 32 (3): 368–393.

Hoagies' Gifted Education: Multi-Cultural Gifted Students (http://www.hoagiesgifted.org/esl.htm).

Iowa Department of Education. (2008). *Identifying gifted and talented English language learners.* Des Moines, IA. Retrieved from http://educateiowa.gov/index.php?option=com_content&view=article&id=421:giftedtalented&catid=58:diverse-learners&Itemid=4865.

Lohman, D.F., Korb, K.A., and Lakin, J.M. (2008). Identifying academically gifted English-language learners using nonverbal tests. *Gifted Child Quarterly,* 52 (4): 275–296. Retrieved from http://faculty.education.uiowa.edu/dlohman/pdf/Comparing%20Raven,%20NNAT,%20&%20CogAT%20.pdf.

Morrison, S. *English language learners with special needs.* Washington, DC: Center for Applied Linguistics. Retrieved from http://www.cal.org/resources/archive/rgos/special.html.

Ortiz, A. (2001). *English language learners with special needs: Effective instructional strategies.* Retrieved from http://www.cal.org/resources/digest/0108ortiz.html.

Park, Y. and Thomas, R. (2012). Educating English-language learners with special needs: Beyond cultural and linguistic considerations. *Journal of Education and Practice,* 3 (9): 52–59.

Teachers' Manuals and Guides

Akhavan, N. (2006). *Help! My kids don't all speak English*. Portsmouth, NH: Heinemann.
  This book explains how to set up a "language workshop" that helps to expand students' language skills and thinking strategies. Although it has an elementary focus, the sample lesson plans, classroom-tested units of study, and ready-to-use graphic organizers included are nonetheless helpful and can be modified for older students.

Brownlie, F., Feniak, C., and McCarthy, V. (2004). *Instruction and assessment of ESL learners: Promoting success in your classroom*. Winnipeg: Portage & Main Press.
  This handbook for teachers provides suggestions for orienting the ELL to a new school, how to assess the ESL learner, how to modify lesson plans, and how to involve parents. Dozens of useful blackline masters are provided as well as suggestions for children's literature and internet resources.

Cary, S. (2000). *Working with second language learners: Answers to teachers' top ten questions*. Portsmouth, NH: Heinemann.
  This easy-to-use book explores topics such as students' cultural backgrounds, encouraging reluctant speakers, and teaching grade-level content to ELLs.

Claire, E., Haynes, J., and Chapman, J. (1994 and 1995). *Classroom Teacher's ESL Survival Kit #1 and #2*. Englewood Cliffs, NJ: Alemany Press, Prentice Hall Regents.
  This teacher's resource book features 130 reproducible activities for both ELLs and mainstream students. Also included are discussions on culture shock, language acquisition, and social and academic adjustment.

Chamot, A. U. (2009). *The CALLA handbook: Implementing the Cognitive Academic Learning Approach*. White Plains, NY: Pearson ESL.
  A resource book for content area teachers who have ELLs in their mainstream classrooms as well as for teachers in bilingual or self-contained EFL classrooms.

Echevarria, J., Vogt, M., and Short, D. (2007). *Making content comprehensible for English learners: The SIOP model*, 3rd edn. Boston, MA: Pearson Allyn & Bacon.
  Using a sheltered instruction approach, the authors offer guidelines for implementing their program. An accompanying CD features classroom clips, reproducible resources, and interviews with the authors.

Einhorn, K. (2001). *Easy and engaging ESL activities and mini-books for every classroom: Terrific teaching tips, games, mini-books and more to help new students from every nation build basic English vocabulary and feel welcome!* New York: Teaching Resources.
  Useful collection of ideas for assessing your ELL students' needs, communicating with family, and creating engaging activities.

Forte, I. (2001). *ESL active learning lessons: 15 complete content-based units to reinforce language skills and concepts*. Nashville, TN: Incentive Publications.

Forte, I., Pangle, M. A., and Drayton, M. (2001). *ESL content-based language games, puzzles, and inventive exercises*. Nashville, TN: Incentive Publications.
  Entertaining strategies to use with ELL students.

Gorea, L. (2005). *ESL games and classroom activities: An interactive activity book for all ages*. Tamarac, FL: Llumina Press.
  Learning activities for various grade levels and differing levels of language ability.

Helmer, S. (2003). *Look at me when I talk to you: ESL learners in non-ESL classrooms*. Toronto: Pippin.

Exploration of the underlying fundamentals of communication and how culture influences messages sent.

Herrell, A. and Jordan, M. (2004). *Fifty strategies for teaching English language learners*, 2nd edn. Upper Saddle River, NJ: Pearson Education.

Josel, C. A. (2002). *Ready-to-use ESL activities for every month of the school year.* Hillsboro, OR: Center for Applied Research in Education.

Kendall, J. and Outey, K. (2006). *Writing sense: Integrated reading and writing lessons for English language learners.* New York: Stenhouse.

Includes dozens of teacher-tested, writing-based lessons for students at all levels of language acquisition.

Law, B. and Eckes, M. (2000). *The more-than-just-surviving handbook: ESL for every classroom teacher.* Winnipeg: Peguis Publishers.

Written for both elementary and secondary school teachers, this book provides strategies for working with ELL students in the regular classroom.

Learning Point Associates. (2009). *Connecting research about English language learners to practice.* Available from: http://www.learningpt.org/pdfs/ConnectResearchPractice_ELL_IntroGuide. pdf.

A review of theories and research related to ELLs but with many district-level and school-level guidelines for implementation.

Peitzman, F. and Gadda, G. (Eds.) (1994). *With different eyes: Insights into teaching language minority students across the disciplines.* White Plains, NY: Longman.

Reiss, J. (2005). *Teaching content to English language learners.* White Plains, NY: Pearson.

This practical book helps content-area teachers to apply second language learning theories in their classrooms. Emphasis is on making content more accessible, strengthening vocabulary, and increasing student participation.

Samway, K. D. and McKeon, D. (1999). *Myths and realities: Best practices for language minority students.* Portsmouth, NH: Heinemann.

This book dispels common myths related to ELL students by providing basic background information on issues such as second language acquisition, legal requirements for educating linguistically diverse students, assessment, and placement.

Short, D. (1996). *Integrating language and culture in the social studies: Teacher training packet.* Washington, DC: Center for Applied Linguistics.

This manual, intended for teachers, administrators, and teacher educators, presents strategies for integrating language and content. Topics include materials adaptations, lesson plan development, and assessment issues.

Vogt, M.E.J. and Echevarria, J.J. (2007). *99 Ideas and Activities for Teaching English Learners with the SIOP Model.* Boston, MA: Allyn & Bacon.

Includes sample lesson plans, step-by-step directions, and classroom-ready activities.

Walter, T. (2004). *Teaching English language learners: The how to handbook.* White Plains, NY: Longman.

This user-friendly book includes discussions on culture, language acquisition, literacy development, and academic/content-area development. A list of resources is also included.

Warschauer, M. and Whittaker, P.F. (1997). The Internet for English teaching: Guidelines for teachers. *ESL Reporter,* 30 (1): 27–33. Available from: http://iteslj.org/Articles/Warschauer-Internet.html.

Although hardly new, this article provides guidelines which are still relevant when using the Internet to teach English to students.

ESOL Textbooks

Brisk, E. (2006). *Bilingual education: From compensatory to quality schooling.* Mahwah, NJ: Lawrence Erlbaum Associates.

Carrasquillo, A. L. and Rodriguez, A. (2002). *Language minority student in the mainstream classroom.* Clevedon, UK: Multilingual Matters.

Carter, R. and Nunan, D. (2001). *The Cambridge guide to teaching English to speakers of other languages.* London: Cambridge University Press.

Diaz-Rico, L. T. and Weed, K. Z. (2006). *The crosscultural, language, and academic development handbook.* Boston, MA: Pearson Allyn & Bacon.

Faltis, C. J. and Coulter, C. A. (2007). *Teaching English learners and immigrant students in secondary schools.* Upper Saddle River, NJ: Prentice Hall.

Garcia, E. (2002). *Student cultural diversity: Understanding and meeting the challenge.* Boston, MA: Houghton Mifflin.

Gonzalez, V., Yawkey, T., and Minaya-Rowe, L. (2006). *English-as-a-second-language (ESL) teaching and learning.* Boston, MA: Pearson Allyn & Bacon.

Hill, J. and Flynn, K. (2006). Classroom instruction that works with English language learners. Alexandria, VA: ASCD.
  Explores nine types of instructional strategies to facilitate and maximize learning in ELLs.

Larsen-Freeman, D. and Anderson, M. (2011). *Techniques and principles in language teaching,* 3rd edn. New York: Oxford University Press.

O'Malley, J. M. (2002). *Authentic assessment for English language learners: Practical approaches for teachers.* Reading, MA: Addison-Wesley.

Ovando, C. J., Combs, M. C., and Collier, V. (2006). *Bilingual and ESL classrooms: Teaching in multicultural contexts.* New York: McGraw-Hill.

Richard-Amato, P. A. (2003). *Making it happen: From interactive to participatory language teaching, theory and practice,* 3rd edn. New York: Longman.

Zainuddin, H., Yahya, N., Morales-Jones, C. A., and Ariza, E. N. (2002). *Fundamentals of teaching English to speakers of other languages in K–12 mainstream classrooms.* Dubuque, IA: Kendall Hunt.

Legal Issues

American Federation of Teachers. (2006). *English language learners and NCLB testing requirements.* Washington, DC: AFT. Retrieved from www.aft.org/topics/ nclb/downloads/QAELL0404.pdf.

American Speech–Language–Hearing Association (no date). *No child left behind: Fact sheet on assessment of English language learners.* Retrieved from www.asha.org/nr/rdonlyres/F6C11387-8290-4613-928D-FDFCD88EF052/0.NCLBELLAssess.pdf.

Education Alliance. (2006). *Linking language policy to practice for English language learners.* Retrieved from http://www.alliance.brown.edu/tdl/policy/index.shtml.

Education Law Center. Law & Policy: English language learners. Retrieved from http://www.elc-pa.org/law/law_english.html.

González, J. M. (2002). *Bilingual education and the federal role, if any . . . .* Tempe, AZ: Language Policy Research Unit, Education Policy Studies Laboratory, Arizona State University. Retrieved from www.asu.edu/educ/epsl/LPRU/features/brief1.htm.

Hakuta, K. (2011). Educating language minority students and affirming their equal rights: Research and practical perspectives. *Educational Researcher,* 40 (4): 163–174.

National Clearinghouse for English Language Acquisition. (2006). *Resources about assessment and accountability for ELLs.* Washington, DC: NCELA. Retrieved from www.ncela.gwu.edu/resabout/assessment/index.html.

Office for Civil Rights. (2012). *Developing programs for English language learners: Legal background.* U.S. Department of Education. Retrieved from http://www2.ed.gov/about/offices/list/ocr/ell/legal.html.

Office of Multicultural Student Language Education (OMSLE). (2000). *Consent decree: League of United Latin American Citizens (LULAC)* et al. v. *State Board of Education Consent Decree, United States District Court for the Southern District of Florida, August 14, 1990.* Tallahassee, FL: Florida Department of Education. Retrieved from www.fldoe.org/aala/cdpage2.asp.

Serpa, M.L. (2005). *Legal provisions affecting English language learners with and without special needs.* Retrieved from http://www.ldldproject.net/legal.html.

State of Maine Department of Education. *Legal provisions for the education of English learners.* Retrieved from http://www.maine.gov/education/esl/LegalProvisionsfortheEducationofEnglish LanguageLearners.html.

U.S. Department of Education, Office for Civil Rights (2000). *The provision of an equal education opportunity to limited-English proficient students.* Washington, DC: Author. Retrieved from www.ed.gov/about/offices/list/ocr/eeolep/index.htm.

Wright, W.E. (2010). *Landmark court rulings regarding English language learners.* Retrieved from http://www.colorincolorado.org/article/49704/.

Home–School Collaboration

Arias, M.B. and Morillo-Campbell, M. (2008). *Promoting ELL parental involvement: Challenges in contested times.* Retrieved from http://greatlakescenter.org/docs/Policy_Briefs/Arias_ELL.pdf.

Chang, J. M. (2004). *Family literacy nights: Building the circle of supporters within and beyond school for middle school English language learners.* Berkeley, CA: Center for Research on Education, Diversity & Excellence.

Colorin Colorado. (2007). *How to reach out to parents of ELLs.* Retrieved from http://www.colorincolorado.org/educators/reachingout/outreach.

Epstein, J. (2001). *School, family and community partnerships: Preparing educators and improving schools.* Boulder, CO: Westview Press.

Gonzalez, N., Moll, L., Floyd-Tennery, M., Rivera, A., Rendon, P., and Amanti, C. (1993). Funds of knowledge for teaching in Latino households. *Urban Education,* 29 (4): 443–470.

Guo, Y. (2006). "Why didn't they show up"? Rethinking ESL parent involvement in K-12 education. *TESL Canada Journal,* 24 (1): 80–95.

King, K. and Fogle, L. (2006). Raising bilingual children: Common parental concerns and current research. Retrieved from http://www.cal.org/resources/digest/raising-bilingual-children.html.

Moll, L., Armanti, C., Neff, D., and Gonzalez, N. (1992). Funds of knowledge for teaching: Using a qualitative approach to connect homes and classrooms. *Theory and Practice,* 31 (2): 132–141.

Schnee, M. and Haynes, J. (2010). *Holding an effective group meeting with parents of ELLs.* Retrieved from http://www.everythingesl.net/inservices/holding_effective_parent_meeti_68636.php.

Teacher Education and Professional Development

Casteel, C.J. and Ballantyne, K.G. (2010). *Professional development in action: Improving teaching for English learners.* Washington, DC: National Clearinghouse for English Language Acquisition. Available from: http://www.ncela.gwu.edu/files/uploads/3/PD_in_Action.pdf.

González, J. and Darling-Hammond, L. (2000). *Programs that prepare teachers to work effectively with students learning English.* Retrieved from www.cal.org/resources/digest/0009programs. html.

Haynes, J. (2004). *Tips on communicating: Show your school's mainstream teachers and students how to communicate with your newcomers from the very first day.* Retrieved from www.every thingesl.net/inservices/tipsoncommunicating.php.

Howard, E. R., Olague, N., and Rogers, D. (2003). *The dual language program planner: A guide for designing and implementing dual language programs.* Berkeley, CA: Center for Research on Education, Diversity & Excellence.
This guide offers a collection of tools (discussion prompts, graphic organizers, and quizzes) to be used by those who are in the process of planning or implementing a new dual language program.

Jameson, J. (2002). *Professional development for bilingual and ESL paraprofessionals.* McHenry, IL: Delta Publishing Group.
Paraprofessional training handbook to support students' language development and academic learning.

McGraner, K.L. and Saenz, L. (2009). *Preparing teachers of English language learners.* Washington, DC: National Comprehensive Center for Teacher Quality. Available from: http://www. tqsource.org/pdfs/PreparingTeachersofELLsprelim%20ed.pdf.

Mihai, F.M. (2010). *Assessing English language learners in the content areas: A research-into-practice guide for educators.* Ann Arbor, MI: University of Michigan Press.

Northwest Regional Educational Laboratory (2001). *Supporting bilingual and minority teachers: How administrators, teachers, and policy makers can help new teachers succeed.* Retrieved from www.nwrel.org/request/may01/bilingual.html.

Short, D. (2000). *Training others to use the ESL standards: A professional development manual.* Alexandria, VA: Teachers of English to Speakers of Other Languages.

Short, D. J. and Boyson, B. A. (2004). *Creating access: Language and academic programs for secondary school newcomers.* Washington, DC: Center for Applied Linguistics.
Designed especially for recent immigrants with limited English proficiency, this book is intended to help district personnel create a newcomer program or enhance an existing program.

Short, D., Hudec, J., and Echevarria, J. (2002). *Using the SIOP model: Professional development manual for sheltered instruction.* Washington, DC: CAL.

Snow, M. (Ed.) (2000). *Implementing the ESL standards for pre-K–12 students through teacher education.* Washington, DC: ERIC Clearinghouse on Languages and Linguistics.

Tarone, E. and Tedick, D. (2000). *Conversations with mainstream teachers: What can we tell them about second language learning and teaching?* Retrieved from http://carla.acad.umn.edu/esl/minnetesol2000.html.

Trickett, E.J., Rukhotskiy, E., Jeong, A., Genkova, A., Oberoi, A., Weinstein, T., and Delgado, Y. (2012). "The kids are terrific: It's the job that's tough": The ELL teacher role in an urban context. *Teaching and Teacher Education,* 28 (2): 283–292.

Villegas, A. M. (2002). *Educating culturally responsive teachers: A coherent approach.* New York: State University of New York Press.

Audio-Visual Materials to Support Instruction

The Adolescent Literacy Case: A Video Ethnography of Teaching Second Language Students Content Through Literacy Development. CD-ROM (2002)
  Stefinee Pinnegar, Annela Teemant, Bobbi Mason, and Carl Harris
  Teachers of English, science, social studies, and mathematics attending to literacy to promote greater academic achievement in their disciplines.
The Craig Cleveland Case. CD-ROM (2002)
  Stefinee Pinnegar, Annela Teemant, and Roland Tharp
  Instruction of high school Mexican American history in a Spanish/English bilingual classroom.
The Second Language Literacy Case: A Video Ethnography of Bilingual Students' Literacy Development. CD-ROM (2003)
  Annela Teemant, Stefinee Pinnegar, and Ray Graham
  This allows mainstream teachers to see and hear the second language literacy accounts of nine diverse second language learners, their teachers, and families. The cases explore who second language readers and writers are, their literacy needs, and their experiences in and outside school.
The SIOP Model: Sheltered Instruction for Academic Achievement. Video (VHS) (2002)
  This 77-minute video illustrates the eight components of the SIOP model for sheltered instruction in detail. The video presents extended footage from middle and high school classrooms. It features interviews with six outstanding teachers and SIOP researchers. It is designed especially for use in sustained programs of staff development and teacher education and is to be used in conjunction with *Using the SIOP Model: Professional Development for Sheltered Instruction.*
Helping English Learners Succeed: An Overview of the SIOP Model. Video (VHS) (2002)
  This 26-minute video provides an introduction to a research-based model of sheltered instruction. The video uses classroom footage and researcher narration to concisely present the eight components of the SIOP model. This video will be useful to administrators, policymakers, and teachers. It also serves as a fitting supplement in teacher methodology courses.

Publishers

Alta Books (www.altaesl.com)
Benchmark Education Company (www.benchmarkeducation.com)
Cambridge University Press (www.cambridge.org/us/esl)
Center for Applied Linguistics (www.cal.org)
Delta Publishing Group (www.delta-systems.com/deltalinks.htm)
Heinemann (http://books.heinemann.com/categories/11.aspx)
Oxford University Press (www.oup.com/us/corporate/publishingprograms/esl/?view=usa)
Pearson ESL (http://www.pearsonelt.com)
Routledge (http://www.routledge.com)
Thomson English Language Teaching (http://elt.thomson.com/namerica/en_us/index.html#)

Resources for Students

In addition to the resources presented here, note that each of the chapters in Part 3 also lists useful resources that may be utilized by students.

Dictionaries

Agnes, M.E. (Ed.) (1998). *Webster's New World Basic Dictionary of American English.* New York: John Wiley.

Cambridge Learner Dictionaries (www.cambridge.org/elt/dictionaries/cld.htm)
   This collection includes beginners' and advanced learners' dictionaries. Pronouncing dictionaries and grammar resources are supplemented with CDs to aid comprehension. *English Grammar in Use* is a self-paced study and reference guide for intermediate and above language learners.

Heinle. (2005). *Heinle Picture Dictionary.* Boston, MA: Heinle Cengage Learning.

Hill, J. and Lewis, M. (Eds.) (1997). *The LTP dictionary of selected collocations.* Sydney: Language Teaching Publications.
   Designed for intermediate and advanced learners; frequently used collocations are grouped by nouns, adjectives, verbs, and adverbs.

Kauffman, D. and Apple, G. (2000). *Oxford picture dictionary for the content areas.* New York: Oxford University Press.
   Color illustrations are used to define over 1,500 vocabulary words from the subjects of social studies, science, and math. Although it is intended primarily for elementary and middle school students, this resource can nonetheless be very useful to recent arrivals. Ancillary materials include a teacher's book, student workbook, wall charts, overhead transparencies, and sound recordings.

Lea, D. (2002). *Oxford collocations dictionary for learners of English.* New York: Oxford University Press.
   This unique dictionary provides over 170,000 common word combinations to help students speak and write English more naturally and fluently.

Longman Learner Dictionaries (www.longman.com/ae/dictionaries)
   This collection offers dictionaries for beginning, intermediate, and advanced language learners. Basic picture dictionaries, pronunciation dictionaries, and bilingual dictionaries are all included in this series. Additionally, the *Longman American Idioms Dictionary* helps students understand common American expressions.

Longman Dictionary of American English (2004). White Plains, NY: Pearson Education.
   Intermediate-level dictionary including full-color pictures and interactive CD-ROM.

Webster's Essential Mini Dictionary. (2011). New York: Cambridge University Press.
   Pocket-sized dictionary that contains basic English words explained in plain language and with illustrations in many cases.

Online Dictionaries

The following is a collection of free-access dictionaries on the World Wide Web.
Alpha Dictionary (www.alphadictionary.com/index.shtml)
Cambridge Dictionaries online (http://dictionary.cambridge.org)
Dictionary.com (http://dictionary.reference.com)
Die.net online Dictionary (http://dict.die.net)
Heinle's Newbury House Dictionary of American English (http://nhd.heinle.com/home.aspx)
Lexicool (www.lexicool.com)
Merriam-Webster Learner's Dictionary (http://www.learnersdictionary.com)
Omniglot (www.omniglot.com/links/dictionaries.htm)
One Look Dictionary Search (www.onelook.com)

Oxford Dictionaries (http://oxforddictionaries.com)
Word2Word (www.word2word.com/dictionary.html)
Yahoo Kids Dictionary (http://kids.yahoo.com/reference/dictionary/english)
Your Dictionary (www.yourdictionary.com)

Online Translation Services

AltaVista Babel Fish (http://www.bablefishfx.com/altavista-babelfish-translation-online)
Applied Language Solutions (www.appliedlanguage.com/free_translation.shtml)
BabelFish (http://www.babelfish.com)
Babylon (http://translation.babylon.com)
Bing Translator (http://www.microsofttranslator.com)
Frengly.com (http://frengly.com)
Google Language Tools (www.google.com/language_tools?hl=en)
Im Translator (http://freetranslation.imtranslator.com/lowres.asp)
Omniglot (www.omniglot.com/links/translation.htm)
World Lingo (www.worldlingo.com/en/products_services/worldlingo_translator.html)

Internet Sites: English Language Support

Digital Dialects (http://www.digitaldialects.com/English.htm)
   Games for learning often-used vocabulary. Some of the games also provide audio for correct pronunciation.
Discovery Education (http://school.discoveryeducation.com/homeworkhelp/socialstudies/social_studies_homework_help.html?campaign=DE&CFID=998671&CFTOKEN=50111402)
   Study tools and learning adventures help students with social studies homework and class work.
EFL/ESoL/ESL Songs and Activities (www.songsforteaching.com/esleflesol.htm)
   Lyrics and sound clips are offered for a variety of songs that help students learn vocabulary for things such as colors, shapes, and food, among many other topics.
English Forum (www.englishforum.com/00/students)
   Online study resources, interactive English language exercises, online dictionaries, and other tools. Full texts of popular novels are also included.
English Online (E. L. Easton) (http://eleaston.com/english.html)
   In addition to language instruction and support, this site offers quizzes, tests, and links to many social studies topics.
ESL Connect (www.eslconnect.com/links.html)
   Student visitors to this gateway site can access links to Homework Help, Crosswords and Puzzles, and other activities that support English language learning.
ESL: English as a second language (www.eslgo.com/quizzes.html)
   Tests students' knowledge of subject–verb agreement, prepositions, punctuation, and vocabulary.
ESL Gold (http://www.eslgold.com)
   An interactive site that allows students to practice and improve their English skills including learning vocabulary, practicing pronunciation, watching videos, and reviewing grammar.
ESL Independent Study Lab (www.lclark.edu/~krauss/toppicks/toppicks.html)
   The ESL Center, housed at Lewis and Clark College in Portland, Oregon, contains speaking and listening exercises and activities that promote learning English as a second language.

ESL Partyland (www.eslpartyland.com)
   Billed as "the cool way to learn English," this website allows users to enter depending on whether they are a teacher or a student. Students can access interactive quizzes, discussion forums, a chat room, and interactive lessons on a variety of topics.
eViews: English Listening Exercises (www.eviews.net)
   Although there is a fee associated with this site, there is a free trial available. The listening exercises are designed for intermediate to advanced English students. English is recorded at normal speed and comprehension checks are included.
Grammar Safari (http://www.iei.illinois.edu/grammarsafari/grammarsafari.html)
   This site provides "grammar safari" activities wherein students "hunt" and "collect" specific common words as they are used in documents accessible on the Internet.
Grammar and ESL Exercises (http://owl.english.purdue.edu/owl/resource/611/01)
   Hosted by Purdue University, this site offers the ELL interactive exercises, printable (offline) exercises, and concise explanations of grammar and punctuation rules.
Intensive English Institute: Study Resources (http://www.iei.illinois.edu/current/studyresources)
   Listening resources, oral communication resources, and a movie guide for English language learners are just a few of the helpful links provided on this site.
Interesting Things for ESL/EFL Students (www.manythings.org)
   This website is for people studying English as a second language (ESL) or English as a foreign language (EFL). There are quizzes, word games, word puzzles, proverbs, slang expressions, anagrams, a random-sentence generator, and other study materials.
Internet Treasure Hunts for ESL Students (http://iteslj.org/th)
   Links to scavenger hunts on the Internet that develop language skills.
iTools (www.itools.com)
   Language tools, translation services, and researching resources.
Learn English (www.learnenglish.de)
   Online games, tests, quizzes, and pronunciation guides assists students learning English.
Merriam-Webster Word Central (http://www.wordcentral.com)
   Students can build their own dictionary, play games, and learn new vocabulary in a "daily wordbuzz" feature.
OWL (Online Writing Lab) (http://owl.english.purdue.edu/handouts/esl/eslstudent.html)
   Help with idioms, grammar, spelling, and vocabulary. Links to quizzes, tests, and interactive sites.
Pearson ELT (http://www.pearsonlongman.com/teens)
   In addition to free access to the *Longman Dictionary of Contemporary English Online*, the ELT Teens Resource Library includes online activities, support materials, and free resources for teenage learners of English.
Randall's ESL Cyber Listening Lab (www.esl-lab.com)
   Listening lab that allows students to practice listening skills, develop a natural accent, and understand slang.
Resources for English as a Second Language (www.usingenglish.com)
   The English Language Reference section provides a glossary of grammar terms, English idioms, and irregular verbs.
Self-Study Quizzes for ESL Students (http://a4esl.org/q/h)
   These self-paced quizzes allow ELLs to test their understanding of language features such as vocabulary, homonyms, grammar, and idioms.
To Learn English (www.tolearnenglish.com)

Social Studies Internet Sites for Students (see also selected sites included in Part 3 chapters)

America's Story from America's Library (www.americaslibrary.gov/cgi-bin/page.cgi)
This interactive site from the Library of Congress provides students with a wide variety of primary sources, including diaries, letters, music, maps, and photographs.

BBC Audio Video Archive (http://esl.about.com/cs/listeningresource/v/v_bbc_archive.htm)
High-quality documentaries and programs on a variety of topics.

Brain Pop (www.brainpop.com/socialstudies/seeall)
Animated shorts teach students about a wide range of social studies topics. Links for teachers and parents are also included.

Dig: The Archaeology Magazine for Kids (www.digonsite.com)

Educational Technology Clearinghouse (http://etc.usf.edu/ss/index.htm)
Social studies sites are annotated to assist in finding resources easily.

History Central (http://www.historycentral.com/dates/Index.html)
Summary of all major world historical events is provided along with associated graphics and images.

History Wired (http://historywired.si.edu)
An interactive site that allows students to take a virtual tour of the Smithsonian's many holdings.

Khan Academy (http://www.khanacademy.org)
Free online library of over 3,000 educational videos on a wide variety of topics.

Kids Psych (http://www.kidspsych.org/index1.html)
A series of interactive games that help students understand psychological principles.

Learning to Give (www.learningtogive.org/students/index.asp)
Interactive games, activities, and ideas for community projects.

National Women's History Museum (www.nmwh.org)
The Cyber Museum on this site offers exhibits on a range of topics, including suffrage, education, sports, and civil rights.

Neuroscience for Kids (http://faculty.washington.edu/chudler/neurok.html)

Social Studies for Kids (www.socialstudiesforkids.com)
Includes glossaries, current events, and connections to all the social studies.

Print Materials that Support English Language and Cultural Learning

Chamot, A. U. (2004). *Keys to learning: Skills and strategies for newcomers.* Upper Saddle River, NJ: Pearson ESL.
This guidebook provides middle and high school newcomers with step-by-step tools for developing academic skills and literacy. Workbook with consumables is also available.

Claire, E. (2004). *American manners and customs: A guide for newcomers.* McHenry, IL: Delta Publishing Group.
The most often required manners and customs are discussed and explained, including greetings, table manners, and body language.

Clark, R. C. and Hawkinson, A. (2006). *Living in the United States.* McHenry, IL: Delta Publishing Group.
Written in language appropriate for intermediate students, this book has information on food and restaurants, communications, and customs and values.

Collis, H. and Kohl., J. (2000). *101 American customs*. Lincolnwood, IL: Passport Books.

Dixson, R. J. (2003). *Essential idioms in English: Phrasal verbs and collocations*. Upper Saddle River, NJ: Pearson Education.

Francis, E. J. (2006). *A year in the life of an ESL student: Idioms and vocabulary you can't live without*. Victoria, BC: Trafford Publishing.

Gaines, B. K. (1997). *Idiomatic American English: A workbook of idioms for everyday use*. Tokyo: Kodansha International.

Gilbert, J. (2004). *Clear speech student's book: Pronunciation and listening comprehension in American English*. London: Cambridge University Press.

Holleman, J. (2006). *American English idiomatic expressions in 52 weeks: An easy way to understand English expressions and improve speaking*. Hong Kong: Chinese University Press.
The meanings of 3,300 commonly used idioms are explained and contextual examples are provided.

Johnston, D. B. (2000). *Speak American: A survival guide to the language and culture of the U.S.A.* New York: Random House Reference.

Lutter, J. G. (1999). *The pronunciation of Standard American English*. Granada Hills, CA: Garrett Publishing.

Orion, G. F. (1997). *Pronouncing American English: Sounds, stress, and intonation*. Belmont, CA: Heinle.

Spears, R. A. (2002). *Common American phrases in everyday contexts: A detailed guide to real-life conversation and small talk*. New York: McGraw-Hill.

Spears, R. A., Birner, B.J., and Kleinedler, S. R. (1995). *NTC's dictionary of everyday American English expressions*. New York: McGraw-Hill.
With more than 7,000 up-to-date phrases, this dictionary covers situations from talking to a doctor to ordering a meal, and helps learners communicate personal feelings, and make small talk.

Swick, E. (2004). *Practice makes perfect: English grammar for ESL learners*. New York: McGraw-Hill.

Yates, J. (1999). *The ins and outs of prepositions: A guidebook for ESL students*. Hauppauge, NY: Barron's Educational Series.

Print Materials that Support Social Studies Learning

Aguilar Lawlor, L. and Mariscal, J. (2005). *Longman social studies*. Upper Saddle River, NJ: Pearson Longman ESL.
A standards-based social studies program for students in grades 6–12. Providing a survey of world and American history, all readings and activities are specifically geared to ELLs.

Bailey, J. (1990). *From the beginning: A first reader in American history*. McHenry, IL: Delta Publishing Group.
Intermediate-level reader written in simple language, summarizing the major issues and controversies of each era.

Becijos, J. (1995). *Global views: A multicultural reader with language exercises*. Upper Saddle River, NJ: Dominie Press.
Biographies, holidays, folktales, and descriptions of people and places from representative areas around the world. Language and content learning are supported through geographic questions, grammar exercises, and language information.

Bernstein, V. (2006). *America's history: Land of liberty*. McHenry, IL: Delta Publishing Group.

Highly readable and interesting text, with special features and activities designed for ELL students.

Cruz, B.C. and Thornton, S.J. (2013). *Gateway to social studies*. Boston, MA: National Geographic/ Cengage.

Designed to support a middle school social studies text. A picture dictionary approach with sections on World Geography, World History, U.S. History, and Civics as well as general social studies resources such as maps and globes, timelines, and primary sources.

English Explorers. Pelham, NY: Benchmark Education Company (www.benchmarkeducation. com)

This series uses a reader's theater format to promote fluency and comprehension through varied social studies topics (e.g., folktales, biographies, and character education).

Lubawy, S. (2006). *World view: A global study of geography, history, and culture*. Palatine, IL: Linmore Publishing.

Written specifically for ELL students at the secondary level, this two-book set develops understanding of geography contexts, vocabulary and grammar practice in social studies, and learning strategies. Book 1 covers the Western Hemisphere (United States, Canada, and Latin America); Book 2, the Eastern Hemisphere (Europe, Africa, Asia, and the Pacific Region). The Teacher's Resource Book includes reproducible worksheets, reviews, and tests.

Ryall, M. (2004). *Legends: Graded reading from American history: 52 people who made a difference*. McHenry, IL: Delta Publishing Group.

Collection of 52 biosketches with illustrations. Also included is a timeline placing the person's life within the context of events and other people in U.S. history.

Sandell, C. (2006). *American history: Supplemental text*. Plano, TX: VIS Enterprises.

United States Citizenship and Immigration Services. (2011). *Citizenship Resource Center*. Washington, DC: Author.

The U.S. government provides free study booklets, CD-ROMs, and flashcards about American government, American history, and integrated civics (which includes geography, symbols, and holidays). http://www.uscis.gov/portal/site/uscis/citizenship.

Audio-Visual Materials for Students

Childs, C. (2003). *Improve your American English accent: Overcoming major obstacles to understanding*. New York: McGraw-Hill.
Audio CD.

Collis, H. (2007). *101 English idioms and CD*. New York: McGraw-Hill.
Book and CD.

Dale, P. and Poms, L. (2004). *English pronunciation made simple*. Upper Saddle River, NJ: Pearson ESL.
Book and two CDs.

Gilbert, J. (2004). *Clear speech from the start: Basic pronunciation and listening comprehension in North American English*. London: Cambridge University Press.
Student's book with audio CD.

Gillett, A. (2004). *Speak English like an American*. Ann Arbor, MI: Language Success Press.
Book and audio CD set.

Yates, J. (2005). *Pronounce it perfectly in English*. Hauppauge, NY: Barron's.
Sound recording (four CDs).

Glossary

Additive bilingualism: Theory that the acquisition of a second language does not interfere in the learning of the native language; second language can be acquired either simultaneously or after native language development.

BICS: Basic interpersonal communication skills; in effect, language skills needed for everyday personal and social communication.

Bilingual education: Although most instruction is in English, concepts are explained in students' primary language and a sheltered English approach is used for academic subjects.

CALP: Cognitive/academic language proficiency; language skills needed for cognitive/academic tasks in the mainstream classroom.

Comprehensible input: Language presented at the student's level of comprehension. Input is made comprehensible through the use of visuals, context, and other cues.

Developmental bilingual education: Instruction is provided in the student's native language for an extended time period while simultaneously learning English, resulting in bilingualism; often used synonymously with "late exit bilingual education."

Dual-language programs: Instruction occurs in both the native language and in English to develop strong skills and proficiency in both. Also known as "two-way immersion."

Early exit bilingual education: Transition to English as quickly as possible, often using sheltered instructional strategies; some content instruction in the native language is provided; transition to mainstream in two to three years.

English language learner (ELL): Student whose limited proficiency in English affects his or her academic achievement in school. Also known as "limited English proficient student."

English learner (EL): Used interchangeably with "English language learner."

English as a new language (ENL): Used by the National Board for Professional Teaching Standards.

English as a second language (ESL): The learning of English by speakers of other languages; often used synonymously with ESOL (see below).

English to speakers of other languages (ESOL): The learning of English by speakers of other languages; often used synonymously with ESL (see above).

Heritage language learner: Student who is exposed to a language other than English at home. Heritage learners usually have varying degrees of knowledge of the home language.

Immersion: Instructional approach wherein 100 percent of the instructional time is spent communicating through the target language; in contrast to submersion, the class is composed mostly of speakers of the target language with only a few non-native speakers.

Immersion language instruction: Instruction—including academic content—in the student's *non-native* language. Students are mainstreamed into regular, English-only classrooms with no special support.

Language minority (LM) student: A student whose primary home language is not English. LM students may have limited English proficiency or may be fluent in English.

Late exit bilingual education: In contrast to early exit bilingual education, transition to mainstream occurs in four to six years; significant amount of instruction is carried out in native language while gradually increasing instruction in English.

Limited English proficiency students: Students whose limited proficiency in English affects their academic achievement in school. Also known as "English language learners."

Mainstreaming: Practice of integrating English language learners into regular classrooms.

Maintenance bilingual education: Instruction is delivered in both native language and target language; often used synonymously with "late exit bilingual education."

Pull-out: Students are pulled out of their regular, English-only classrooms for special instruction to develop English language skills.

Self-contained: ELL classrooms located in "regular" schools but separate from regular education classrooms; ELLs are provided special instruction apart from their peers.

Sheltered English instruction: Using comprehensible content and strategies to teach grade-level subject matter in English while simultaneously also developing English language skills. Also known as "specially designed academic instruction in English."

Sheltered immersion: Instructional approach that promotes English language development while providing comprehensible grade-level content.

Silent period: Common, varying period of time during which a new language learner listens to, but does not speak in, the new language.

Specially designed academic instruction in English (SDAIE): Using comprehensible content and strategies to teach grade-level subject matter in English while simultaneously also developing English language skills.

Structured immersion: Students' proficiency levels in English are taken into account so subject matter is comprehensible.

Submersion: Instructional approach wherein the class is composed entirely of students learning a target language; 100 percent of the instructional time is spent communicating through the target language.

Subtractive bilingualism: When the acquisition of a second language interferes with the maintenance of the native language, effectively replacing the first language.

Total physical response: Instructional approach integrating both verbal and physical communication (and often movement) so that students can internalize and eventually "code break" a new language; especially effective with beginning language students, vocabulary instruction, and with students who are primarily kinesthetic learners.

Transitional bilingual education: Language acquisition theory emphasizing fluency in learner's native language first, before acquiring fluency in second language.

Two-way immersion: Instruction occurs in both the native language and in English to develop strong skills and proficiency in both. Also known as "dual-language programs."

Notes

Introduction

1 Although other terms are used (e.g. limited English proficient, English as a second language), we will use the term English language learner (ELL) throughout the book, mostly because of its widespread use and acceptance.

1.1 Orientation

1 Proposition 227 was part of a referendum in California to abolish bilingual education for ELLs in favor of more instruction in English. The *No Child Left Behind* legislation is a federal initiative to oversee teacher performance and student improvement in literacy and numeracy through such accountability measures as standardized testing in schools.

1.7 Not All Parents Are the Same: Home–School Communication

1 Two research studies from the Center for Research on Education, Diversity & Excellence (CREDE) have recently been published through the Center for Applied Linguistics. The two books, arising out of a four-year and a three-year study respectively, center on the solidification of home–school ELL communication. The first, entitled *Creating Access: Language and Academic Programs for Secondary School Newcomers*, describes the ins and outs of an effective education model—newcomer programs for immigrant students—and is designed to help district personnel create a newcomer program or enhance an existing program. The second book, called *Family Literacy Nights: Building the Circle of Supporters within and beyond School for Middle School English Language Learners*, discusses a project to improve students' education through a home–school collaboration called "Family Literacy

Nights." The program brought parents of linguistically and culturally diverse students together with teachers and students, resulting in greater parental involvement and improved student learning. This report offers practitioners strategies for implementing similar programs.

3.2 Geography

1 Based on information taken from Coonrod (1998).

3.4 World History

1 Reproduced with permission from National Council for the Social Studies.
2 Based on the account in Enloe (1989: 169–171). Lesson reproduced and modified with permission from Cruz and Bermúdez (1997).

3.5 Government and Civics

1 Used and modified with permission from Caroline Parrish, based on a lesson of her creation.

3.6 Economics

1 Text and visual reprinted with permission by National Geographic/Cengage Learning. Cruz, B.C. and Thornton, S.J. (2013). *Gateway to social studies*. Boston, MA: National Geographic/Cengage Learning, pp. 16–17.
2 Reprinted and modified with permission from Cruz and Bermúdez (1997).
3 Used and modified with permission from Caroline Parrish, based on a lesson of her creation.

3.7 Anthropology, Sociology, and Psychology

1 Lesson reproduced with permission from Cruz and Bermúdez (1997).

3.8 Controversial Issues in the Social Studies Classroom

1 Reproduced with permission from Cruz *et al.* (2003).
2 The strategy used in this activity is loosely based on Population Connection's (www. populationeducation.org) "Take a Stand." This organization offers an excellent program for teachers and students, including workshops, a curriculum, and classroom-ready materials.

References

Series Introduction

CREATE. (2012). *Addressing the challenges of educating English language learners in the middle grades: Research*. Retrieved from www.cal.org/create/research/index.html#studies.

Ladson-Billings, G. (2001). *Crossing over to Canaan: The journey of new teachers in diverse classrooms*. San Francisco, CA: Jossey-Bass.

Introduction

Ballantyne, K. G., Sanderman, A. R., and Levy, J. (2008). *Educating English language learners: Building teacher capacity*. Washington, DC: National Clearinghouse for English Language Acquisition. Available at: http://www.ncela.gwu.edu/practice/mainstream_teachers.htm.

Calderón, M., Slavin, R., and Sánchez, M. (2011). Effective instruction for English learners. *The Future of Children, 21* (1): 103–127.

Cho, S. and Reich, G. A. (2008). New immigrants, new challenges: High school social studies teachers and English language learner instruction. *The Social Studies,* 99 (6): 235–242.

Clair, N. (1995). Mainstream classroom teachers and ESL students. *TESOL Quarterly*, 29: 189–196.

Menken, K. and Antunez, B. (2001). *An overview of the preparation and certification of teachers working with limited English proficient (LEP) students.* Washington, DC: U.S. Department of Education Office of Bilingual Education and Minority Languages Affairs in cooperation with the ERIC Clearinghouse on Teaching and Teacher Education & Center for the Study of Language & Education Institute for Education Policy Studies, Graduate School of Education and Human Development, The George Washington University.

National Center for Education Statistics (2002). *1999–2000 schools and staffing survey: Overview of the data for public, private, public charter and Bureau of Indian Affairs elementary and secondary schools.* Washington, DC: U.S. Department of Education, Office of Educational Research and Improvement.

National Center for Education Statistics. (2008). *The Condition of Education*. NCES 1008-031. Washington, DC: U.S. Government Printing Office.

Noddings, N. (2006). *Critical lessons: What our schools should teach*. New York: Cambridge University Press.

Rumbaut, R. G. and Portes, A. (2001). *Ethnicities: Children of immigrants in America*. Berkeley, CA: University of California Press.

Short, D. J. (1993). *How to integrate language and content instruction: A training manual.* Washington, DC: Center for Applied Linguistics.

Watson, S., Miller, T. L., Driver, J., Rutledge, V., and McAllister, D. (2005). English language learner representation in teacher education textbooks: A null curriculum. *Education,* 126 (1). Retrieved from http://findarticles.com/p/articles/mi_qa3673/is_200510/ai_n15641937.

Part 1

Baca, L. and Cervantes, H. (2004). *The bilingual special education interface.* Columbus, OH: Merrill.

Bailey, A. L., Butler, F. A., Borrego, M., LaFramenta, C., and Ong, C. (2002). Towards a characterization of academic language. *Language Testing Update,* 31: 45–52.

Baker, C. (2001). *Foundations of bilingual education and bilingualism,* 3rd edn. Clevedon, UK: Multilingual Matters.

Bassoff, T. C. (2004). Three steps toward a strong home–school connection. *Essential Teacher,* 1 (4). Retrieved from www.tesol.org/s_tesol/sec_document.asp?CID=659&DID=2586.

Boscolo, P. and Mason, L. (2001). Writing to learn, writing to transfer. In P. Tynjälä, L. Mason, and K. Lonka (Eds.), *Writing as a learning tool: Integrating theory and practice.* Dordrecht, The Netherlands: Kluwer Academic Publishers, pp. 83–104.

Brinton, D. (2003). Content-based instruction. In D. Nunan (Ed.), *Practical English language teaching.* New York: McGraw-Hill, pp. 199–224.

Carrasquillo, A. L. and Rodriguez, V. (2002). *Language minority students in the mainstream classroom,* 2nd edn. Boston, MA: Multilingual Matters.

Clark, D. (1999). *Learning domains or Bloom's taxonomy.* Retrieved from www.nwlink.com/~donclark/hrd/bloom.html.

Coady, M., Hamann, E. T., Harrington, M., Pacheco, M., Pho, S., and Yedlin, J. (2003). *Claiming opportunities: A handbook for improving education for English language learners through comprehensive school reform.* Providence, RI: Education Alliance at Brown University.

Collier, V. P. (1995). Acquiring a second language for school. *Directions in Language and Education,* vol. 1 (4). Washington, DC: National Clearinghouse for Bilingual Education.

Collier, V. and Thomas, W. (1997). *School effectiveness for language minority students.* Washington, DC: National Clearinghouse for Bilingual Education. Retrieved from www.ncela.gwu.edu/pubs/resource/effectiveness.

Consent Decree (1990). Retrieved from www.firn.edu/doe/aala/lulac.htm.

Crawford, J. (2004). *Educating English learners: Language diversity in the classroom,* 5th edn. Los Angeles, CA: Bilingual Educational Services.

Cummins, J. (1979). Cognitive/academic language proficiency, linguistic interdependence, the optimum age question and some other matters. *Working Papers on Bilingualism,* 19: 121–129.

Cummins, J. (1980). The cross-lingual dimensions of language proficiency: Implications for bilingual education and the optimal age issue. *TESOL Quarterly,* 14 (2): 175–187.

Cummins, J. (1981). The role of primary language development in promoting educational success for language minority students. In C. F. Leyba (Ed.), *Schooling and language minority students: A theoretical framework.* Los Angeles, CA: California State University, Evaluation, Dissemination and Assessment Center.

Cummins, J. (1986). Empowering minority students: A framework for intervention. *Harvard Educational Review,* 56 (1): 18–36.

Cummins, J. (1992). Bilingual education and English immersion: The Ramírez report in theoretical perspective. *Bilingual Research Journal,* 16: 91–104.

Cummins, J. (2001). *Negotiating identities: Education for empowerment in a diverse society.* Los Angeles, CA: California Association for Bilingual Education.

Diaz-Rico, L. and Weed, K. Z. (2006). *The crosscultural, language and academic development handbook,* 3rd edn. Boston, MA: Pearson Education.

Echeverria, J. and McDonough, R. (1993). *Instructional conversations in special education settings: Issues and accommodations.* Educational Practice Report 7. National Center for Research on Cultural Diversity and Second Language Learning. Retrieved from www.ncela.gwu.edu/pubs/ncrcdsll/epr7.htm.

Ellis, R. (2005). *Instructed second language acquisition: A literature review.* Report to the Ministry of Education, New Zealand. Retrieved from www.educationcounts.edcentre.govt.nz/publications/downloads/instructed-second-language.pdf.

Gay, G. (2000). *Culturally responsive teaching: Theory, research, and practice.* New York: Teachers College Press.

Genesee, F. (Ed.) (1999). *Program alternatives for linguistically diverse students.* Santa Cruz, CA: Center for Research on Education, Diversity and Excellence. Retrieved from www.cal.org/crede/pubs/edpractice/Epr1.pdf.

Gold, N. (2006). *Successful bilingual schools: Six effective programs in California.* San Diego, CA: San Diego County Office of Education.

Gollnick, D. M. and Chinn, P. C. (2002). *Multicultural education in a pluralistic society,* 6th edn. New York: Merrill.

Hakuta, K. (2011). Educating language minority students and affirming their equal rights: Research and practical perspectives. *Educational Researcher,* 40 (4): 163–174.

Hakuta, K., Butler, Y. G., and Witt, D. (2000). *How long does it take English learners to attain proficiency?* Santa Barbara, CA: University of California Linguistic Research Institute Policy Report (2000–2001).

Hoover, J. J. and Collier, C. (1989). Methods and materials for bilingual education. In M. Baca and H. T. Cervantes (Eds.), *The bilingual special interface.* Columbus, OH: Merrill, pp. 231–255.

Kern, R. (2000). *Literacy and language teaching.* Oxford, UK: Oxford University Press.

Krashen, S. (1981). *Principles and practice in second language acquisition.* English Language Teaching series. London: Prentice-Hall International.

Krashen, S. D. and Terrell, T. D. (1983). *The natural language approach: Language acquisition in the classroom.* London: Prentice Hall Europe.

Long, M. (1996). The role of the linguistic environment in second language acquisition. In W. Ritchie and T. Bhatia (Eds.), *Handbook of second language acquisition.* San Diego, CA: Academic Press, pp. 413–468.

Long, M. H. (2006). *Problems in SLA.* Mahwah, NJ: Lawrence Erlbaum Associates.

Lyster, R. (1998). Recasts, repetition and ambiguity in L2 classroom discourse. *Studies in Second Language Acquisition,* 20: 51–81.

Lyster, R. (2001). Negotiation of form, recasts, and explicit correction in relation to error types and learner repair in immersion classrooms. *Language Learning,* 51 (Suppl. 1): 265–301.

Lyster, R. (2004). Differential effects of prompts and recasts in form-focused instruction. *Studies in Second Language Acquisition,* 26: 399–432.

Lyster, R. (2007). *Learning and teaching languages through content: A counterbalanced approach.* Amsterdam: John Benjamins.

Lyster, R. and Mori, H. (2006). Interactional feedback and instructional counterbalance. *Studies in Second Language Acquisition,* 28: 321–341.

Lyster, R. and Ranta, L. (1997). Corrective feedback and learner uptake: Negotiation of form in communicative classrooms. *Studies in Second Language Acquisition,* 19: 37–66.

Meltzer, J. (2001). *The adolescent literacy support framework.* Providence, RI: Northeast and Islands Regional Educational Laboratory at Brown University. Retrieved from http://knowledgeloom.org/adlit.

Meltzer, J. and Hamann, E. T. (2005). *Meeting the literacy development needs of adolescent English language learners through content-area learning. Part two: Focus on classroom teaching strategies.* Providence, RI: Education Alliance at Brown University.

National Clearinghouse for English Language Acquisition. (2006). *How many school-aged English language learners (ELLs) are there in the U.S.?* Washington, DC: U.S. Department of Education. Retrieved from http://www.ncela.gwu.edu/expert/faq/01leps.html.

National Clearinghouse for English Language Acquisition. (2011). *The growing numbers of English learner students.* Washington, DC: U.S. Department of Education. Retrieved from http://www.ncela.gwu.edu/files/uploads/9/growingLEP_0809.pdf.

Oberg, K. (1954). *The social economy of the Tlingit Indians of Alaska.* Unpublished doctoral dissertation. University of Chicago.

Ortiz, A. (1984). Language and curriculum development for exceptional bilingual children. In C. P. Chinn (Ed.), *Education of culturally and linguistically different exceptional children.* Reston, VA: Council for Exceptional Children–ERIC Clearinghouse on Handicapped and Gifted Children, pp. 77–100.

Ovando, C. and Collier, V. (1998). *Bilingual and ESL classrooms: Teaching in multicultural contexts.* Boston, MA: McGraw-Hill.

Pienemann, M. (1988). Determining the influence of instruction on L2 speech processing. *AILA Review*, 5: 40–72.

Pienemann, M. (1989). Is language teachable? Psycholinguistic experiments and hypotheses. *Applied Linguistics*, 10 (1): 52–79.

Pienemann, M. (2007). Processability theory. In B. van Patten and J. Williams (Eds.), *Theories in second language acquisition: An introduction.* Mahwah, NJ: Lawrence Erlbaum Associates, pp. 137–154.

Ragan, A. (2005). Teaching the academic language of textbooks: A preliminary framework for performing a textual analysis. *The ELL Outlook.* Retrieved from www.coursecrafters.com/ELL-outlook/2005/nov_dec/ELLoutlookITIArticle1.htm.

Richards, H. V., Brown, A. F., and Forde, T. B. (2004). *Addressing diversity in schools: Culturally responsive pedagogy.* Tempe, AZ: National Center for Culturally Responsive Educational Systems. Retrieved from www.nccrest.org/Briefs/Diversity_Brief.pdf.

Ruiz, N. T. (1989). An optimal learning environment for Rosemary. *Exceptional Children*, 56 (2): 130–144.

Ruiz, N. T. (1995a). The social construction of ability and disability: I. Profile types of Latino children identified as language learning disabled. *Journal of Learning Disabilities*, 28 (8): 476–490.

Ruiz, N. T. (1995b). The social construction of ability and disability: II. Optimal and at-risk lessons in a bilingual special education classroom. *Journal of Learning Disabilities*, 28 (8): 491–502.

Scarcella, R. (2003). *Academic English: A conceptual framework.* Technical Report 2003-1. Irvine, CA: University of California Linguistic Minority Research Institute. Retrieved from www.ncela.gwu.edu/resabout/literacy/2_academic.htm.

Skehan, P. (1998). *A cognitive approach to language learning.* Oxford, UK: Oxford University Press.

Swain, M. (1995). Three functions of output in second language learning. In G. Cook and B. Seidlhofer (Eds.), *Principle and practice in applied linguistics.* Oxford, UK: Oxford University Press, pp. 125–144.

U.S. Census Bureau. (2010a). *Language use in the United States: 2007.* Washington, DC: U.S. Department of Commerce. Retrieved from http://www.census.gov/prod/2010pubs/acs-12.pdf.

U.S. Census Bureau. (2010b). *Language spoken at home.* Report S1601. Retrieved from http://factfinder2.census.gov/faces/nav/jsf/pages/index.xhtml#none.

U.S. Census Bureau. (2010c). *Place of birth for the foreign-born population in the U.S.* Report B05006. Retrieved from http://factfinder2.census.gov/faces/nav/jsf/pages/index.xhtml#none.

Valdez, G. (2000). Nonnative English speakers: Language bigotry in English mainstream classes. *Associations of Departments of English Bulletin*, 124 (Winter): 12–17.

de Valenzuela, J. S. and Niccolai, S. L. (2004). Language development in culturally and linguistically diverse students with special education needs. In L. Baca and H. Cervantes (Eds.), *The bilingual special education interface*, 4th edn. Upper Saddle River, NJ: Merrill, pp. 125–161.

Zamel, V. and Spack, R. (1998). *Negotiating academic literacies: Teaching and learning across language and cultures.* Mahwah, NJ: Lawrence Erlbaum.

Zehler, A. (1994). *Working with English language learners: Strategies for elementary and middle school teachers.* NCBE Program Information Guide, No. 19. Retrieved from www.ncela.gwu.edu/ pubs/pigs/pig19.htm.

Part 2

Aguirre, N. (2003). ESL students in gifted education. In J. A. Castellano (Ed.), *Special populations in gifted education: Working with diverse gifted learners.* Boston, MA: Pearson Education, pp. 17–27.

Anstrom, K. (1999). *Preparing secondary education teachers to work with English language learners: Social studies.* NCBE Resource Collection Series 13. Washington, DC: NCELA. Retrieved from www.ncela.gwu.edu/pubs/resource/ells/social.htm.

Asher, J. J. (1982). *Learning another language through actions.* Los Gatos, CA: Sky Oaks Productions.

Au, K. H. (2010). Isn't culturally responsive teaching just good teaching? In W. C. Parker (Ed.), *Social studies today: Research and practice.* New York: Routledge, pp. 77–86.

Ballenger, C. (1997). Social identities, moral narratives, scientific argumentation: Scientific talk in a bilingual classroom. *Language and Education*, 11 (1): 1–13.

Barnes, D. (1992). *From communication to curriculum*, 2nd edn. Portsmouth, NH: Boynton/Cook Publishers.

Barnes, D. (1995). Talking and learning in classrooms: An introduction. *Primary Voices*, 3 (1): 2–7.

Barton, K. C. and Levstik, L. S. (2004). *Teaching history for the common good*. Mahwah, NJ: Erlbaum.

Berger, E. and Winters, B. A. (1973). *Social studies in the open classroom*. New York: Teachers College Press.

Brinton, C. (1965). *The anatomy of revolution*, rev. edn. New York: Vintage.

Brinton, D. and Gaskill, W. (1978). Using news broadcasts in the ESL/EFL classroom. *TESOL Quarterly*, 12 (4): 403–413.

Brooks, G. J., Libresco, A. S., and Plonczak, I. (2007). Spaces of liberty: Battling the new soft bigotry of NCLB. *Phi Delta Kappan*, 88: 749–756.

Brophy, J. (2001). Introduction. In J. Brophy (Ed.), *Subject-specific instructional methods and activities*. Oxford, UK: Elsevier Science, pp. 1–23.

Brown, C. L. (2007). Specific strategies for making social studies texts more comprehensible for English language learners. *The Social Studies*, 98 (5): 185–188.

Bruner, J. (1960). *The process of education*. Cambridge, MA: Harvard University Press.

Calderón, M., Slavin, R., and Sánchez, M. (2011). Effective instruction for English learners. *The Future of Children*, 21 (1): 103–127.

Cantoni-Harvey, G. (1987). *Content-area language instruction*. Reading, MA: Addison-Wesley.

Cardoso, W. (2006). Review of the Heinle Picture Dictionary-Interactive CD-ROM. *Language Learning and Technology*, 10 (3): 27–35. Retrieved from http://llt.msu.edu/vol10num3/review2/default.html.

Case, R. and Obenchain, K. M. (2006). How to assess language in the social studies classroom. *The Social Studies*, 97 (1): 41–48.

Chamot, A. and O'Malley, J. (1994). *The CALLA handbook*. Reading, MA: Addison-Wesley.

Chartock, R. K. (2010). *Strategies and lessons for culturally responsive teaching: A primer for K-12 Teachers*. New York: Pearson.

Cohen, E. G. (1994). *Groupwork*. New York: Teachers College Press.

Common Core State Standards Initiative. (2012). *English Language arts standards: history/social studies, grade 6–8*. Retrieved from http://www.corestandards.org/ELA-Literacy/RH/6-8.

Crandall, J. (1994). Content-centered instruction in the United States. *Annual Review of Applied Linguistics*, 13: 111–126.

Cruz, B. C. and Thornton, S. J. (2012). Visualizing social studies literacy: Teaching content and skills to English language learners. *Social Studies Research and Practice*, 7 (3), http://www.socstrpr.org.

Danielson, C. (1996). *Enhancing professional practice: A framework for teaching*. Alexandria, VA: Association for Supervision and Curriculum Development.

Danker, A. C. (2006). *Multicultural social studies: Using local history in the classroom*. New York: Teachers College Press.

Duplass, J. A. (2008). *Teaching elementary social studies*, 2nd edn. Boston, MA: Houghton Mifflin.

Echevarria, J., Vogt, M., and Short, D. (2000). *Making content comprehensible for English learners: The SIOP model*. Boston, MA: Allyn and Bacon.

Echevarria, J., Vogt, M., and Short, D. J. (2004). *Making content comprehensible for English learners: The SIOP model*, 2nd edn. Boston, MA: Pearson.

Egbert, J. and Simich-Dudgeon, C. (2001). Providing support for non-native learners of English in the social studies classroom: Integrating verbal interactive activities and technology. *The Social Studies*, 92 (1): 22–25.

Eisner, E. W. (2002). *The arts and the creation of mind*. New Haven, CT: Yale University Press.

Elhoweris, H., Muta, K., Alsheikh, N., and Holloway, P. (2005). Effect of ethnicity on teachers' referral and recommendation decisions in gifted and talented programs. *Remedial and Special Education*, 26 (1): 25–31

Fox, J. and Fairbairn, S. (2011). Test review: ACCESS for ELLs. *Language Testing*, 28 (3): 425–431.

Fraenkel, J. (1992). Hilda Taba's contribution to social studies education. *Social Education*, 56 (3): 172–178.

Fregeau, L. A. and Leier, R. D. (2008). Assessing ELLs in ESL or mainstream classrooms: Quick fixes for busy teachers. *The Internet TESL Journal*, 14 (2). Retrieved from http://iteslj.org/Techniques/Fregeau-AssessingELLs.html

rdner, H. (2006). *Multiple intelligences: New horizons*. New York: Basic Books.

Gay, G. (2000). *Culturally responsive teaching: Theory, research, and practice.* New York: Teachers College Press.

Genesee, F. (2011). *Myths and realities about educating English language learners.* Address given at Princeton University. Retrieved from futureofchildren.org/futureofchildren/events/.../practice.../genesee.pdf

Gewertz, C. (2011). Specialists weigh common core standards in social studies. *Education Week,* May 18, http://www.edweek.org/ew/articles/2011/05/18/32socialstudies.h30.html.

Goodlad, J. I. (1984). *A place called school.* New York: McGraw-Hill.

Granada, A. J. (2002). Addressing the curriculum, instruction, and assessment needs of the gifted bilingual/bicultural student. In J. A. Castellano and E. I. Díaz (Eds.), *Reaching new horizons: Gifted and talented education for culturally and linguistically diverse students.* Boston, MA: Allyn and Bacon, pp. 133–153.

Harmon, J. M. and Hedrick, W. B. (2000). Zooming in and zooming out: Enhancing vocabulary and conceptual learning in social studies. *The Reading Teacher,* 54 (2): 155–159.

Harvey, K. D., Harjo, L. D., and Jackson, J. K. (1997). *Teaching about Native Americans,* 2nd edn. Washington, DC: National Council for the Social Studies.

Haynes, J. (2004). *How to develop questioning strategies.* Retrieved from www.everythingesl.net/inservices/questioning_strategies.php.

Haynes, J. (2005). *Challenges for ELLs in content area learning.* Retrieved from www.everythingesl.net/inservices/challenges_ells_content_area_l_65322.php.

Henze, R. and Hauser, M. (2000). *Personalizing culture through anthropological and educational perspectives.* Retrieved from http://calstore.cal.org/store/detail.aspx?ID=137.

Hess, D. E. (2004). Discussion in social studies: Is it worth the trouble? *Social Education,* 68 (2): 151–155.

Hinde, E. R., Osborn Popp, S. E., Jimenez-Silva, M., and Dorn, R. I. (2011). Linking geography to reading and English language learners' achievement in US elementary and middle school classrooms. *International Research in Geographical and Environmental Education,* 20 (1): 47–63.

Hoose, P. (2001). *We were there, too! Young people in U.S. history.* New York: Melanie Kroupa Books.

Irvin, J. L., Lunstrum, J. P., Lynch-Brown, C., and Shepard, M. F. (1995). *Enhancing social studies through literacy.* Washington, DC: National Council for the Social Studies.

Jacobs, E., Rottenber, L., Patrick, S., and Wheeler, E. (1996). Cooperative learning: Context and opportunities for acquiring academic English. *TESOL Quarterly,* 30 (2): 253–280.

Jones, E. B., Pang, V. O., and Rodriguez, J. L. (2001). Social studies in the elementary classroom. *Theory into Practice,* 40: 35–41.

Koenigsberg, S. P. (1966). "See and suppose": Learning through discovery in the social studies. *The Social Studies,* 57: 257–262.

Kopriva, R. J., Emick, J. E., Hipolito-Delgado, C. P., and Cameron, C. A. (2007). Do proper accommodation assignments make a difference? Examining the impact of improved decision making on scores for English language learners. *Educational Measurement: Issues and Practice,* 26 (3): 11–20. Retrieved from http://onlinelibrary.wiley.com/doi/10.1111/j.1745-3992.2007.00097.x/full.

Krashen, S. (1985). *The input hypothesis: Issues and implications.* Beverly Hills, CA: Laredo Publishing Company.

Larsen-Freeman, D. and Anderson, M. (2011). *Techniques and principles in language teaching,* 3rd edn. New York: Oxford University Press.

Lindholm-Leavy, K. and Borsato, G. (2006). Academic achievement. In F. Genesee (Ed.), *Educating English language learners.* New York: Cambridge University Press, pp. 176–211.

Mansilla, V. B. and Gardner, H. (2008). Disciplining the mind. *Educational Leadership,* 65 (5): 14–19.

Marzano, R. J., Frontier, T., and Livingston, D. (2011). *Effective supervision: Supporting the art and science of teaching.* Alexandria, VA: Association for Supervision and Curriculum Development.

Mihai, F. M. (2010). *Assessing English language learners in the content areas.* Ann Arbor, MI: University of Michigan Press.

Moline, S. (1995). *I see what you mean: Children at work with visual information.* York, ME: Stenhouse.

Montecel, M. R. and Cortez, J. D. (2002). Successful bilingual education programs. *Bilingual Research Journal,* 26: 1–22.

National Council for the Social Studies. (2001). *Preparing citizens for a global community.* Retrieved from http://www.socialstudies.org/positions/global.

National Council for the Social Studies. (2008). *A vision of powerful teaching and learning in the social studie* Retrieved from http://www.socialstudies.org/positions/powerful.

National Council for the Social Studies. (2010). *National curriculum standards for social studies.* Silver Spring, MD: National Council for the Social Studies.

Noddings, N. (2005). *The challenge to care in schools,* 2nd edn. New York: Teachers College Press.

Ogle, D. (1986). K-W-L: A teaching model that develops active reading of expository text. *The Reading Teacher,* 39, 564–570.

Oller, D. and Eilers, R. (2000). An integrated approach to evaluating effects of bilingualism in Miami school children. In D. Oller and R. Eilers (Eds.), *Language and literacy of bilingual children.* Clevedon, UK: Multilingual Matters, pp. 12–21.

Olmedo, I. M. (1997). Family oral histories for multicultural curriculum perspectives. *Urban Education,* 32 (1): 45–62.

Pang, V. O., Stein, R., Gomez, M., Matas, A., and Shimogori, Y. (2011). Cultural competencies: Essential elements of caring-centered multicultural education. *Action in Teacher Education,* 33 (5–6): 560–574.

Partnership for 21st Century Skills. (2012). *A framework for 21st century learning.* Retrieved from http://www.p21.org.

Pew Internet & American Life Project. (2010). *Internet and American Life Project.* Retrieved from http://www.pewinternet.org/Reports/2010/Teens-and-Mobile-Phones.aspx.

Pike, K. L. (1967). *Language in relation to a unified theory of the structure of human behavior.* 2nd edn. The Hague: Mouton. (First edition in three volumes: 1954, 1955, 1960.)

Ramirez, J. and Yuen, S. (1991). *Longitudinal study of structured English immersion strategy, early-exit, and late-exit transitional bilingual education programs for language minority children.* Report prepared for the United States Department of Education under Contract No. 300–87–0156. Retrieved from www.nabe.org/documents/research/Ramirez.pdf.

Salinas, C., Fránquiz, M. E., and Guberman, S. (2006). Introducing historical thinking to second language learners: Exploring what students know and what they want to know. *The Social Studies,* 97 (5): 203–207.

Sanchez Terrell, S. (2011). Integrating online tools to motivate young English language learners to practice English outside the classroom. *International Journal of Computer-Assisted Language Learning and Teaching,* 1 (2): 16–24.

Schön, D. A. (1983). *The reflective practitioner: How professionals think in action.* New York: Basic Books.

Selwyn, D. (2009). *Following the threads: Bringing inquiry research into the classroom.* New York: Peter Lang.

Shaftel, F. R. and Shaftel, G. (1967). *Role-playing for social values.* Englewood Cliffs, NJ: Prentice-Hall.

Shand, K, Winstead, L., and Kottler, E. (2012). Journey to medieval China: Using technology-enhanced instruction to develop content knowledge and digital literacy skills. *The Social Studies,* 103 (1): 20–30.

Short, D. J. (1991). *How to integrate language and content instruction: A training manual.* Washington, DC: Center for Applied Linguistics.

Short, D. J. (1994) The challenge of social studies for limited English proficient students. *Social Education,* 58 (1): 36–38.

Short, D. J. (1997). *Teacher discourse in social studies classrooms: How teachers promote academic literacy for English language learners.* Unpublished manuscript. Fairfax, VA: George Mason University.

Short, D. J. (1998). Social studies instruction and assessment: Meeting the needs of students learning English. In S. H. Fradd and O. Lee (Eds.), *Creating Florida's multilingual global work force: Educational policies and practices for students learning English as a new language.* Tallahassee, FL: Florida Department of Education.

Short, D. J. (2002). Language learning in sheltered social studies classes. *TESOL Journal,* 11 (1): 18–24.

Short, D., Echevarria, J., and Ruchards-Tutor, C. (2011). Research on academic literacy development in sheltered instruction classrooms. *Language Teaching Research,* 15 (3): 363–380.

Simich-Dudgeon, C. (1998). *Classroom strategies for encouraging collaborative discussion.* Directions in Language and Education, 12. Washington, DC: NCBE. Retrieved from www.ncela.gwu.edu/pubs/directions/12.htm.

Sleeter, C. E. (1995). *Multicultural education, critical pedagogy, and the politics of difference.* New York: SUNY Press.

Smith, L. J. and Smith, D. L. (1990). *Social studies: Detecting and correcting special needs.* Boston, MA: Allyn and Bacon.

ahl, R. J., VanSickle, R. L, and Stahl, N. N. (Eds.). (2009). *Cooperative learning in the social studies classroom.* Silver Spring, MD: National Council for the Social Studies.

Sweller, J. (1988). Cognitive load during problem solving: Effects on learning. *Cognitive Science,* 12 (2): 257–285.

Szpara, M. Y. and Ahmad, I. (2007). Supporting English-language learners in social studies class. *The Social Studies,* 98: 189–195.

Taba, H. (1967). Implementing thinking as an objective in social studies. In J. Fair and F.R. Shaftel (Eds.), *Effective thinking in the social studies.* Washington, DC: National Council for the Social Studies, pp. 25–49.

Tannenbaum, J. (1996). *Practical ideas on alternative assessment for ESL students.* ERIC Digest. ED 395 500.

Thomas, W. and Collier, V. (2001). *A national study of school effectiveness for language minority students' long-term academic achievement final report: Project 1.1.* Center for Research on Education, Diversity & Excellence. Retrieved from www.crede.org/research/llaa/1.1_final.html.

Thornton, S. J. (1994). The social studies near century's end: Reconsidering patterns of curriculum and instruction. In L. Darling-Hammond (Ed.), *Review of Research in Education,* vol. 20. Washington, DC: American Educational Research Association, pp. 223–254.

Thornton, S. J. (2005). *Teaching social studies that matters: Curriculum for active learning.* New York: Teachers College Press.

Tomlinson, C. and Imbeau, M. (2010). *Leading and managing a differentiated classroom.* Alexandria, VA: Association for Supervision and Curriculum Development.

Tishman, S. (2008). The object of their attention. *Educational Leadership,* 65 (5): 44–46.

Truscott, D. and Watts-Taffe, S. (1998). Literacy instruction for second-language learners: A study of best practices. *National Reading Conference Yearbook,* 47: 242–252.

Truscott, D. and Watts-Taffe, S. (2000). Using what we know about language and literacy development for ESL students in the mainstream classroom. *Language Arts,* 77 (3): 258–265.

Udall, A. J. (1989). Curriculum for gifted Hispanic students. In C. J. Maker and S. W. Schiever (Eds.), *Critical issues in gifted education: Defensible programs for cultural and ethnic minorities.* Austin, TX: Pro-Ed, pp. 41–56.

Valenzuela, A. (1999). *Subtractive schooling: U.S.-Mexican youth and the politics of caring.* Albany, NY: State University of New York Press.

Webb, W. P. (1960). Geographical-historical concepts in American history. *Annals of the Association of American Geographers,* 50: 85–93.

Weisman, E. M. and Hansen, L. E. (2007). Strategies for teaching social studies to English language learners at the elementary level. *The Social Studies,* 98 (5): 180–184.

Werner, W. (2006). Reading pictures of people. In E. W. Ross (Ed.), *The social studies curriculum.* Albany, NY: State University of New York Press, pp. 217–239.

White, J. J. (1986). Decision-making with an integrative curriculum. *Childhood Education,* 62: 337–343.

White, J. J. (1990). Involving different social and cultural groups in discussion. In W. W. Wilen (Ed.), *Teaching and learning through discussion: The theory, research and practice of the discussion method.* Springfield, IL: Charles C. Thomas, pp. 147–174.

Williamson, R. and Johnston, J. H. (2012). *The school leader's guide to social media.* Larchmont, NY: Eye on Education.

Yano, Y., Long, M. H., and Ross, S. (1994). The effects of simplified and elaborated texts on foreign language reading comprehension. *Language Learning,* 44 (2): 189–219.

Yell, M. M., Scheurman, G., and Reynolds, K. (2004). *A link to the past: Engaging students in the study of history.* Silver Spring, MD: National Council for the Social Studies.

Part 3

Beyer, B. K. (1969). *Africa south of the Sahara: A resource and curriculum guide.* New York: Thomas Y. Crowell.

Billman, L. W. (2002). Aren't these books for little kids? *Educational Leadership,* 60 (3): 48–51.

Brinton, D. and Gaskill, W. (1978). Using news broadcasts in the ESL/EFL classroom. *TESOL Quarterly,* 12 (4): 403–413.

Brophy, J., Prawat, R., and McMahon, S. (1991). Social education professors and elementary teachers: Two purviews on elementary social studies. *Theory and Research in Social Education,* 19: 173–188.

Carr, K. S., Buchanan, D. L., Wentz, J. B., Weiss, M. L., and Brant, K. L. (2001). Not just for the primary grades: A bibliography of picture books for secondary content teachers. *Journal of Adolescent and Adult Literacy*, 45 (2): 146–153.

Christian, D. (2008). *This fleeting world: A short history of humanity*. Great Barrington, MA: Berkshire Publishing Group.

Coonrod, C. S. (1998). *Chronic hunger and the status of women in India*. Retrieved from www.thp.org/reports/indiawom.htm.

Cruz, B. and Bermúdez, P. (1997). *Latin America and the Caribbean for the 21st century: A resource guide for Florida teachers*. Miami, FL: Florida Caribbean Institute.

Cruz, B.C. and Thornton, S. J. (2012). Visualizing social studies literacy: Teaching content and skills to English language learners. *Social Studies Research and Practice*, 7 (3), http://www.socstrpr.org.

Cruz, B. C., Nutta, J. W., O'Brien, J., Feyten, C. M., and Govoni, J. M. (2003). *Passport to learning: Teaching social studies to ESL students*. Silver Spring, MD: National Council for the Social Studies.

Danker, A. C. (2005). *Multicultural social studies: Using local history in the classroom*. New York: Teachers College Press.

DeGroot, G. J. (1996). *Blighty: British society in the era of the Great War*. London: Longman.

Dewey, J. (1966, first published 1916). *Democracy and education*. New York: Free Press.

Dewey, J. (1991, first published 1910). *How we think*. Amherst, NY: Prometheus Books.

Downing, F. (Ed.) (1945). *Cactus blossoms*. Pasadena, CA: b.s.n.

Drake, F. D. and Nelson, L. R. (2005). *Engagement in teaching history: Theory and practices for middle and secondary teachers*. Upper Saddle River, NJ: Pearson.

Egbert, J. and Simich-Dudgeon, C. (2001). Providing support for non-native learners of English in the social studies classroom: Integrating verbal interactive activities and technology. *The Social Studies*, 92 (1): 22–25.

Enloe, C. (1989). *Bananas, beaches, and bases: Making feminist sense of international politics*. Berkeley, CA: University of California Press.

Gillespie, C. A. (2010). How culture constructs our sense of neighborhood: Mental maps and children's perceptions of place. *Journal of Geography*, 109 (1): 18–29.

Grant, S. G. (2001). It's just the facts, or is it? Teachers' practices and students' understandings of history. *Theory and Research in Social Education*, 29: 65–108.

Hahn, C. L. (1996). Research on issues-centered social studies. In R. W. Evans and D. W. Saxe (Eds.), *Handbook on teaching social issues*. Washington, DC: National Council for the Social Studies, pp. 25–41.

Hahn, C. L. (2001a). Democratic understanding: Cross-national perspectives. *Theory into Practice*, 40 (1): 14–22.

Hahn, C. L. (2001b). What can be done to encourage civic engagement in youth? *Social Education*, 65 (2): 108–110.

Hanvey, R. G. (1982). An attainable global perspective. *Theory into Practice*, 21 (3): 162–167.

Hardwick, S. W. and Davis, R. L. (2009). Content-based language instruction: A new window of opportunity in geography education. *Journal of Geography*, 108 (4–5): 163–173.

Hardwick, S. W. and Holtgrieve, D. G. (1996). *Geography for educators: Standards, themes, and concepts*. Upper Saddle River, NJ: Prentice Hall.

Harwood, A. M. and Hahn, C. L. (1990). *Controversial issues in the classroom*. ERIC Clearinghouse, ED 327 453.

Herber, H. L. (1970). *Reading in content areas*. Englewood Cliffs, NJ: Prentice-Hall.

Hertzberg, H. W. (1966). *Teaching a pre-Columbian culture: The Iroquois*. Albany, NY: University of the State of New York, the State Education Department, Bureau of Secondary Curriculum Development.

Hess, D. E. (2004). Discussion in social studies: Is it worth the trouble? *Social Education*, 68 (2): 151–155.

Hess, D. E. and Posselt, J. (2002). How high school students experience and learn from the discussion of controversial public issues. *Journal of Curriculum and Supervision*, 17 (4): 283–314.

Kobrin, D. (1996). *Beyond the textbook: Teaching history using documents and primary sources*. Portsmouth, NH: Heinemann.

Lacina, J. G. (2004). Designing a virtual field trip. *Childhood Education*, 80 (4): 221–222.

Levstik, L. S. and Barton, K. C. (2001). *Doing history*, 2nd edn. Mahwah, NJ: Erlbaum.

Levy, P. (1994). *Switzerland.* New York: Marshall Cavendish.

Loewen, J. W. (1995). *Lies my teacher told me.* New York: Touchstone.

Marcus, A. S., Stoddard, J. D., and Woodward, W. W. (2012). *Teaching history with museums: Strategies for K-12 social studies.* New York: Routledge.

Marino, M. (2011). World History and teacher education: Challenges and possibilities. *The Social Studies,* 102: 3–8.

Marx, K. and Engels, F. (1848 [1998]). *The Communist Manifesto.* New York: Verso.

Merryfield, M. M. (2000). How can electronic technologies promote equity and cultural diversity? Using threaded discussion in graduate courses in social studies and global education. *Theory and Research in Social Education,* 28 (4): 502–526.

Merryfield, M. M. and Wilson, A. (2005). *Social studies and the world: Teaching global perspectives.* Silver Spring, MD: National Council for the Social Studies.

Mitchell, L. S. (1991). *Young geographers: How they explore the world and how they map the world,* 4th edn. New York: Bank Street College of Education.

Naimark, N. M. (2001). *Fires of hatred: Ethnic cleansing in twentieth-century Europe.* Cambridge, MA: Harvard University Press.

National Council for the Social Studies. (2006). *About NCSS.* Retrieved from www.ncss.org/about.

National Council for the Social Studies. (2010). *National curriculum standards for social studies,* 2nd edn. Silver Spring, MD: National Council for the Social Studies.

National Council on Economic Education. (2007). *Survey of the states: Economic, personal finance, and entrepreneurship education in our nation's schools in 2007.* Retrieved from www.ncee.net/news/story.php?story_id=108.

Neustadt, R. E. and May, E. R. (1986). *Thinking in time: The uses of history for decision-makers.* New York: Free Press.

Noddings, N. (2004). War, critical thinking, and self-understanding. *Phi Delta Kappan,* 85 (7): 488–495.

Noddings, N. (2006). *Critical lessons: What our schools should teach.* New York: Cambridge University Press.

Nystrom. (2009). *Nystrom atlas of United States history.* Indianapolis, IN: Nystrom.

Olmedo, I. M. (1996). Creating contexts for studying history with students learning English. *The Social Studies,* 87 (1): 39–44.

Osborn, E. R. (2006). The Seneca Falls Convention: Teaching about the rights of women and the heritage of the Declaration of Independence. ERIC Digest. Retrieved from www.ericdigests.org/2002–1/women.html.

Oxfam. (2006). *Teaching controversial issues.* London: Author. Retrieved from www.oxfam.org.uk/cool planet/teachers/controversial_issues/index.htm.

Parker, W. C. (2001). Classroom discussion: Models for leading seminars and deliberations. *Social Education,* 65 (2): 111–115.

Pike, K. L. (1967). *Language in relation to a unified theory of the structure of human behavior,* 2nd edn. The Hague: Mouton. (First edition in three volumes, 1954, 1955, 1960.)

Ponzi, P. H.. (1974). The Sacred Rac. In S. Fersh (Ed.), *Learning about peoples and cultures.* Evanston, IL: McDougal, Littell and Co., pp. 37–38. Retrieved from www.drabruzzi.com/sacred_rac.html.

Potter, L. A. (2003). Connecting with the past. *Social Education,* 67 (7): 372–377.

Ramirez, A. D. (2012). Mexican Americans in the era of World War II: Studying the Sleepy Lagoon case and Zoot Suit Riots. *Social Education,* 76 (3): 151–156.

Rossi, J. A. (1996). Creating strategies and conditions for civil discourse about controversial issues. *Social Education,* 60 (1): 15–21.

Rossi, J. A. (2006). The dialogue of democracy. *The Social Studies,* 97 (3): 112–120.

Salinas, C., Franquiz, M., and Reidel, M. (2008). Geography approaches for second language learners: Highlighting content and practice. *The Social Studies,* 99 (2): 71–76.

Schmidt, S. J. (2011). Who lives on the other side of that boundary: A model of geographic thinking. *Social Education,* 75 (5): 250–255.

Schug, M. C. (2007). Why did the colonists fight when they were safe, prosperous, and free? *Social Education,* 71: 61–65.

Segall, A. (2003). Maps as stories about the world. *Social Studies and the Young Learner,* 16 (1): 21–25.

Short, D. J. (1991). *How to integrate language and content instruction: A training manual.* Washington, DC: Center for Applied Linguistics.

Short, D. J. (1994). The challenge of social studies for limited English proficient students. *Social Education,* 58 (1): 36–39.

Short, D. J. (1998). Social studies instruction and assessment: Meeting the needs of students learning English. In S.H. Fradd and O. Lee (Eds.), *Creating Florida's multilingual global workforce: Educational policies and practices for students learning English as a new language.* Tallahassee, FL: Florida Department of Education.

Simich-Dudgeon, C. (1998). *Classroom strategies for encouraging collaborative discussion.* Directions in Language and Education, 12. Washington, DC: NCBE.

Stevens, R. L. and Fogel, J. A. (2007). Using music to teach about the Great Depression. *Social Education,* 71 (1): 15–20.

Thornton, S. J. (2006). What is history in U.S. history textbooks? In J. Nicholls (Ed.), *School history textbooks across cultures: International debates and perspectives.* Oxford, UK: Symposium Books, pp. 15–25.

Thornton, S. J. (2007). Geography in American history courses. *Phi Delta Kappan,* 88 (7): 535–538.

Torney-Purta, J., Lehman, R., Oswald, H., and Schultz, W. (2001). *Citizenship and education in twenty-eight countries: Civic knowledge and engagement at age 14.* Amsterdam, The Netherlands: IEA.

United States Citizenship and Immigration Services. (2011). *Learn about the United States: Quick civics lessons for the naturalization test.* Washington, DC: Author.

Wade, R. C. (Ed.) (2007). *Community action rooted in history.* Silver Spring, MD: National Council for the Social Studies.

Watzman, H. (2007). Israel's incredible shrinking sea. *New York Times,* July 29, p. WK 11.

Wiegand, P. (2006). *Learning and teaching with maps.* London: Routledge.

Wilkins, K. H., Sheffield, C. C., Ford, M. B., and Cruz, B. C. (2008). Using picture books to teach about the Civil Rights Movement in the secondary classroom. *Social Education,* 72 (3): 178–181.

Williams, M., Ratte, L., and Andrian, R. K. (2001). *Exploring world history: Ideas for teachers.* Portsmouth, NH: Heinemann.

Zax, D. (2007). When Portugal ruled the world. *Smithsonian,* 38: 74–79.

Index

academic literacy: Cummins' conception of 26–27; definition of 13
adolescence, relevance of social studies to 52, 191, 199
American history *see* United States history
anthropology *see* behavioral sciences
assessment 69–71; in ELL's native language; modified for ELLs 194; varied for individualization 60
assumptive teaching 75
authentic text *see* content-centered language learning

behavioral sciences: activities and resources on 192–203; subject matters of 191–2
BICS (basic interpersonal communication skills) 27, 57, 58, 61, 63
bicultural affirmation 56
bilingualism, consequences of 26–27

CALP (cognitive academic language proficiency) 27, 57, 61, 63
civics *see* government and civics; controversial issues
cognitive demand or load 27–29; reduction of 59, 68
Common Core Standards (CCS) 49–50, 52
comprehensible input 18, 58, 59, 62, 71
conceptual learning 48, 81–82, 96–97
content-centered language learning 56–57, 58–59

controversial issues: activities and resources on 206–220; subject matters of 204–206
cooperative learning 57, 63, 71, 85, 101
culturally responsive pedagogy 35–37, 55–56
Cummins, Jim 26–27; quadrants showing cognitive demand, 27–29
curriculum standards *see* social studies programs

demonstrations and total physical response (TPR) 66–67
Dewey, John 80–81
dioramas 68, 100, 101
discovery approaches 62–63, 91
discussion and questioning 61–62, 90; and controversial issues 204–206

economics: activities and resources on 178–90; subject matter of 177–178
ELLs databases online 18–19, 79
English language learners (ELLs): cultural adjustment stages of 32–33; diversity among 30–32; gifted 77; MLA Language Map of 21; numbers and location of 9–10; parents of 38–40; with special needs 41–43
ESOL programs, types of 22–25
exploration approaches *see* discovery approaches

feedback strategies 15–16

Gay, Geneva 35
geography: activities and resources on 82–94;
    Dewey on 80–81; integration with history 82;
    learning through observation in 80; subject
    matter of 80–82
gifted students 43–44, 77
globalization 51
government and civics: activities and resources on
    158–176; subject matter of 157–158
graphic organizers 65–66

Hahn, Carole, 158, 204–205, 206
Haynes, Judie 56, 62
historical documents: teaching with 163–164
history *see* United States history; world history
home–school communication 38–40

individualized instruction 59–60
instructional materials modified for ELLs 57–58,
    65

Kobrin, David 96, 164

Ladson-Billings, Gloria xiv
language acquisition, stages of 12–13, 17–18,
    77–78; principles of 13–17
lesson plan with ELL modifications template 78
listening centers 57–58

maps and globes 77, 81
Mihai, Florin 58, 68–69

National Council for the Social Studies (NCSS) 48,
    49, 51, 79, 157, 164, 177
Nutta, Joyce 77–78

Oxfam 205

photographs 50, 57, 67–68, 80, 112
picture books 113
picture dictionaries 68
Pienemann, Manfred 12–13
political cartoons 146, 158, 161, 162
political science *see* government and civics;
    controversial issues

primary sources *see* historical documents
psychology *see* behavioral sciences

questioning *see* discussion and questioning

realia 57, 65, 66, 124
research on ELLS in social studies 54–71
role playing and simulations 67, 70, 71, 101
Rossi, John 205, 206

sheltered instruction 58–59
Short, Deborah 55, 57, 58, 64–65, 69, 71
simulation *see* role playing and simulations
social studies programs 46–71; and the Common
    Core 49–50; curriculum standards in 49;
    desirable elements of 47–53; ELL research on
    54–63; national curriculum standards for
    49; relationship to the academic disciplines
    47, 49
sociology *see* behavioral sciences
special needs students 41–4
speech emergence *see* language acquisition
standards *see* social studies programs
study skills 50

Taba, Hilda 48, 53
technology-based approaches 60–61, 206
textbooks 64–65, 80
total physical response (TPR) *see* demonstrations
    and total physical response
trade books 64–65
Twenty-first Century Skills *see* globalization

United States history: activities and resources
    on 97–121; and assumed cultural knowledge
    95; and citizenship test 95; integration with
    civics and geography 97; subject matter of
    95–97

visual resources 67–68, 80; *see also* photographs;
    picture books

White, Jane 61
word wall 123, 127
world history: activities and resources on 124–156;
    conflict over curricular perspective 122–123;
    subject matter of 122–124